HARDWIRED
HUMANS

Also by Andrew O'Keeffe
The Boss

HARDWIRED HUMANS

Successful Leadership
Using Human Instincts

Andrew O'Keeffe

Roundtable Press

Published by Roundtable Press
PO Box R1944
Royal Exchange NSW 1225
Australia

Phone: +61 2 8246 6363

Distributed by Dennis Jones and Associates
Telephone: +61 3 9762 9100
Email: theoffice@dennisjones.com.au
Website: www.dennisjones.com.au

Design and composition by Greenleaf Book Group LLC and Alex Head
Cover design by Greenleaf Book Group LLC
Proof reading by Tim Learner

National Library of Australia Cataloguing-in-Publication entry
O'Keeffe, Andrew.
Hardwired humans : successful leadership using human instincts / Andrew O'Keeffe.
First Edition
9780646551746 (hbk.)
Leadership—Psychological aspects.
Evolutionary psychology.
Organizational behavior.
658.409

Printed in Australia by McPherson's Printing Group

11 12 13 14 15 16   10 9 8 7 6 5 4 3 2 1

Contents

A Note From Dr Jane Goodall   vii

Why We Behave the Way We Do   1

Instinct 1. Social Belonging   5
The paradox that comes with the job of leader

Instinct 2. Hierarchy and Status   27
Avoiding chaos in families, clans and tribes

Instinct 3. Emotions Before Reason   43
It's not just for fight or flight

Instinct 4. First Impressions to Classify   59
Why a bank CEO got out of a Mumbai hotel just ahead of the terrorists

Instinct 5. Loss Aversion   89
Busting the myth that people resist change

Instinct 6. Gossip   111
Gossip is grooming without the fleas

Instinct 7. Empathy and Mind Reading   137
It's always good to put a face to a name

Instinct 8. Confidence Before Realism   167
Why 155 people on flight 1549 survived landing in an icy Hudson River

Instinct 9. Contest and Display   187
Looking good to get ahead

Organisational Behaviours that Now Make More Sense   207

Appendix: The 9 Human Instincts Defined   211

Acknowledgments 213

Notes 217

References 225

Index 229

A Note From Dr Jane Goodall

WHEN I FIRST SET FOOT on what is now the Gombe National Park on the shores of Lake Tanganyika in Tanzania it was to fulfil my childhood dream—to live with animals and write books about them. That was in 1960. I could not have imagined then that my study of the Gombe chimpanzees, now in its 50th year, would also provide information that would be used by other people writing their own books—such as Andrew's *Hardwired Humans*.

So many people are obsessed with how we are *different* to other animals, but chimpanzees impress us with the *similarities* in their behaviour and our own. They have many of the attributes that used to be considered uniquely human—such as using and making tools, intellectually solving problems, expressing emotions such as anger, sadness, happiness, despair. This should not surprise us since we differ, in structure of DNA, by only just over one percent. Indeed, we are part of and not separated from the rest of the animal kingdom.

Yet we are different in one way—the explosive development of the human intellect. We are thus able to analyse those traits that we share with chimpanzees and other animals and use this knowledge to help us better understand why we behave the way we do. Based on lessons learned from the chimpanzees we can, Andrew suggests, develop strategies for successful interactions with others. An understanding of the complex ways in which chimpanzees maintain social harmony within their community can provide valuable insights for dealing with tensions in a group of humans. And this, along with an understanding of the social skills required by (in their case, male) chimpanzees to become successful alphas, will help humans to become better leaders.

As well as reading about the Gombe chimpanzees, Andrew has spent many hours watching and learning from the wonderful chimpanzee group at the Taronga Zoo in Sydney. It is his fascination for these apes, the knowledge he has gained first hand and from talking to the keepers that make this a compelling book. You will get many insights into your own behaviour and that of your friends and colleagues.

Dr Jane Goodall
Gombe Stream Research Centre, Tanzania

Why We Behave the Way We Do

ON ONE SIDE OF SYDNEY HARBOUR is the city's business district. If you started work in any of the high-rise buildings, there are some things you would want to know about your new organisation. Like who's the big boss. That wouldn't be too hard to figure out. They're the one occupying the corner office on the top floor.

On the opposite side of the harbour, a short ferry ride from the iconic Opera House, a similar scene unfolds every day at Taronga Zoo, home to one of the world's best captive communities of chimpanzees. If you know what to look for it's easy to spot the leader of this community. We take business leaders to visit the chimps, and leaders always want to know which one is the alpha male. The keeper will point to a chimp some twenty paces away. 'That's him sitting on the rock near the waterfall.' The keeper continues, 'We think he sits on that particular rock because that's the rock the prior alpha male used to sit on.' It's the 'corner office'. In this community, when you've got claim to that rock, baby, you've made it!

Our natural behaviours—behaviours that come as part of being human—have significant implications for leaders. The two great benefits of knowing about instincts is that first, we can better make sense of why we humans behave the way we do at work so that second, we can make more informed leadership choices.

Comparing human behavioural characteristics to those of chimpanzees is revealing because their social structure, behavioural strategies and community politics are so similar to ours. The chimpanzee stories woven into the book come from the chimps at Taronga Zoo and from Dr Jane Goodall's experiences at Gombe Stream Chimpanzee Reserve in Tanzania.

The knowledge, application and value of our basic instincts have largely been ignored in the practice of leadership. Understanding those instincts can provide the missing link to effective people leadership. Most leaders find the toughest part of their job—the one more likely to keep them awake at night—is the 'people' dimension. As one manager said to me, 'The numbers are easy; it's the people stuff that's hard.' This book will help ensure that managing people isn't as hard as it tends to be.

Behaviours that frustrate organisational performance are uncannily similar from one organisation to another. Irrespective of their organisation, their industry or country, most leaders say that in our organisation:

- There's a lot of silo behaviour and internal competition.
- Change is difficult to manage and often resisted or derailed.
- The informal gossip grapevine is incredibly effective and is generally faster and regarded as more reliable than the formal channels.
- Our performance appraisal system doesn't deliver what it should and Human Resources is redesigning the system just one more time!
- Managers find it hard to give negative feedback and often procrastinate on managing poor performers.

Given that these experiences and many more are common to most organisations then they are not explainable at the organisational level. They can only be explained by a common factor—we all employ humans! Likewise, the solutions to these common issues will not be found at the organisational level. They can only be solved if we understand the human condition that both explains the behaviours and provides the solutions.

There's a suite of behaviours that come with being born human. Irrespective of whether our belief systems are more aligned to evolution or creation, the point is that when we're born human there's a package of behaviours that come with being human and that out of the whole period of human history we have only recently popped up in offices and factories.

From an evolutionary view, *Homo sapiens* emerged on the plains of Africa around 200,000 years ago and it's only 250 years ago with the Industrial Revolution that (in Western cultures) we left our hunting, gathering and village societies to work in offices and factories. A mere 250 years is no time at all for our ingrained behavioural instincts to change. Little surprise, therefore, that the behaviour that ensured our survival on the savannah plains of Africa over the millennia is alive and well in the corridors, meeting rooms and offices of today's organisations!

And early *Homo sapiens* were shaped by their pre-human ancestors. The evolutionary theory is that pre-humans emerged around 5 million years ago in the form of *Australopithecines* who had a similar skull structure to humans and walked upright on two legs. The 23 metres of hominoid footprints preserved in volcanic ash at Laetoli in Tanzania date from around 3.7 million years ago.

Homo habilis appeared around 2 million–1.5 million years ago and then *Homo erectus* emerged around 1.5 million years ago, walking upright, with a large brain and engaged in tool making. Evidence of the use of fire first appears at this time. The oldest fossil of modern humans has been found at Herto in Ethiopia that dates back to around 160,000 years ago. From separate studies of genetic code scientists date *Homo sapiens* from around 200,000 years ago which fits the fossil evidence.

Generations of early hominoids have been a key force in shaping what it means to be human. Even the transition to agricultural communities occurred only around 10,000 years ago. Then suddenly our grandparents' grandparents were the first to find themselves in offices and factories.

While our habitat might have changed 250 years ago—the equivalent of a nanosecond on the evolutionary clock—our hardwired behaviour, the way we process information and the way the brain works, has not.

The definition of instincts, courtesy of Robert Winston, is, 'That part of our behaviour that is not learned.' For the list and explanation of the nine human instincts we rely on the research of a number of people. The key source and inspiration for the instincts comes from Professor Nigel Nicholson from London Business School, who first inspired me to see and apply instincts to solve practical leadership challenges, along with Professor Robert Winston of Imperial College London and Professor Robin Dunbar from the University of Oxford amongst others.

People who have learned about instincts find that workplace behaviour suddenly makes a lot more sense, they are more in control of their environment, better able to influence things and to be more effective. Leaders who have acquired the insight into human instincts say that the knowledge has transformed their ability to lead. They report that confusion about why people think and behave as they do has been significantly reduced. And as a consequence they are able to make better leadership choices so that managing people is easier, less stressful, more satisfying and more successful.

By understanding and reconnecting with the nine instinctive behaviours, you will realise that this valuable knowledge was already tucked inside your subconscious, exactly where you would expect to find instinctive behaviour. By making this knowledge explicit you will be better able to predict what will work and what won't, and to avoid the perennial derailers of leadership and life in organisations.

Instinct 1. Social Belonging

This instinct helps explain why:
- people talk about a great team being just like a family
- teams have a natural size
- 80% of people who resign do so because of their manager
- conflict in our team drives us crazy
- silo behaviour emerges as organisations grow beyond a moderate size.

JANE GOODALL WATCHED FLINT die. Dr Goodall first began studying the chimpanzees at Gombe Stream National Park in Tanzania in 1960. One of her early observations was that chimps, like us, have strong bonds between family members and those bonds endure for life. Flint's reaction to his mother's death shows how strong this bond can be. His mother Flo died when Flint was eight and a half years old. So traumatised was the youngster with the loss of his mother he died within three weeks.

Some 35 years after Flint's death Dr Goodall was telling me about Flo and Flint's deaths. In October 2008 Dr Goodall and I had just concluded a three week tour speaking to business audiences about the implications of instincts for leaders. In vividly recalling Flint's death, Dr Goodall said that she could describe it as nothing other than grief. Upon Flo's death Flint stopped eating and with his immunisation system so weakened he quickly deteriorated. Back closer to the time she wrote, 'The last short journey he made, pausing to rest every few feet, was to the very place where Flo's body had lain. There he stayed for several hours … he struggled on a little further, then curled up—and never moved again.'

The first of our nine instincts is *social belonging*. We are a social animal; we are not loners. As a social animal, we gain our sense of identify from our membership of two groups: our family group that naturally numbers about seven people, and our extended clan which can number up to around 150.

Let's make concrete the connection between instincts and organisational life. The building block of human communities is family groups. Given that we have just recently emerged into offices and factories, it follows that the building blocks of organisations are, or should be, small family-sized teams. With our need to connect intimately with a small group of others numbering around seven, it also means that nothing drives us to distraction faster than if our immediate work team is dysfunctional. It means that as organisations grow towards 150, people will begin to say, 'It's not as friendly as it used to be.' And when numbers go significantly beyond 150 we will have stronger bonds to our department or subsidiary than to the whole organisation to the extent that silos and internal competition will tend to occur as departments compete for resources and recognition.

Family

Our strong sense of community and lifetime family bonds comes from our reproductive strategy as a species. There are not many animals on the planet that have this lifetime family bond as their survival strategy.

Our strategy is to invest everything in the raising of a few offspring—we focus our reproductive energy on just a few children. Some animals adopt a strategy at the other extreme. A mother turtle, for example, swims up to the beach during the night, digs a shallow hole and lays her eggs. She covers her eggs with sand, and that's her mothering duty done! The hatchlings have all the information they need to survive and the species plays the numbers game where enough hatchlings—around one in a thousand—hopefully survive through to adulthood to reproduce.

We humans don't play the numbers game. Human parents, particularly mothers, invest heavily in raising an infant to reproductive age. After birth, a human baby's brain takes another year to complete its physical growth and quite a few years before the youngster could hope to survive on their own. The human mother has the capacity to give birth to only a handful of children over her lifespan. With this incredible investment in an offspring, it's not surprising that the bond between parents and offspring, and between direct family members, are for life.

There is something special about families and our primary sense of identify that comes with being part of a family. In April 1846, the Donner party consisting of 87 men, women and children set off from Illinois en route inland to California on the west coast of the USA. Unfortunately for the group they reached the Sierra Nevada mountains later than expected and became trapped by an October snow storm and camped to face the winter. Come spring, 40 of the party had died due to the atrocious conditions. But curiously, a high proportion of people who survived were members of family units and a high proportion who died were young men travelling alone. Only three of the 15 single men survived and the only woman who died was travelling in a small group of four.

We're just not loners and family holds a special place. James Bain spent 35 years in a Florida gaol wrongly sentenced for a crime he didn't commit. When he was freed in December 2009 he was asked on the steps of the court house how he got through so many years in prison. He answered with his engaging smile, 'By maintaining myself and to get home to my mum.' When asked what he planned to do now he was out, he said, 'I'm going home with my family. I'm going to see my mum. That's the most important thing in my life right now.'

We are not surprised by this human response. It is a key part of what it means to be human and an instinct we share with chimpanzees.

Taronga chimpanzees

Through my work using zoos as a base, I have become friendly with a number of wonderful primate keepers. Louise Grossfeldt is head of primates at Sydney's Taronga Zoo and her colleague, Allan Schmidt, is a senior member of her team. They generously share their stories of their chimp community to assist leaders gain insight into the natural condition for social animals.

The chimpanzee community at Taronga is one of the best zoo-based communities in the world, mainly due to the size and complexity of the group that reflects the wild condition of chimps. There are 19 individuals in the chimp community at Taronga. The 19 chimps represent six families. There are three adult males, and the multi-male, multi-family nature of chimpanzee communities is a key part of the social complexity, coalitions and politics in the life of a chimp.

In November 2009 the chimps at Taronga were temporarily relocated while their exhibit underwent a major refurbishment. The relocation was as sensitive as an office move, planned with as much thought as we would expect our office move to be managed. Louise and her team planned the move around family groups. The politics amongst the male chimps also featured prominently in the keepers' planning. Adult males are almost always rivals for the top job, and the relationships between males is observably more intense and more dynamic than between the females.

The first group moved the 200 metres to the temporary exhibit was the alpha male, Lubutu, and his family along with the two oldest females. Lubutu was comfortably established in his new territory when on the third day the second of the adult males arrived.

Chimbuka, this second male, was still unconscious and in the care of the vets when Lubutu spotted him. All hell broke loose. Lubutu went into a wild display, hair hackled so he looked twice his size, screaming and banging on walls and screens. A fully-grown adult chimp with around five times the strength of a human male creates an awesome display. Arrivals of females over the previous two days had not created such a response from Lubutu.

After his health check Chimbuka was left to wake up in the den. When he did wake Chimbuka freaked out. In the wild, male chimps never leave their territory so being moved to a strange location would indeed be instinctively frightening. The keepers opened an access raceway so the females might greet and comfort him.

But the females were reluctant to go to him, presumably frightened by Chimbuka's frenzied display and presumably torn by the decision confronting them—on the one hand, if they left him alone his mood might deteriorate and he might become more dangerous, yet if they went to him they might be attacked. The group of seven females plus juveniles and infants wavered at the edge of the raceway some ten metres away. They oscillated, teetering on going forward and then shrinking back. Individual chimps, not moving themselves, encourage others to go forward. No one moved. The group was frozen.

From the back of the pack comes Bessie, Chimbuka's 60-year-old grand-mother. She wants to get to her grandson. Bessie is frail, stooped and moves awkwardly. She is blocked by the band of petrified observers. Like Moses, she parts a path and makes her way through the group. Finally, she gets to the front of the pack. She crosses the precipice and reaches her grandson. She pauses just before him as if saying, 'Come here, Sweetie' and gives him a big hug. The reassuring effect is instant—Chimbuka quickly calms down. The other females now gather round and reassure him. There are some things only a mother or grandmother can provide.

Family as the organisation building block

Given that we humans moved from villages into offices and factories only 250 years ago (and for many countries outside the Western world, many years fewer than that) we bring the basic construct with us to work—our need to bond intimately with a few people. These people become our 'as if' family and we want that group to be close-knit and functional. Many of us even describe our teams as being 'just like family'.

Given the critical role of family for the human condition, it is not surprising that our organisations are, or at least should be, built upon family-sized work groups of around seven people. This was the natural size of family in primitive days—mum and dad, perhaps a grandparent and a few children. The range in this group is five to nine, or seven plus or minus the standard deviation of two.

'Seven' is significant for the human brain. The working memory of the brain has, on average, the capacity to handle seven items. After seven, plus or minus two, we tend to make mistakes. Seven digits of a telephone number are quite easy to remember, while eight is challenging for the average human. Up to seven is the number of people that work in a syndicate team at a conference—eight is quite dysfunctional due to the increased mathematical combinations. In a study by physicist Peter Kline of Medical University of Vienna analysing the size of a committee that is the most dysfunctional, the number that stood out as the worst was the committee size of eight.

Seven or so people as a group is the size that can best create a sense of intimacy. *The Economist* magazine asked Facebook to test whether the technol-ogy of social networking revealed any trend of people's intimate contacts. In the research conducted by Dr Cameron Marlow, the 'in-house sociologist' at Facebook, *The Economist* reported:

> ... What also struck Dr Marlow ... was that the number of people on an individual's friend list with whom he or she frequently interacts is remarkably small and stable. The more 'active' or intimate the interaction, the smaller and more stable the group.
>
> Thus an average man—one with 120 friends—generally responds to the postings of only seven of those friends by leaving comments on the posting individual's photos, status messages or 'wall'. An average woman is slightly more sociable, responding to ten. When it comes to two-way communication such as e-mails or chats, the average man interacts with only four people and the average woman with six ...

The analysis concluded that despite the capacity of online social networking sites, humans 'still have the same small circles of intimates as ever'.

The family paradox

There's a paradox in this instinct for leaders and team members. On the one hand we have this instinctive need to bond closest with around seven people. We want our work team to be *as if* it is family. We know that nothing drives us to distraction faster than if our team is dysfunctional. And in turn, if it *is* dysfunctional we hold our leader most responsible. This is our natural model.

Yet on the other hand, and here's the paradox, our work team *cannot* be our family. Our true family is our immediate family with whom we have our closest genetic bond. Nothing replaces kin, and it is our real family alone that, in the normal condition, endures a lifetime. Our work team cannot fill that role. So when people refer to their team as 'family', it's important not to take that literally. A team leader needs to manage this paradox. People want to work in a functional team where they are secure in their relationships with each other and confident in the support the leader gives them. But there is a line the team leader can't cross. For example, the team leader shouldn't talk to people at work with the same candour that they would use with their immediate family. If the leader did, there is a good chance the staff would be aggrieved and resentful—and the leader might be counselled.

Here is an example of the family paradox. Say you are a team leader and you have someone in your team with powerful body odour. Other team members constantly complain to you about the obnoxious smell of their colleague.

If the situation involved direct family members the matter wouldn't be a problem and would be solved without great thought or sensitivity. A parent or sibling says to the smelly individual, 'Johnny, you stink. Go take a shower.' Johnny is unlikely to be seriously offended and the parent/offspring/sibling relationship is at no risk of being damaged. While we want to experience a strong connection with our work team *as if* we are family, our social boundaries forbid us to talk as directly as this at work, at least without risking offence. The manager in this particular situation must find a more careful and sensitive approach. The stakes are high in the conversation when it occurs.

When I mentioned this scenario to a group of leaders, one of them confessed that this exact situation confronted him some years before and that the way be managed it was not one of his better moments. Unable to find a way to pluck up the courage to raise it with the employee, he left a note on the person's car windscreen that would be seen after work. The individual never appeared back in the office, no doubt embarrassed by the complaint and probably angry with the manager. Few managers would handle this challenge well. That's how delicate it can be when we are managing non-family.

Awareness of the implications of this paradox assists leaders to be grounded in the reality of what's possible and what's not, and as a consequence, to overcome one of the inhibitors to effective leadership.

Dynamics of a newcomer

Managers and zoo keepers have a lot in common. A newcomer to a small group affects the team's dynamics. We've all noticed team members sizing up a newcomer and the new person working out where they fit in. After all, it's *as if* someone has joined our family. Even the power of the boss can be affected, for better or worse, by a new arrival. With social animals, like chimps, gorillas and humans, things can get pretty tricky when introducing a new member into the group.

In April 2010 the keepers at Melbourne Zoo began managing the introduction of a gorilla to the zoo's gorilla community. Damian Lewis is a primate keeper at the zoo and one of the generous keepers who share their experiences with our clients. Several months after the introduction he was sharing the story with a group of leaders—who could readily identify with the dynamics in the family group associated with a new 'team' member.

At the time of the introduction the group comprised a silverback male and four females. A fifth female, Mbeli, was transferred from Taronga Zoo. One of the reasons for the transfer was the 'team' dynamics of the group. The silverback, Rigo, was not a very dominant leader—not as dominant as you would expect in the normal course of things for gorillas. As a consequence of this lack of power by the silverback, the most dominant female, Yuska, pretty much ran the show. She henpecks Rigo and dominates the females—who support her against Rigo. His lack of leadership confidence reflects his upbringing. He grew up alone, which for social animals like gorillas has left him lacking social skills and not well adjusted to living in a group, let alone being the dominant and mating male. While he got the job of silverback because of his technical capability (his genes), he has shortcomings in terms of interpersonal and leadership skills. Young Mbeli, aged seven at the time, was a socially confident individual and the plan was that she would make a positive impact on the dynamic of the group. What unfolded was startling, yet not so different to a workplace team.

Now, the keepers don't just throw the individuals together. It's very carefully planned. For the first month the interaction was limited to visual contact through a glass window so they could see each other but not touch and then with a mesh between them so they could just touch. Then the physical contact started first with the youngest member of the group, 10-year-old Johari, then Rigo and then two of the three adult females. Only the dominant female, Yuska, remained.

At this point Mbeli had been present for over two months. Throughout that time Yuska was aggressively demonstrating, screaming and banging on the mesh. A gorilla with any social awareness would know that Yuska was threatening and trying to put Mbeli in her place. Well, when the keepers opened the mesh to finally allow them to meet, Mbeli took the initiative. She charged Yuska and punched her in the face! Yuska retreated. For good measure, Mbeli took a bite out of Yuska's shoulder. It was a cat fight.

After three months of separate introductions the group was finally allowed to be together. Yuska chose an interesting strategy to retain her dominant position. At the time of the group first being together, Yuska was in oestrous—the sexually receptive stage of her cycle. For the three years since Rigo had joined the group as the silverback, Yuska had shown no sexual interest in him and for that whole time had refused to mate with him. Suddenly, with the introduction of Mbeli, she changed her strategy and presented herself for mating. She has continued to regularly mate with Rigo even when she is not in oestrous.

Even within a month of Mbeli's arrival the keepers observed a positive impact on the culture of the group. Rigo's position was enhanced and Yuska's much reduced. The females were less inclined to support Yuska so she was no longer able to run the show. It seemed to be a more stable, harmonious group. Rigo was more in charge, which is what a gorilla group expects from its silverback.

It sounds like just another day in the office, right? Well, maybe not in every respect. Damian makes the point that the objective of this gorilla team is simple and straightforward: to reproduce. Yet even such a natural objective gets complicated and derailed by the dynamics and politics of the group.

IMPLICATIONS OF THIS INSTINCT FOR LEADERS

Here's a snapshot of what we have learned about the family element of the instinct of *social belonging*.

1. We gain our identity as a member of a small intimate group of around seven people.
2. We carry this *as if* family model with us into our workplaces.
3. Yet our work team cannot really be family—that's the preserve of direct family members.
4. Hence a leader in modern workplaces is challenged with a paradox of leading a family size group which desires to act as if it is family but can never be and should not be so.

There are significant practical implications of our natural family condition which, if incorporated into your toolkit, will make managing people easier.

Implication 1. Team size

The size of a team determines whether it is set to be functional or dysfunctional. To be designed to be functional, teams should number around seven members.

If a manager is leading a team much smaller than five or larger than nine, it's useful to know that there will be some unnatural challenges.

A small team of, say, two people is too small for those two individuals to feel a sense of belonging. Typically, small teams suffer a sense of isolation. Small teams should be merged or at least connected at the next level so that individuals have a sense of belonging to a family-sized unit.

Teams can be too big. If a team is larger than nine people then the team is too large for people to have an intimate sense of connection and too large for the manager to lead.

In some organisations teams swell to 15, 20 or even 30 people. Be aware that such over-sized teams create a foundation of dysfunction. The leader is not able to spend the necessary time with each person. The team will struggle to deliver outputs. Team members become frustrated that the leader can't respond to their requests fast enough. Factions or cliques will emerge in the team. This group is way beyond the size with which we bond intimately.

A group of middle managers of a manufacturing business shared with me their recent experience. They had teams of around 30 people reporting to their team leaders. The teams were structured around this size in order to save 'unproductive headcount' of managers. The assumption was that because the work of the 30 staff was routine production work, the structure could work. Frustrated with the low level of productivity in the group and after trying a range of possible solutions, the managers finally changed the structure and appointed team leaders to lead teams of around seven. Instantly the facility became more productive. Decision-making sped up, production obstacles were removed, groups were more efficiently in touch with each other and resources were more appropriately allocated.

The ideal is seven, plus or minus two, meaning between five and nine. This team size applies irrespective of the level of the organisation. A senior team of 14 will be too big for the executive members to gain a sense of intimate connection. Cliques will most likely form. A team this size will have duplicated functions and a width of coverage too broad for the head of the team to sufficiently cope. For senior executives a team size of five to nine is functional for another reason—such a team will naturally represent the range of functions that the CEO will need a line of sight to. These roles will represent the voices the CEO needs at the table for effective decision making. If the CEO has many more than nine voices, it can almost be guaranteed that voices will be duplicated and energies diluted. With such a large team the CEO will also be trying to skate across too many subjects and the operation will be hampered.

Flight Centre is a global organisation employing around 14,000 people in the travel industry. The company is regularly awarded Best Employer status in countries where it operates. One reason for its ongoing success is that it bases its organisational structure on human instinct principles which it calls 'family, village and tribe'. In its retail travel stores, call centres and central functions, Flight Centre has teams of no more than seven staff. According to the Human Resources Director, Michael Murphy, 'Any time we compromised the rule of seven and even had eight staff in a store, productivity dropped. From painful experience, we will not compromise team size, our family team, of seven in number. This family unit is a foundation of our business, both in terms of the connection of people and the accountability of managers.'

For Flight Centre, if a store is generating business that justifies more than seven people then the company opens another store in the same neighbourhood. The company will pay the extra infrastructure costs of a second store rather than suffer the predictable decline in productivity that accompanies a team larger than seven.

Flight Centre wisely knows that it's impossible for staff to connect to a human group of 14,000. However, they also know that they *can* have a highly engaged group of staff if there is a strong sense of belonging. If staff members are highly connected at the local level within their team of seven and in their village of around 80 people then the company has a band of loyal, energetic people. The company has replicated this model around the world and attributes its growth, stability and sustainability to this principle.

Implication 2. Role of leader

The human instinct to connect with a small group of others gives clarity to the critical role of the team leader.

The natural condition for human family groups is to have a leader. This need for a leader of work teams applies irrespective of whether you manage a team of front-line sales staff, call centre operators or lead the top team. The team leader's task is to be the effective leader of a family-sized group.

This role as the leader of a group of humans is both empowering and also carries with it obligations. It is indeed empowering for a leader to know that their people want someone in the leader role. Our natural model for our small group of intimates is to have a leader. The single leader model is still present in the natural family of mum and dad because both parents need to work as one and not allow mum to be played off against dad and vice versa—in functional families the two parents act 'as if' there was one leader/parent.

New managers are often uncertain of their role and power, so this insight should help them to have increased confidence in their leadership role. The team wants and needs them to be the leader. It also helps leaders promoted from within the team to make a quick transition from peer to leader. If the new manager continues to act as peer versus leader, they are leaving a leadership vacuum.

Yet there are also certain obligations that come with the team leader role. If the leader doesn't fill those obligations then there can be only one result for human groups—without a leader the group will become dysfunctional. The same thing happens to chimpanzees in the absence of a single leader. Dr Goodall witnessed a two-year period amongst the Gombe chimps when there was no single leader of the community. There were two males competing for the top position, so during those two years the community was in chaos. One of the measures of dysfunction, she says, was that the other males used the opportunity to try to improve their social position and mating success. Only when one of the males achieved dominance did the community return to normal and harmony was restored.

So on the one hand people are fine about having a person fill the role of leader. But the leader also needs to sign up for the obligations that come with the leader role. The leader must:

- set the vision and direction for the team so people have context for their role
- connect the group to the rest of the organisation so they can see the value they provide
- be an advocate for the team
- provide appropriate resources so people can succeed

- defend the team against unreasonable demands of others
- set goals so people have clarity in their role
- give feedback to help people learn and grow
- value people's contributions
- provide an environment where people can progress to enhance their social standing
- take care in bringing new members into the team
- set the standards of behaviour and performance
- hold to account those people who don't work to those standards
- minimise rivalries, address any conflict within the team and ensure harmony.

If the leader doesn't deliver on these dimensions the group will be weakened, will be dysfunctional, performance will suffer, the leader will be considered inadequate and members of the team will want out to go join a functional team that acts *as if* it's a family.

Implication 3. Gaining loyalty as though people elected the leader

Repeatedly, we are reminded of the impact managers have on staff engagement and retention. The Corporate Leadership Council conducted a study on the work attribute that most causes people to stay with their current organisation. The study explored 23 job attributes to find what people are least likely to trade off to leave one organisation to join another. It might surprise that the one attribute least likely to be traded wasn't work challenge or location or company reputation or base salary. The attribute least likely to be traded off was manager quality. That is, if a person works for a good boss then they are not likely to change jobs, and as the study showed, if a person works for a good manager then any next employer has to offer so much more to attract that person away from their current job.

It's clear that bosses are important and have a significant impact on people's morale and output. Leaders should maintain a focus on serving their team. While it's most likely that the team leader was appointed to their role by their own boss, a guiding principle should be that if the team was asked, they would elect their boss to indeed be their leader and along the way would re-elect them to remain in office.

Implication 4. Protection of the family unit

An extension of our mental framework of belonging to a small intimate work group *as if* we are family is that we expect the leader to protect members of the team. We *expect* a manager not to compromise the interests of the group in favour of their own. We *expect* a manager to protect us from criticism, to protect our resources and keep us from being overloaded and under-appreciated.

Of course, we shouldn't expect managers to fight for us as much as they would their real family. For primates, protection of family is also primal. Close family genetic ties can sometimes lead to dark behaviour. Taronga chimps Koko and her daughter Kamili on one occasion attacked Shabani when he was an infant. Shabani's mother, Shiba, came to her son's rescue. A year later Kamili had her first offspring. Shiba, presumably holding a grudge that had festered over the year, attacked and killed Kamili's newborn. Perhaps the score was settled, or perhaps the family feud was consolidated.

Implication 5. Integrating new members

Like the gorilla Mbeli joining the group, the dynamics of a newcomer to a team can be delicate and the leader plays a key role in effectively integrating new members to the team.

Primates have a cute way of signalling that a youngster needs to be given time to learn the society's ways. Chimps and gorillas are born with a tuft of white hair around their bottom. The infant will have this white tuft until around the age of four or five. The keepers call this tuft a 'learner's plate'. While they have this tuft of hair they are given great latitude by the adults. They are allowed to take food, to jump on the adults, punch the alpha and generally run amuck. After all, the little chimp doesn't know any better. It's like the latitude we give to a toddler. But when the young chimp starts losing its tuft of white hair, then it's welcome to the adult world! As the youngster starts to be disciplined and first incurs the wrath of an adult, this can be quite a shock.

New members need to be integrated into the work group. In instincts terms the challenge is to quickly move new members from stranger status to in-group status. Through the lens of human instincts, leaders need to look after the basics of integration: of having equipment and space ready for the person on their first day, of informal introductions to break the ice, of providing clarity of the group's purpose and values and to facilitate the new person becoming an immediate contributor to the group's purpose. The lens also explains why the team leader should take the lead in the integration and not be too quick to pass the person to others, a theme we return to at various places in this book.

Implication 6. Freeloaders and social rejection

For a social animal, rejection from the group is of ultimate significance. On the savannah plains to be stranded alone or with just your family without group support would most likely be catastrophic. No wonder managing poor performers to the point of dismissal is one of the hardest things a manager gets to do. A social animal would not take such a situation lightly.

Yet as long as we have been around human societies have needed to respond when it has a freeloader in its ranks, when someone is flouting group culture or harming group success. In his book *Hierarchy in the Forest*, anthropologist Christopher Boehm outlines the four levels of increasing sanction that human groups traditionally deploy to discipline a difficult member. First the person might be treated as a nonperson (ignored). If that didn't do the trick, then the person might be shunned (ostracised so nobody cooperates with them) after which they might be expelled from the group and the 'ultimate distancing is execution'. As we might talk about at work that the objective of attending to a poor performer is to try to correct their behaviour rather than result in termination, Boehm points out that, 'Social control … is often about pro-socially oriented manipulation of deviants so that they can once more contribute usefully to group life.'

Instincts helps explain a leader's discomfort in confronting and perhaps threatening termination of employment of a team member, yet also provides a message to leaders that every so often a leader might need to address asocial behaviour of an individual for the benefit of the group. This has been an aspect of human living and a leader's lot for the duration of our history.

Clan

Apart from our family-sized group, there is a second group that gives us our sense of identity and which is critical to humans as social animals. This group is known as our clan and, in the natural course, comprises up to 150 people.

Social living was the key survival strategy for early humans. The savannah was a hostile and short-lived place for a solitary human or even a small lonely family. Compared to other animals on the plains of Africa also battling to survive, humans don't have the same natural survival tools—we're not strong like an elephant, we don't run fast like a cheetah, we don't fly like eagles or vultures, we don't have sharp night vision like a cat and we're not armed with poison like a scorpion. Our method of survival was social living—our families gathered in groups.

Group size is related to the size of the human brain. Our brain size allows us to associate with groups of up to around 150 others. Oxford professor Robin Dunbar is an expert on the topic. He argues that living in complex social groups demands a significant amount of intellect. Being a social animal, to get on you need to know who's connected to whom, which family is not getting on so well with another, who is on the outer with the leaders and who recently won favours. This takes a fair amount of brain power. Dunbar has found a link between the ratio of brain to body size and the group size of animals (well, more accurately the ratio of the neocortex and body size). Humans have the biggest brain per body size of any animal on the planet. This larger brain allowed us to live in bigger groups than, say, chimpanzees, gorillas or monkeys. On Dunbar's analysis the brain per body ratio of humans correlates to a community size of 150, which is indeed the size of primitive, or natural, human groups.

Chimpanzees are the second brainiest animals on the planet. They have the second largest brain per body size. On Dunbar's analysis, chimpanzees would live in groups of around 55 on average in the wild, which is what happens. The main Gombe community, the Kasekela clan, numbers around 50 chimps.

For animals with a survival strategy based on family groups, there are great incentives for families to gather together. For starters, it's the best defence against predation where bigger numbers can protect each other. There's also attraction in sharing duties and sharing the search for food. In sourcing food, there's a fair chance that if you miss out on finding food for a few days your family might not starve because another family will have enough to share, as yours did last time or might do next time.

The magical 150 appears in various places.

- On Facebook the average number of friends in a network is 120.
- For most people, if you take the time to list your friends and acquaintances your list will total around 150.
- The ex-global CEO of Proctor & Gamble was personally involved in the career planning for a key group of 150 high potential people.
- The prehistoric Tonga navy, a highly effective conquering force, built war canoes that were powered by 150 rowers.

If 150 is the number of people we naturally associate with, we have a fundamental challenge when our organisation grows beyond that size. Our brains are just not large enough for individuals to associate with and gain identity in organisations of 2,000, 20,000 or 200,000. Our brains are not big enough to manage the social and political complexities in groups significantly beyond 150. In larger organisations, then, people will naturally associate with their department, subsidiary or geography of a human scale of up to 150. 'Silos' will naturally occur in large organisations, so any search for an organisational structure that removes silos in large organisations will be rather fruitless (although senior leaders can mediate to reduce the natural sub-allegiances and selfish rivalry). The better organisational design question is to ask, 'Where do we want the silos to form?' Large organisations numbering way beyond the normal human number for connectedness will fracture into groups that individuals can most associate with.

The significance of 150 is further demonstrated by what repeatedly happens when small organisations grow towards that number. Consistently, people in organisations experiencing growth toward and beyond that threshold start to say, 'It's not as friendly as it used to be', and, 'We don't know everyone like the old days'. Often in these smaller organisations the founders sense but don't consciously realise the increased complexity that occurs when the organisation grows closer and then beyond the 150 mark. At this point the complexity is not linear—it's exponential. When the organisation was 20 people then 30 then even 70 the founder knew each person well and was close to the job each person performed. As the organisation grows beyond 100 or so the founder can't be across the level of detail that they used to be. They also start to rely, or should rely, on another level of management. Often the founder, not realising the significance of the growth, has not put in place the necessary processes, systems and capabilities to manage the growth in a sustainable way.

A significant implication of our clanning instinct is that we have an inherent fear of strangers. Over the millennia of our hardwiring circuitry, strangers mostly meant no good. More likely than not, they represented disputes over territory and competing claims over resources. In large organisations, colleagues outside *our* clan are *like* strangers. A 'them and us' occurs within the organisation, usually on geographical, functional or business unit lines.

Chimpanzees also display strong 'them and us' behaviours. At one point Dr Jane Goodall observed the Gombe community fracture into two groups, perhaps due to the increased population beyond the natural sized group. The smaller breakaway group took up occupation of a neighbouring territory. Competitive group rivalries boiled over into brutal warfare. Over the following two years, the main established group hunted down and killed all members of the splinter group. And these were individuals that up until recently had been part of their community.

While in organisational life our response might be more subtle, the intent is not such a long way from the Gombe chimp actions—we become protective of our in-group, we battle for resources, we talk disparagingly of the *other* department and conflicts can be more emotional with intra-organisation groups that we should by rights be friends with!

We will talk more about silos and the implications for leaders in the next chapter. At this point let's look at the implications of the clan size of 150. I won't go into as much detail as I did for the family-sized leader because the focus of this book is the role of the leader of immediate teams rather than leaders of the 'village' or the 'tribe'.

The implications for leaders

First, the decision-makers in charge of organisational design should take into account natural clan formation in the structure of the organisation. We can create structures where the organisation uses group size advantageously. If we design our organisation according to human instincts we will harness natural energy. If we ignore human nature there's a good chance we will design dysfunction into the system.

Gore Associates is the highly regarded firm and maker of Gore-Tex. Gore deliberately uses group sizes of 150. When Gore builds a new facility it provides car spaces for only 150 cars. When the car park starts to reach capacity, it's time to build a new facility.

I referred earlier to Flight Centre. With its 'family, village, tribe' strategy, Flight Centre groups a certain number of family-sized stores or teams together in their geography so that there are around 80 to 100 people in a village. These village groups are encouraged to select nicknames for themselves, to create an identity, and the annual primary recognition awards go to a village group. Flight Centre in effect uses the clan-size concept to foster a healthy sense of rivalry rather than allow the rivalry to emerge in an unplanned and unmanageable way.

Second, senior executives, knowing the natural inclination for bonding is around 150, can guard against behaviours that undermine the cohesion of larger groups. Knowing that intra-organisational rivalries will tend to appear, a chief executive can choose to be watchful and move quickly to stop the behaviour. And for a CEO it's handy to know that intra-group rivalries are accelerated because of the behaviour of the CEO who favours one division or function over the others which quickly causes cliques within the top team that cascade through the organisation (we will return to this point under the instinct of *gossip*).

Third, the role of department leaders—leaders of the village-sized group of up to 150 staff—is critical. After a person's immediate manager, the divisional leader is the next most critical person who provides people with a sense of belonging within their work community. The divisional and department leader sets the culture and provides harmony within the clan. The department leader needs to:

- know the names of all their people
- know the important things that define them as individuals
- know their role and they must know the leader values their role
- establish the direction, goals and purpose of the clan
- create an environment where the managers pull together
- convene social functions so people have a sense of community

- coach their first-level managers to address any community freeloaders who are diminishing the community's efforts and interests.

Fourth, for hierarchical animals like humans, team leaders (including senior executives) should be conscious of the distribution of power in their team. In particular, leaders (and designers of organisations) should avoid the concentration of power in a single direct report. That is, avoiding the formal or informal deputy or 2IC ('second in charge') where one person in the team of reports carries extra power differentiating them from the rest.

One CEO shared with me the negative consequences of a structure where a Chief Operations Officer reporting to him had much more power than the rest of his direct reports. The COO had the key operating units and most of the organisation's staff reporting to her. The imbalance of power in the hands of one direct report weakened both the CEO and also the functioning of the organisation.

Fifth, the first-level leaders of family-sized groups need to connect their team to other family groups in the clan. Team leaders need to manage the natural tension of both providing for their family (so they are not taken for granted or lose out on resources) while ensuring they deliver the outputs on which other family groups within the clan are relying. Team leaders need to ensure that their people are seen and valued by higher-level managers as part of the individuals' social progression, and to ensure that higher-level management is seen and involved with the team so the team members feel connected and well regarded.

Genghis Khan

Genghis Khan knew the importance of organisational structure. In 1203 he undertook a major restructure of his army using principles closely aligned to human instincts as the basis.

The results of Genghis Khan's restructure were spectacular. Applying today's business terminology, we would say he was the leader of a high performing organisation! Here are the highlights of his performance review: He united the Mongol people for the first time in their history. In a 25 year period his army conquered more people than the Romans conquered in 400 years. He organised history's largest free trade zone (the famous Silk Road). He created the first international postal system. He created a system of international law. He recognised religious freedom and financially supported Christian, Buddhist and Moslem faiths. His creative and fearsome military capability made walled cities redundant as a defence against attack. On the balanced scorecard, his staff were highly engaged and no general ever deserted him throughout his six decades as a warrior.

His organisational challenges were as complex as a modern global CEO's, with 100,000 warriors spread from China through India and the Middle East across to Hungary and Russia.

Genghis Khan used family-sized groups as his organisational foundation, arranging warriors into squads of ten (*arban*; granted, slightly more than the ideal 5–9 range). No matter what their kin group or tribal origin, they were ordered to live and fight together as loyally as brothers. No one could ever leave another behind in battle as a captive. As in the family model of the day, the eldest took the leadership position in the group of 10, but the men could also choose another to be their leader.

This legendary warrior was serious about the role of the family-sized group. His law recognised group responsibility and group guilt. The family group was responsible for ensuring correct behaviour of its members. Giving a whole new dimension to performance management, a crime by one could bring punishment to all!

He used clan-sized groups as his next layer. Ten of the squads formed a company (*zagun*) of 100 men, one of whom they selected to be their leader. Ten companies formed a battalion (*mingan*) of 1,000 men. Ten mingan formed a *tumen* of 10,000, the leader of whom was chosen by Genghis.

He also had an elite personal bodyguard numbering … wait for it … 150 soldiers!

It's really not surprising that Genghis Khan would organise his 'workforce' according to human instincts. Given that we are talking about the human condition, that knowledge was as available then, 800 years ago, as it is today. It's just that sometimes we forget and tend to overcomplicate things.

Families and clans are a key part of our survival strategy as a species. But social groups of smart animals can only function through a hierarchy or a pecking order. We now turn to that aspect of human instincts.

Instinct 2. Hierarchy and Status

This instinct helps explain why:
- my boss keeps me waiting but never keeps their own boss waiting
- status symbols keep popping up
- technical professionals with little interest in the 'people stuff' still accept a promotion to manager
- powerful people can do strange things.

IT WAS LIKE THE PLOT out of a bad movie. In November 2008 the CEOs of the three US automotive companies (Ford, General Motors and Chrysler) went to Washington seeking government funds to keep their organisations out of possible bankruptcy. Despite the desperate state of their businesses driving them to beg for money, they each flew in and out of Washington in corporate luxury jets. Not a good look.

On one level their behaviour was just plain dumb. On another level it reveals a significant human dimension that not just one, but all three no doubt highly intelligent leaders demonstrated such astonishing behaviour that was so out of touch with the moment.

The three CEOs arriving in their $36M aircraft at a round trip cost of 70 times more than a commercial flight begins to make sense if we look through the lens of power and status. The thought of taking a commercial flight like everyone else was obviously something they couldn't contemplate, and even if their advisors were brave enough to suggest it, the advice was obviously rejected. Yet still they didn't get it. From the frosty reception they received, one would presume that the CEOs would make a wiser choice next time. Well, hardly. The second time they travelled to Washington they went in hybrid vehicles, still wanting to differentiate themselves from ordinary folk. While we might marvel at their insensitive behaviour, it can be explained if we understand the tendencies of those who hold high-power positions.

Power is central to the functioning of human groups. Human groups function *because* of hierarchy. The same is true of chimpanzees. Chimps are hierarchical animals, meaning that within their community there is a pecking order. In chimp society the top of the hierarchy is occupied by a male, the so-called alpha male.

Lubutu, the current alpha male of the chimps at Taronga Zoo, became the alpha at the young age of eight years. He was the oldest male at the time when Gombe, the then alpha, died. Lubutu's acclimatisation to power gives first time leaders some valuable lessons. When Lubutu became the alpha he appeared to lack confidence. His leadership style was best described as passive. He did not exert the appropriate power of his position and he refused to intervene in squabbles amongst members of his community; he would literally look the other way! Like the experience of many a first-time leader, some of the members of his community supported his 'appointment' and some didn't. One of the females, Shiba, for instance refused to accept him as alpha, indicated by her refusal to submit to him—she refused to be dominated by him. He was still just a boy, so he didn't have the physical strength to back himself and exert his position. But as he physically matured he grew into his role and appeared more comfortable in using the power of his position. Now almost ten years in the role, he has grown into a very constructive leader who uses power appropriately to the apparent benefit of his community—the Taronga group is a productively reproducing, reasonably harmonious group that replicates behaviours typical of wild chimps.

Lubutu's key leadership strategy is to be friendly to the females and their offspring. He invests time in grooming sessions with the females. He lets the infants play with him and spends time with the teenagers. Consequently, the females (the majority of his community) appear to like Lubutu. Certainly they get to show their preference for him over the rival males.

One day in August 2009 Lubutu was temporarily absent from his 'organisation'. Lubutu's absence reminded me of a conversation with a HR director when she told me what happens when her CEO is away from the office on business trips: 'When our CEO is away the executives go feral!'

Lubutu had gone to the vet for a vasectomy. He was out of the community for a mere half day. But that's long enough for aspirational males to take advantage. Beta male, Shabani, seemed to rejoice in his good fortune to have Lubutu out of the way. When Lubutu did return to the exhibit he was no doubt uncomfortable from the operation. Shabani, presumably sensing his discomfort, displayed aggressively over Lubutu who had a reduced capacity to fight back. With hair hackled in a fierce display, Shabani screamed at Lubutu then chased the weakened alpha and, when he caught him, bashed him.

Lubutu may have thought his days as alpha were over as he hung on by a thread late into the afternoon. With night approaching, the 19 chimps filed into their night den. What happened next is fascinating and reveals the benefits of Lubutu's friendly leadership style. Shabani is habitually and unpredictably aggressive, often attacking the females and infants to force his will. In the night den the female chimps expressed their preference for their leader by gathering around Lubutu and groomed him reassuringly. They turned their backs to Shabani who was ostracised like an unwelcome stranger. By the next day Lubutu had regained his strength, was still the alpha and continued the unending task of holding the top job.

This demonstration of support by the chimp community might explain Dr Goodall's observation that constructive alphas usually endure as leaders for around ten years, but bullying and intimidating alpha males tend to last for only about two years.

One of the most constructive leaders of the Gombe chimps was Figan, and the one who appeals to me as the standout leader over these 50 years of Gombe research. When Dr Goodall and I met in late 2008 I was keen to hear more about Figan and she added to what I already knew from her books. Figan was alpha in the late 1970s and early 80s and one of the most powerful males Dr Goodall has observed (he also had the support of his brother, Faben, so anyone who challenged Figan had to be prepared to take on both brothers in coalition). Figan's outstanding attribute was that he used his power constructively and did not bully or intimidate his community (at least relatively speaking for an alpha chimp). But he did use his power to insist on appropriate behaviour. As Dr Goodall wrote, 'I suspect that many would-be aggressors, anticipating the displeasure of their boss, exercised more self-restraint when he was around.'

The observed outcome of Figan's leadership style is persuasive. Dr Goodall writes that his style 'helped to promote and maintain an atmosphere of social harmony among the members of his group'. During Figan's reign most of his interactions with members of his community were relaxed and friendly. 'He was so clearly dominant over them that, except when there were moments of tension such as during a reunion, he had no need for violent demonstrations of strength and mastery.'

Not all alpha male chimps are as constructive as Figan in the way they exercise power. Figan's nephew, Frodo, became alpha male some years later. Frodo was one aggressive alpha, leading through bullying and intimidation. When I asked Dr Goodall about Frodo, she replied that he always showed the personality of a bully. Even as a youngster, when the other young chimps his age were playing and saw Frodo approach, they would suspend their game because they knew the tyrant was about to destroy their fun. The bully of a kid grew up to be a bully of a leader.

Power is a natural dimension to life for hierarchical social animals. It comes with the domain. The challenge for leaders is to use power effectively. This means using just the right amount of power that is appropriate for your position. We will come back to this and other implications for leaders later. First, we need to discuss the importance of social standing for humans—our standing in the pecking order.

Social standing

With so much riding on our position in the hierarchy, it is little wonder that we place such an emphasis on signs of our social standing and so much energy on progressing in our social group. Social standing, or status in the hierarchy, explains a number of curious behaviours in organisations.

Hierarchy and status explains who keeps who waiting. The team leader might keep a staff member or external supplier waiting yet would not keep their CEO waiting for a second. The CEO might keep a lower level manager waiting, yet this same executive would not dream of doing the same to a Board member. That's life for social primates. We can of course choose to treat people equally and not keep lower ranking people waiting! They'll appreciate it.

Hierarchy and status explains why people who have their own office often fight and scream against any move into open-plan design. And it's why, when forced into an open-plan configuration, some might collect bigger and better pot plants than their neighbours ... or they gain the preferred position by the window ... or mysteriously procure a leather chair ... or sit closer to the Director (who retained their office).

Hierarchy and status explains why in organisational life we naturally tend to have grades and job titles, and along with the instinct of *contest and display*, it's why people can be touchy about job titles—especially how their title compares with their peers.

Early in my career I worked as a human resources officer in a manufacturing firm. At the factory there were two car parking areas—one for managers and one for the workers. The managers' car park was located, not surprisingly, in the privileged position alongside the office block. The employees' car park was at the edge of the site. Being an eager young HR professional, I had in mind that it would be a grand sign of equality if we removed the managers' car park.

When one particular young and extremely capable engineering manager heard about my proposal he quickly sought me out. He'd only just gained access to the managers' car park through a recent promotion and passionately argued to retain it. He enthusiastically made his point: 'When I first joined this firm as an apprentice I had aspirations to progress. I would know that I had made it when I gained rights to park in the managers' car park.' The equivalent to Lubutu's rock at Taronga Zoo.

Years later, armed with the insight of instincts, I could see his point. It doesn't mean that there is not a case for egalitarian leadership. It does mean, though, that try as we might to remove symbols of position in the pecking order, they will keep popping up. And any opportunities to progress in our social group are generally extremely motivating.

Hierarchy provides a vital function for complex social animals. It provides the means by which social animals can live and function. Human groups are able to coordinate their efforts because of hierarchy. This applies to work organisations, to church groups, to sporting groups and to political parties. The largest organisation in the world is reportedly the Chinese army with 1 million people and a human group that size can still function—because of hierarchy.

Political parties are a useful study because they are so on display. If hierarchical power is not clearly in the hands of a single dominant individual, then the political party is weakened until that situation is resolved. In the Primaries leading up to the 2008 US Presidential elections, the Democrat Party had two primary contenders in Senators Obama and Clinton. For the time that the candidature was unresolved the party was divided into two factions. There was rumour and innuendo directed from one candidate to another. There were coalitions and alliances. And the situation continued until Senator Obama pulled away as the preferred candidate and then the party was able to settle its differences and unite. Senator Hillary and ex-President Bill Clinton swung behind candidate Obama. The party became united and the single leader had the power and authority to harness the resources and energy for the campaign.

For organisations, it is reassuring for leaders to know that the natural and necessary pattern is that people work for a manager, the manager in turn works for a boss and on up to the CEO. This reporting hierarchy, formalising the pecking order, allows organisations to function. But it also means that if each leader does not deliver what they need to at their level then the organisation will rapidly become dysfunctional.

Indicators of power

A key aspect underpinning *hierarchy and status* is the dimension of power differences in groups. In making sense of *hierarchy and status* in organisations, it's handy to know the behaviours that are typically displayed by people with high power or low power.

Researchers from Stanford University and the University of California studied the positive and negative indicators of power. They found 'striking differences in how powerful and less powerful individuals perceive and act within the social environment'. They hypothesised that elevated power provides rewards and freedoms while reduced power is associated with increased threat and punishment.

They listed the attitudes and behaviours typical of powerful people. Some are positive and some are negative. Not all leaders in high-power positions demonstrate these behaviours, but the research revealed the strong tendency for them to do so.

Positive implications of power

On the positive side, when people are in positions of relative power they are more likely to:

- initiate ideas and be more direct in their expression of ideas
- engage in group activity
- express approval and affection
- show more gestures and less facial construction
- display smiles of pleasure
- feel and display positive emotions.

Negative implications of power

But when people are in positions of relative power, they are also more likely to:

- take what they want for themselves and be quicker at detecting material rewards
- treat any situation or person as a means of satisfying their own needs
- talk more, speak out of turn and interrupt more
- ignore what other people say and want
- ignore how less powerful people react to their behaviour
- act rudely and be more aggressive
- enter the social space of others
- tease and be more aggressive in their teasing
- stereotype others
- eat with their mouths open and get crumbs on their face and table!

Eating and leaving crumbs on their face and table? When I mentioned this one day to a group of business people on one of our zoo workshops, one participant laughed and told a story about her CEO who never interrupts his lunch routine but continues to eat ravenously, always makes a terrible mess of his chin, tie and table in apparent oblivion to his hungry visitor watching on.

The point behind these negatives is that high-power people *can*. They *can* talk when they want to even if that means interrupting others; they *can* detect and take rewards for themselves. Because they *thought* they could, the three CEOs of the US automotive companies were preoccupied with their own interests—but got a rude shock when the reaction of the public reduced their chances of gaining government support.

Of course, we appreciate working for people who demonstrate the positive dimensions of power and who contain or avoid the negative tendencies of power.

Managing power in organisations

The famous Milgrim research is a sobering reminder to leaders of the power of their position. In 1974 Stanley Milgram conducted studies of positional power. One of his studies involved a 'teacher' administering electric shocks of increasing voltage to a 'learner' each time the learner made a mistake. The subjects, filling the role of teacher, believed that the experiment was a study of the effect of punishment on learning, when in fact it was a study of the influence of authority.

The individual subjects in the role of teacher were unaware that the learner subjects were actors who feigned the pain of the electric shocks. While the teachers hated what they were doing and pleaded with the researcher that they be allowed to stop, no teacher steadfastly refused to administer the shocks *before* the 300 volt level. Notwithstanding their anxiety, the teachers abided by the instruction to keep delivering the electric shocks. About two-thirds of the teachers pulled every one of the 30 shock switches up to the last switch (450 volts) until the researcher ended the experiment.

Milgrim explained that this was indicative of a deep-seated sense of duty that people have to those in authority and a reluctance not to defy the wishes of the boss.

Organisations with good cultures implement systems to constrain inappropriate use of power by managers. For ten years from the mid-80s I worked for IBM. Here was an organisation with effective systems to manage power. The systems constrained managers by equipping staff with ways to complain of alleged inappropriate use of power by leaders. The systems included open door reviews, anonymous 'speak-ups' and regular employee surveys. Leaders in the organisation knew that if they abused their power they would likely be found out and the issue addressed, including possibly being moved from their leadership role. There were consequences. Leaders were appropriately constrained.

Motivation to lead

A potential tension associated with the status drive explains why some people accept management roles but have little interest in the people aspects of their elevated job. The natural way to progress in the organisational hierarchy is through the management line. And not surprisingly, strong technical performers are naturally promoted to lead the team of technical professionals. The problem arises when people with little interest in leading are promoted. People without an interest in managing people might accept the manager role because it provides for them the desired elevation in their social group. It is often the fastest way up the pecking order. But while their status is enhanced, leaders with little interest in managing people will struggle with this key dimension of their job.

Professor Nicholson calls this interest in leading a 'motivation to lead'. He points out that some people, through the make-up of their personality, just don't have an interest in leading and that such folks should not be put in charge of other people.

Chimps, too, seem to vary in terms of individual interest in leading or not leading. Dr Goodall could see whether an individual male from a young age appeared to have the personal drive—the personality—to seek to be alpha.

When Figan was a youngster, Dr Goodall saw from his form of play that he had the personality to try to be the alpha. As a youngster, Figan was apparently impressed with how Mike rose to become the alpha. Mike, at the time the lowest ranked male, became skilled at using empty kerosene cans that were stacked near Dr Goodall's camp at the time. Mike developed a technique of incorporating these cans into his dominance display and became so skilled using three cans as props that he rose through the ranks until he reached the alpha position. (We'll come back to Mike's display later.)

Like a human child kicking a soccer ball and imagining World Cup glory, young Figan practised using the cans. He was the only one that Dr Goodall observed playing with the cans. She would sometimes see him all alone, in a clearing in the jungle, skilling himself with the cans. He appeared to be readying himself for the contests he would need to take on as an adult. Years later he was ready to rise through the ranks and did so to become the alpha male.

IMPLICATIONS OF THIS INSTINCT FOR LEADERS

Here's a snapshot of what we have learned about the instinct of *hierarchy and status*.

1. Hierarchy helps complex social animals function in their communities.
2. Progression in the pecking order is a strong motivator.
3. Leaders should have the most power in their group.
4. There are positive and negative tendencies associated with power.
5. The appropriate use of power is a key leadership dimension.

There are significant practical implications of *hierarchy and status* which, if incorporated into your toolkit, will make managing people easier.

Implication 1. Licence to lead

A reassuring implication of this instinct is that the natural order of human groups is to indeed have a leader. The leader has a licence to lead. Without leadership, human groups become dysfunctional.

Knowing that leaders have a licence to lead is of particular importance for first time managers and managers appointed from within their team. First time managers are often uncertain in their role. *Hierarchy and status* should give them confidence that the team wants them to lead. But if the leader doesn't lead, someone else will assert themselves to fill the void.

Implication 2. Motivation to lead

We just covered the possible tension caused by a team leader who is driven by status to accept the job of leader but has little or no interest in doing the 'people stuff'.

How appealing to you are the tasks outlined in Instinct 1 and repeated below? These are the people-leadership tasks that come with being the leader of a family-sized team:

- set direction for the team so people have context for their role
- connect the group to the rest of the organisation so they can see the value they deliver

- be an advocate for the team
- provide appropriate resources so people can succeed
- defend the team against unreasonable demands of others
- set goals so people have clarity in their role
- give feedback to help people learn and grow
- value people's contribution
- provide an environment where people can progress to enhance their social standing
- take care in bringing new members into the team
- set the standards of behaviour and performance
- hold to account those who don't work to those standards
- minimise rivalries, address any conflict within the team and ensure harmony.

It's a demanding list. To repeat, the good news is that people *want* an effective leader. The bad news is that if the leader doesn't deliver on these responsibilities, the group will become dysfunctional.

If the list of activities doesn't appeal to a prospective team leader, they should either re-evaluate whether people management is for them or accept that they need to take an interest in providing these responsibilities to the team and acquire the skills to do so. Motivation alone to progress in the hierarchy is not enough.

Implication 3. Use of power

Power can be underused or overused.

Overuse of power by the boss can drive compliance. Most people want to keep in sweet with the boss. Why wouldn't they? It's the surest way to keep your job, get a pay rise and progress in the organisation. The trap to avoid is where the boss drives compliance by being dismissive of contrary views. The more sensitive the boss is to disagreement, the more people wisely avoid debate. As a consequence, the boss creates distance between themselves and their followers and denies themselves useful information.

Underuse of power by the boss can drive confusion, ill-discipline and disharmony, where people are uncertain of the expectations and standards of the group. In this case, someone else will likely emerge as the actual leader in the boss's place.

The leader's goal is to use just the right amount of power for their level—not too much and not too little. Following the lead from Lubutu, a good dose of friendliness is a useful leadership strategy. If the leader is unfriendly then, being human, team members will respond by keeping out of harm's way. It only takes one event of intimidation for people to keep their distance. A reassuring sign that people perceive their leader as friendly is whether they express disagreement when they hold a view different to their leader. They can only afford to do so if they hold no fear of retribution.

Implication 4. Allocation of resources

One of the ways leaders get to exercise power is in the allocation of resources. Leaders should be comfortable in doing so and in using this power thoughtfully. Resources have value if the item is valued by the receiver and the giver.

In the wild, chimps hunt meat. But they seem to hunt for social rather than nutritional reasons. For Dr Goodall's Gombe chimps the most common prey is a red colobus monkey. For the energy expended for the meagre 1 kg of meat on a baby monkey, chimps would be better off foraging for nuts and fruit if the purpose was nutritional. But chimps appear to hunt for social reasons. A hunting party is most successful when there are between four and ten gang members. When a kill is made the prey is appropriated by the alpha male. The prey becomes a resource. At Gombe the alpha male shares the meat in a deliberate, consistent way—he gives a greater share to his allies and he ignores his rivals.

In organisational life there are a range of 'resources' that the boss gets to allocate. Just to name the most common: grades, promotions, appraisal ratings, salary reviews, bonuses, sales quotas and territories, projects, budgets, office space and development opportunities. Use them well.

Implication 5. Three warnings by the silverback

A silverback gorilla provides a model in socially constructive discipline and maintaining acceptable standards of behaviour. A leader on one of our programs at Melbourne Zoo asked the keeper, 'What does Rigo do if one of his group is misbehaving?'

The keeper, Damian Lewis, nodded knowingly. He tells how Rigo, the silverback, has a three-step warning process! His first step, the bottom of the disciplinary stage and the lightest touch, is just his mere presence. Damian described how two female gorillas were bickering, and Rigo strutted past them as though he just wanted his presence noted. That is usually enough to stop the offending behaviour. If that doesn't work, his next warning is verbal—he coughs at the offending individual(s). That's often as far as he needs to go in signalling his displeasure. The point of the escalating warnings is that the ultimate discipline, a physical reprimand such as a slap or a hit, is rarely required. However, if the short sharp cough doesn't work, then the next step, just short of the ultimate leadership discipline, is a charging display. One hundred and sixty-five kilograms (363 lbs) of charging silverback generally works. But if not, on those rare occasions when steps one to three don't work, Rigo will use his ultimate disciplinary act and hit the offender.

Maybe there is a natural pattern for social animals where 'anti-social' behaviour is corrected in an orderly fashion and ultimate acts (physical for gorillas and termination of employment for us in organisational life) is reserved for rare occasions when verbal and written warnings don't do the trick. One can imagine the chaos, though, if Rigo either doesn't use his position to stay on top of group standards or if he is too quick to race to the ultimate discipline act and misses out on the first few steps.

Implication 6. Social standing

After the wellbeing of our immediate family the second most important motivation for humans is our standing in our social group. The team leader has significant impact on the regard in which their people are held in the eyes of others, both within the team and in the wider organisation. It's little wonder that 80% of people who resign from organisations do so because of an unsatisfactory relationship with their immediate manager.

To deliver on this key motivation a leader needs to provide their people with opportunities to grow and impress, to protect and enhance the reputations of individuals on the team and to acknowledge their achievements so confidence is enhanced.

Implication 7. Regular review meetings

The single most important technique that I recommend to leaders is to hold regular individual reviews with their people. This means scheduling an hour's review no less frequently than once every two weeks with each of their direct reports. A meeting lasting less than one hour is unlikely to cover the subjects that should be covered. In Instinct 7 on Empathy we cover this topic in more detail and include a possible agenda for the reviews.

Implication 8. Making sense of the matrix

Anyone who has managed within a matrix will know its complexity. In case you are not familiar with matrix reporting (and you're fortunate if you don't operate within this structure) it means that a person reports to two bosses, where one boss is the business unit or functional boss and the other boss is perhaps the location manager. The business unit boss is often based at a different location to his or her direct reports. The structure expects us to be part of two teams and to attend to the requirements of both bosses.

This dual reporting is unnatural for humans, as it would be for chimps. Our natural pattern, being an animal where a pecking order is natural, is that we screen for a single line of reporting based on power. A key issue with matrix reporting is that it denies reality (we will discuss the instinct of *confidence before realism* in Instinct 8). Expecting people to report to two bosses is unrealistic. The real line of power is the boss who has the control of resources (budgets and headcount) and the primary financial reporting responsibility. People work this out incredibly quickly.

The person primarily frustrated in the matrix is the less powerful boss, for example the location boss. This person is trying to fulfill their responsibilities as the location executive, but they have little or no formal power to cause others to respect their power and to abide by the normal reporting protocols. The location manager might even have trouble insisting that people attend location meetings.

Given that you are probably not the designer of the organisation, an implication for a leader working in a matrix is to be aware of your natural tendency to focus on only one line of reporting (the boss who has the control of resources) so that you deliver in a leadership sense what your organisation needs of you right now. In this situation you need to be a balanced member of two teams.

Implication 9. Managing up and down

In my book, *The Boss*, one of the characters makes the observation that managers tend to be good at either managing up or managing down, but rarely both. Staff members are quick to spot if their boss prioritises managing up.

A leader good at managing up will tend to:
- focus most on the needs of their superiors
- spend a disproportionate amount of time grooming their boss and other people higher in the hierarchy
- probably sit close to their boss's office even if that means being further away from their people
- demand outputs from their people with insufficient resources
- be prepared to compromise the team's interests to protect their own
- avoid challenging the system.

These behaviours erode the loyalty of their people. But it does mean that the leader is probably well connected with people in power, which will be of some benefit to the team (and may well enhance the leader's chances of progressing in the hierarchy).

A leader good at managing down will tend to:
- focus most on the needs of their people

- spend a fair amount of time with the team
- sit close to them
- give them resources
- protect them from unreasonable demands
- challenge the system where necessary
- decline to turn a blind-eye.

While the team will appreciate their style, the downside is that such a leader might be seen by people higher in the organisation as difficult.

In many organisational cultures, it is difficult for a leader to be good at managing both up and down. The ability to do so, apart from the leader's own bias, will be driven by the culture of those in the high-power positions and whether those people are easy to please and expect managers to be effective at leading their people. Politics for social animals can be quite a challenge!

So far we have covered how humans *live*. Together, the first two instincts describe a species that lives in hierarchical social groups. We have covered how leaders can use that natural orientation to make their job as a leader easier and more successful. The remaining chapters can be categorised as instincts that reflect the way humans *think and feel*. They relate to how we process information, how we make decisions and, in an evolutionary sense, how we make ourselves attractive to a member of the opposite sex as a potential mate. We'll build up the picture as we go.

Instinct 3. Emotions Before Reason

This instinct helps explain why:
- we jump to conclusions
- the meaning we attach to other people, and they to us, is based on emotion
- people are predictably irrational
- we produce more on days of positive emotion

A FRIEND ONCE TOLD me a story about a small business. This business was owned by a husband and wife and employed eight workers. One Monday morning just after 9 o'clock the couple made an announcement: 'Could everyone please stop work. We have some important news.' They asked the employees to immediately join them in the kitchen at the round table they use for lunch and tea breaks. The workers obediently stopped what they were doing and filed into the kitchen with puzzled looks on their faces. Such an impromptu staff meeting this early on a Monday was unusual. When everyone had gathered the husband began. 'Thanks everyone. We have some important news.' He paused to let his wife continue. People tensed. 'We've had a terrific last quarter financially,' she said with a big smile, 'and we want to share our success with you!' The husband waved eight small envelopes. 'These are for you,' he said, 'one each. Inside your envelope is five hundred dollars! Now you can take your envelope, but on one condition—that you leave work *right now*, spend your money *today* and come back at 3 o'clock and show the rest of us what you bought.'

That's a nice story, but where did your mind go first when you read, *Could everyone please stop work. We have some important news?* What did you think the news might be? I have told this story to hundreds of people and almost always the reaction is to assume the worst—something bad is about to happen. That's natural and expected. At the end of the story people say, 'I thought the business was about to close.' Someone else nods and says, 'I thought the husband and wife were separating.' Another might say they thought the business was being sold.

Due to the way our brains are wired and from our instinctive behaviour, we can predict two reactions to this story as it begins.

First, we jump to conclusions. We do not suspend judgment waiting in a neutral state for the story to unfold. This is because we process information based first on emotion. If we were rational beings we would stay in a neutral state until all is revealed. As emotional beings we don't do that. We race ahead and anticipate.

Second, the conclusion we jump to will overwhelmingly be negative. We assume the worst. From a survival instinct that is just as well. Assuming the worst will tend to keep us out of harm's way. As neuroscientist Antonio Damasio says, he can't imagine an individual being wired other than for first screening for pain and danger. If we were wired for pleasure above pain we could not survive at all, he says. (We will talk more about *loss aversion* in Instinct 5.)

In the modern workplace we tend to think of ourselves as rational beings. This assumption both misleads us in our thinking about people and limits our effectiveness as leaders. Humans are primarily *emotional*. The basis on which we make sense of our world and the way in which we make decisions is overwhelmingly emotional. The best leaders and most effective business professionals are acutely aware of the primacy of emotions and consciously use the role of emotions in the way they operate and how they relate to and seek to influence others.

There are two key dimensions driving the dominant role of emotions in how we process information. One is the role that emotions play in the way we create meaning in our world. The other is the actual wiring of the brain.

Imprinting

The meaning we attach to words, to other people, to places and to our experiences reflects the emotion that those words, places and people generate for us. Without emotion there is no meaning.

In May 2009 I was explaining this central role of emotions to my 15-year-old niece Heather, 12-year-old nephew David and one of their friends, 14-year-old Rachel. Heather, David and Rachel are Americans and live in Milwaukee. I was visiting from Australia and my brother and I thought it would be handy for the kids to know about human instincts. That evening while my brother and sister-in-law prepared dinner we held a 'Human Instincts for Kids' session!

We got to the stage where I was teaching them the prime role that emotion plays in the human condition and how the meaning we attach to people and places is emotional. To demonstrate the point I asked them, 'What meaning does the following word have for you ... Tonga—T-O-N-G-A?' I suspected what their respective reactions would be.

The point of the exercise is that the five letters, T-O-N-G-A strung in that particular *rational* order has no meaning by itself. The meaning relates to the emotion attached to the word from each person's experience.

As though a fun switched had been flicked, Heather instantly burst into laughter. David smiled, though not as intensely as Heather. Rachel looked blank. These were indeed the reactions I had anticipated.

I turned to Rachel, with her blank look mixed with confusion as to what this strange word had triggered in the other two. I asked again what Tonga meant to her. 'It means nothing,' she said, shrugging her shoulders. That's fair enough because up until this point she had not heard of the Pacific Island country so it had no meaning at all. There was for Rachel an absence of emotion.

Heather was still beaming, unable to wipe the smile from her face. I asked her what Tonga meant to her. 'Fun, happiness, joy!' she laughed. I knew she would say this not just because it was written on her face but because she was nine years of age when she first came across the word and I was with her at the time, six years before. I asked her to explain.

'We were holidaying in Australia a few years ago,' she started, grinning broadly and just getting the words out between giggles. 'It was Christmas Eve and we wanted to open the presents but Grandma has a strict rule that there are no presents opened before Christmas Day. David and I were very disappointed. You (nodding at me) and Aunty Jude (my wife) were there with us. You looked at your watch and it was just after 9 pm, still a long way off midnight and Christmas Day. But then you declared that with the time difference it was just past midnight somewhere in the world. It was Christmas Day in Tonga! We pleaded with Gran that we should therefore be permitted to open at least one present. Like the good sport she is, Gran relented. It was fun!'

Tonga became the humorous Christmas theme that year and Heather was still laughing at the memory. The memory has been consolidated along the way as whenever I see Tonga in the news I email Heather and David the clip.

I turned to David, who was only six at the time of the Christmas experience. 'What does Tonga mean to you?' I asked. 'Fun!' he answered. 'I don't remember the present opening. But I do remember that Christmas we made Tonga ice cream. We stuck chocolate Tim Tam biscuits in the ice cream. The Tim Tams were palm trees. It was fun!'

I'd forgotten that bit, but hey, who can blame a little boy for attaching meaning through an ice cream experience!

Rachel may in time attach meaning to Tonga (and in fact the meaning will have started from that discussion), but for Heather and David, it is highly likely that Tonga will retain its positive meaning for all time—all from one first and significant experience. The only thing that would change their meaning is if they one day visit Tonga and are let down for any reason.

This process by which we create meaning is termed *imprinting*. Imprinting occurs on the first occasion we experience a person, a word, an activity or place. From the first experience we start to create meaning and if the second and subsequent experience is similar to the first then the meaning is consolidated and unlikely to change.

The point for leaders is that your people's view about you is emotional and based on the meaning they have attached to you. You might call it your 'Tonga moment'. If your people were asked the 'Tonga question', *what's it like working for your boss?* their reaction is unlikely to be neutral—it will be either positive or negative reflecting how you lead and what you have done or not done as the leader.

Those who study chimps observe a similar emotional repertoire. Dr Goodall and the chimp keepers at Taronga Zoo say that chimps experience emotions which we label as pleasure, joy, anger, boredom and sorrow. The Taronga chimps displayed sorrow or grief in July 2007 when an old female died. Fifi was 60, a fine old age for a chimp. She had been ailing for a few days when the keepers allowed her to stay in the night den rather than continuing with the normal practice of being outdoors on display during the day. Fifi had prepared her nest and died peacefully.

At this point every other chimp, all 19, made their way back into the night den. They lingered in the raceway a slight distance from Fifi's body. Fifi's family members were the only ones who touched her, the others remaining a respectful few metres away. Kuma, her 16-year-old daughter, sat with her and touched her hand. Four-year-old grandson Furahi jumped up and down on her motionless body.

After a short time the rest of the community drifted off while Fifi's family lingered. Kuma waited until after the keepers had removed Fifi's body, watching her mother being taken away.

Normally, chimps are loud and active. On this morning there was very little noise and no 'wah barking'. For the next week or so the community was subdued. About a week later I was hosting a group of leaders at the zoo. The chimps were noticeably sombre and unusually quiet. They moved more slowly and even the youngsters were subdued.

The brain

The second dimension explaining the primary role of emotions is the wiring of the brain. Recent discoveries of the functions of the brain support the role of emotions in how we make sense of the world and make decisions.

Antonio Damasio is a leading neurologist. He studies brains. In his book, *Descartes' Error*, he guides us through the connection between decisions and emotions. A key discovery of his research is the link between reasoning, emotions, feelings and decisions. The parts of the brain involved in emotion and decision making are generally involved in social cognition and behaviour. In short, emotions and feelings are part of a normal, healthy brain and a normal, socially adjusted individual.

As a neurologist, Damasio gets to study people with brain damage. One such patient he calls Elliot. Prior to his brain tumour and subsequent brain damage, Elliot was a well-adjusted husband, father and employee. When surgeons operated and removed Elliot's tumour they subsequently discovered damaged frontal lobe tissue in his brain, so in removing the tumour the surgeons also had to remove the damaged tissue.

Elliot's change in personality was profound and the reason he was referred to Damasio. While Elliot retained normal capacity for facts and figures, he had a much changed personality. He was unable to make decisions and he also showed an absence of emotion. Damasio was intrigued to find if there was a connection between the two symptoms: absence of emotion and inability to make decisions.

As Damasio describes Elliot, 'his ability to reach a decision was impaired, as was his ability to make an effective plan for the hours ahead of him, let alone to plan for the months and years ahead of his future.' Indeed, 'the machinery for his decision making was so flawed that he could no longer be an effective social being.' Elliot's decision making capability was so impaired that in the simple task of writing a note he could not decide which colour pen to use.

To get a glimpse of Elliot's life, imagine you're a friend of Elliot's and you suggest to him that you go out for dinner. He's hungry so it's easy to agree that you should eat. Then his inability to decide becomes disabling. He can't decide on a restaurant. You finally go to a neighbourhood of restaurants to try to help him decide. You park the car and you walk up and down the street but he just can't make up his mind. Finally, you make the decision on the restaurant. You sit down and the waiter hands you both a copy of the menu. Elliot looks at the menu and just can't decide what to order. He looks at what other people are eating. He can see and understand the ingredients in the various dishes—fish, chicken, beef and various vegetables. He just can't decide what he feels like tonight. Elliot's problem is that he is receiving no emotional signals to help him make decisions, even decisions as routine as deciding what to eat.

One can only begin to imagine how he struggled to function at work and make the hourly and daily decisions one needs to make. He lost his job. Business ventures failed. His wife divorced him. As Damasio describes Elliot, 'he was unable to make choices' and not able to function as a normal human being.

Damasio found the same abnormal behaviour in other patients with prefrontal brain damage. He describes the day when a patient visited his laboratory, and at the end of the session Damasio was discussing with the patient an appropriate time for the next appointment. Damasio suggested two possible dates, both in the coming month and just a few days apart from each other. 'The patient pulled out his appointment book and began consulting his calendar. The behaviour that ensured, witnessed by several investigators, was remarkable. For the better part of half an hour, the patient enumerated reasons for and against each of the two dates: previous engagements, proximity to other engagements, possible meteorological conditions, virtually anything that one could reasonably think about concerning a simple date ... he was now walking us through a tiresome cost-benefit analysis, an endless outlining and fruitless comparison of options and possible consequences.' When finally Damasio suggested the date, 'his response was equally calm and prompt. He simply said: "That's fine." Back the appointment book went into his pocket, and then he was off.'

Damasio's studies of people like Elliot reveal the neurological conditions in which reasoning and decision making, emotion and feeling figure prominently. 'First, there is a region of the brain, the ventromedial prefrontal cortices, whose damage consistently compromises ... both reasoning/decision making, and emotion/feeling, especially in the personal and social domain. One might say, metaphorically, that reason and emotion "intersect" in the ventromedial prefrontal cortices, and that they also intersect in the amygdala.

'Second, there is a region of the human brain, the complex of somatosensory cortices in the right hemisphere, whose damage also compromises reasoning/ decision making and emotion/feeling, and, in addition, disrupts the processes of basic body signals ... (a third brain dimension is explained that we don't need to cover here).

'In short, it appears a collection of systems in the human brain are consistently dedicated to the goal-oriented thinking process we call reasoning, and to the response selection we call decision making, with a special emphasis on the personal and social domain. This same collection of systems is also involved in emotion and feeling ...'

In workplaces we might consider ourselves primarily rational beings, unaffected by or understating the role of emotions. Not so. At least not if you are a normal functioning human being. Our humanness involves this automatic interweaving of reasoning, decision making, emotions and feelings.

Damasio and his colleagues devised a set of experiments to study the interplay of emotions and decisions and to assess decision-making performance. The set of tasks became known as the 'Gambling Experiments'. How would people with damage to the prefrontal cortices compare to normal people, and how about people with damage to their brain other than to prefrontal cortices?

Damasio describes the basic experiment. The subject, known as the 'Player', sits in front of four decks of cards labelled A, B, C and D. The Player is given a loan of $2,000 (play money but looking like the real thing) and told that the goal of the game is to lose as little as possible of the loan and try to make as much extra money as possible. Play consists of turning cards, one at a time, from any of the four decks until the experimenter says to stop. The Player thus does not know the total number of turns required to end the game. The Player is told also that turning each and every card will result in earning a sum of money and that every now and then turning some cards will result in having to pay a sum of money to the experimenter.

The turning of any card in decks A and B pays a handsome $100, while turning of any card in decks C and D only pays $50. The problem is that certain cards in decks A and B (the high-paying decks) require the Player to make a sudden high payment, sometimes losing as much as $1,250. Likewise, certain cards in decks C and D (the low-paying decks) also require a payment or loss, but the sums are much smaller, less than $100 on average.

Unbeknown to the Player, the game will be terminated after 100 plays. There is no way for the Player to predict, at the outset, what will happen, and no way to keep in mind the precise tally of gains and losses as the game proceeds.

In this way the experiment replicates critical elements of our everyday life—we gain bits of information as events unfold, we develop hunches (refer to the next instincts where we discuss *gut feelings*), we steer away from loss (refer to the instinct of *loss aversion*), and favour reward over punishment.

Damasio says that 'what regular folks do in the experiment is interesting. They begin by sampling from all four decks, in search of patterns and clues. Then, more often than not, perhaps lured by the experience of high reward from turning cards in the A and B decks, they show an early preference for those decks. Gradually, however, within the first thirty moves, they switch the preference to decks C and D. In general, they stick to this strategy until the end ... There is no way for players to carry out a precise calculation of gains and losses. Rather, bit by bit, they develop a hunch that some of the decks—namely, A and B—are more 'dangerous' than others ... I suspect that before and beneath the conscious hunch there is an unconscious process gradually formulating a prediction for the outcome of each move ...'

What about frontal damaged individuals like Elliot? Damasio says, 'Their behaviour was diametrically opposed to that of normal individuals.' He describes what happens.

After an early general sampling, the frontal damaged patients systematically turned more cards in the A and B decks, and fewer and fewer cards in the C and D decks. Despite the higher amount of money they received from turning the A and B cards, the penalties they kept having to pay were so high that halfway through the game they were bankrupt and needed to obtain extra loans from the experimenter. In the case of Elliot, this behaviour is especially remarkable because he still describes himself as a conservative, low-risk person, and because even normal subjects who described themselves as high-risk and as gamblers performed so differently, and so prudently. Moreover, at the end of the game, Elliot knew which decks were bad and which were not.

Damasio says that Elliot was fully engaged in the task, fully attentive, cooperative and interested in the outcome. In fact, he wanted to *win*. He just chose disastrously. He didn't develop hunches on imprecise probabilities. He couldn't make good use of uncertainty and he could not make the choices that would be to his advantage and to reduce his loss and maximise his gain.

Individuals like Elliot with frontal lobe damage 'persisted in making the least advantageous choices for longer than any other group of patients so far observed in this task, including several patients with brain damage outside the frontal lobes ... patients with large lesions elsewhere in the brain (not in the frontal lobes) can play the gambling game as normals do provided they can see and can understand the instructions.'

Clearly, the frontal lobe plays a key role in the function of choice in humans. The part of the brain that connects reasoning and emotion plays a significant part in making choices about consequences of future possibilities.

But the link of emotions to the processing of choices was to be even more convincingly demonstrated. A second step of the experiment was introduced. While they played the gambling game, subjects were connected to a polygraph to monitor their 'skin conductance responses'. Skin conductance is the sensation signalled on the skin from emotional stimulation, such as sweaty palms and goose bumps. Skin conductance measures the often subtle secretions of fluid in the skin's sweat glands generated by the autonomic nervous system in response to a thought generated in the subject. The thought will affect the bodily state of the subject which is why polygraphs are used as lie-detectors.

The researchers monitored normal subjects and subjects with frontal lobe damage. Initially both sets of subjects generated skin conductance responses as reward or punishment occurred with each turn of a card. In other words, 'within a few seconds immediately following their receiving the monetary reward or having to pay the penalty, normal subjects as well as frontally damaged subjects were suitably affected ...'

Damasio explains an intriguing discovery of how the response of normal and frontal lobe damaged subjects differed within a few card-turns into the game. 'In the period immediately preceding their selection of a card from a bad deck, that is, while the subjects were deliberating or had deliberated to pick from what the experimenter knew to be a bad deck, a skin conductance response was generated, and its magnitude increased as the game continued. In other words, the brains of normal subjects were gradually learning to predict a bad outcome, and were signalling the relative badness of the particular deck before the card turning.'

A key function of the emotional message the subjects were receiving from their experience was to avoid choices and situations that would be bad for the person.

The further fascinating discovery was that subjects with frontal lobe damage *showed no anticipatory responses whatsoever* ... the neural systems that would have allowed them to learn what to avoid or prefer are malfunctioning, and are unable to develop responses suitable to a new situation.' (Italics in original)

In the uncertain world in which we live a key function of the complex brain systems connecting reasoning, decision making, emotions and feelings appears to serve us well by helping us develop hunches, to avoid loss and pain and to keep out of harm's way. The brain is wired to put the avoidance of loss at a greater premium than the opportunity to gain through the classifying of experiences into good or bad. We will return to these concepts in the next two chapters.

The link between emotion and work output

It won't come as a great surprise that our boss has a significant impact on our energy and output. It's handy to know, especially if you are a boss, that there is one thing that most distinguishes a good boss. To discover what makes a good boss we need to know what goes on in people's heads during a typical day at work. This is what Harvard professor Teresa Amabile and her colleague Steven Kramar set out to discover; they sought to explore what goes on in the 'black box' of people's heads as they experience daily events at work.

Amabile and Kramar had 238 people keep a daily diary of work events. The participants made about 12,000 diary entries that the researchers analysed. The authors found that there is a clear cycle that occurs in people's daily work experiences. A 'daily event' might be from the mundane (a task review, a conversation in a corridor, receiving an email or phone call) to a significant event (the annual appraisal, a presentation to a top team, a major project). The research found a predictable pattern of how people process these daily events. What happens inside the black box? Amabile and Kramar describe four steps.

First, people perceive the meaning of the event. The function of *perception* is sense-making—in human instinct terms, *classifying* (which we'll cover in the next chapter). As we would expect from instincts, this step of sense-making is, as the researchers identified, inexorably connected with the second dimension of *emotion*. People make sense of the event based on how it makes them feel. The emotional reaction immediately affects the third step, *motivation*—if the emotion is positive, then motivation is lifted but if the emotional reaction is negative, then motivation is reduced. The final step in the cycle is that motivation affects *performance outcomes*—a lift or drop in motivation affects outcomes such as productivity, creativity, collegiality and commitment to work.

The authors make the point that work events are happening all the time, so our emotional radar is switched on all the time which is indeed what we would expect from human instincts. It means that our motivation and output are affected constantly by what's happening around us at work. For example, they found that a positive work experience lifts one's creativity by 50 per cent; people are much more likely to have a creative idea on days when something 'good' happens and that this positive impact on creativity can continue for two days.

Not surprisingly from the perspective of human instincts, the researchers found that managers have a major impact on this perception-emotion-motivation-output cycle—causing the cycle to be positive or negative.

The good news is that the authors discovered the *one* most important thing that managers can do to make the cycle a positive one. The finding is this: *enable your people to move forward in their work*. That is, be the sort of manager who enables people to make progress in their daily work! It can be that simple.

This is a wonderful, reassuring message for two reasons. First, any manager is capable of being an *enabling* manager. You don't need to be a certain personality type and you don't need to be a charismatic leader holding mysterious powers. You just need to help people move forward in their work.

Second, the enabling requirement fits the natural pattern of why a manager was appointed as the manager in the first place. Generally, an individual is chosen to manage a team because of their technical expertise—they know the work of the people they will manage. This natural pattern is sensible. To manage a team of engineers you need to know engineering. To be a manager of a team of nurses you need to know nursing and it helps if you're a good nurse. There is sense in this natural order because the organisation and the client or other users of the outputs of the team are best served if the team manager has the technical expertise to lead the team delivering the outputs. The opposite would lead to chaos. So, the best (or near best) technical person gets to be the leader of the team. The good news with the Amabile and Kramar discovery is that a manager is naturally well placed to be the sort of boss who enables their people to make progress in their daily work.

Helpfully, the authors listed *enabling* leadership behaviours. To enable their people to make progress in their daily work a leader needs to:
- set clear goals (what is expected and why it matters)
- provide adequate resources and time for people to do their job
- remove barriers that hinder people
- provide feedback from a learning perspective (not a blame perspective)
- give sincere appreciation for the work people do well.

The fundamental point is that people are continually interpreting events at work through their emotional processes and the events have a consequential impact on a person's energy and output. This flow is going to be either positive or negative, rarely neutral. The actions of the leader have a major influence on whether the flow is positive or negative.

IMPLICATIONS OF THIS INSTINCT FOR LEADERS

Here's a snapshot of what we have learned about the instinct of *emotions before reason*.
1. Our brains are wired to process emotions before reason.
2. Individuals who have suffered damage to their emotional processors don't function normally in terms of social skills and decision making.
3. The meaning we attach to our world is emotional.

4. People's opinion about their boss and their organisation is based on emotion, and is rarely neutral.
5. At times of positive motivation people have higher outputs and creativity.

There are significant practical implications of *emotions before reason* which, if incorporated into your toolkit, will make managing people easier.

Implication 1. Your emotional meaning

Given that we are a species that uses emotion to attach meaning to our world, it follows that for leaders the meaning people attach to the leader is emotional—the 'Tonga test'. If you're a leader, here's a way to test the meaning your people attach to you. Imagine that you are calling each person who reports to you. The staff member is sitting with a friend when you call. Your name appears on their mobile phone screen. What emotion is triggered when they see it's you calling? What do they say to their friend? Do they say negatively, 'Oh, rats, it's my boss.' Or do they say happily, 'Hey, it's my boss!'

What have you done to cause the reaction to be as you would want it to be and what will you do from this point to influence the relationship constructively for people to attach positive emotion to you?

Implication 2. Proactively using positive emotion

A number of leaders I know have thoughtfully used emotions and imprints to create constructive connections with their people. These might trigger ways in which you can proactively use the primary role of emotions to your advantage.

There is the manager who, the evening after interviewing strong candidates for a role, calls the candidate to thank the person for the meeting that day and to have a brief pleasant conversation. This creates positive feelings from the outset.

There is the manager who, conscious that one of their team is spending significant time away from their family on an urgent work assignment, sends a 'thank you' letter home to the person's spouse.

There is the new manager who recognises quickly that her new team has strong negative feelings attached to work, primarily because of the undermining and intimidating tactics of the prior manager. She realises that she'll need to show a lot of care, and give a little time, for the emotional state of the team to shift.

Implication 3. The 'five word' test

Decide the words you would want people to use in describing you.

Readers of my book *The Boss* will be familiar with the 'five word test'. The test is: what five words would you want people to say about you in a conversation with their friends and family? Of course, given human nature, you know people have an opinion of you. It will be positive or negative, and in large degree that opinion is caused by how you relate to your people. Write down the five words you want people to attribute to you as the manager. The five words should be different from each other so there is no repetition and hence wastage of five words. They should be words that you would very much want people to use. Having written the words, all you have to do now is live them. Act according to your aspiration.

A few years ago I gave this 'five words' advice to a leader we'll call Peter who was about to move to Malaysia to lead the company's business in that part of the world. In assisting Peter to prepare for his new role, I asked him, 'What five words would you want the staff to say about you soon after taking up your new role?' He reflected for a moment and then answered, 'Smart (as in intelligent and quick), visionary, caring, a good listener and approachable.' I said, 'Great. A month after you've started I'll ask "Alice", our Kuala Lumpur HR manager, what words people are using to describe you.' About a month after Peter took up the role I called and asked Alice how Peter was going. She answered that he was going really well and the staff appreciated him being in the leadership role. I asked her what the staff were specifically saying about Peter. Alice answered, 'They are saying he is really bright, he's quick at picking up things, that he has a good sense of where the business should be going, that he's a caring sort of person and is impressing people with being approachable and getting back to them. He's a good communicator and when people are with him they say that they always feel they have his attention because he listens.'

Implication 4. Enabling management

To return to the message from the Amabile and Kramar research, the one most important thing a leader can do to make a virtuous cycle out of the connection of emotion and output and how the brain works is to *enable* people to move forward in their daily work. In turn, the most important enabling behaviour is to set clear goals and a clear purpose for the person's work.

There is indeed a reason why HR teams often remind leaders to set job goals for their people at the beginning of the year or soon after a new person starts. When people have clarity about what is expected of them and how their tasks fit into the purpose of the organisation they feel energised and motivated and their performance is enhanced. With this knowledge, for a leader to now choose not to spend time giving people clarity would not be a sensible or informed choice!

Implication 5. Agreement and disagreement is emotional

Dr John Evans works in the field of cross-cultural imprints, where the meaning that we attach to our world is associated with the emotions connected to our experiences. He once gave me some good advice. When we seek agreement with someone, it's handy to know that the other person's agreement or disagreement is emotional; does our proposition *feel* okay to the other person? But if the other person disagrees they won't declare, as they might not even know, that their disagreement is emotional. They will express their disagreement and counter-arguments as rational. Yet, they won't change their mind and agree with us unless we can shift the emotion that they are associating with our argument. So while in the modern workplace our debates are rational, there is an unarticulated undercurrent of emotion.

The benefit of this tip is that you'll need to find the key to shifting the person's feelings so that your proposition begins to *feel* okay.

Implication 6. The power of laughter

Laughter is a great barometer of the emotional environment of a team. It is a good sign if a team is often laughing. People only laugh when they feel safe and secure. The Amabile and Kramar research shows that people will produce more and be more creative on days when they feel good.

We should use laughter as a measure of a team's spirit.

The opposite of laughter is fear, and fear in the workplace is often created by an intimidating boss. Intimidation causes weaker individuals to seek protection and reassurance. While Lubutu, the alpha male of the chimps at Taronga, is generally a constructive and friendly fellow, he uses the tendency of a powerful person to throw his weight around. One morning while the chimps were still in their night den, he kicked off his display ritual, scattering chimps as they sought to escape danger and an unfortunate smack or worse. Fifty-nine-year-old Bessie and 35-year-old Koko were sitting close to each other and out of range of Lubutu's fearsome display. The keeper observed Bessie and Koko look at each other and quickly reach out, putting a hand up to the other's mouth. Putting fingers into another chimp's mouth is a sign of trust, on this occasion presumably signalling in effect, 'We're okay, we'll stick together here and keep out of danger.'

The primary role of emotion is just the start of the story on how we process information. The next two chapters complete the picture. First we'll look at the fundamental purpose of our emotion-before-reason processing to make sense of things, and then in the following chapter we'll turn to what happens if we are unable to make sense of something.

Instinct 4. First Impressions to Classify

This instinct helps explain why:
- we're guided by gut feelings
- people are quick to judge
- anxiety increases if we can't make sense of something
- one department might not get along with another
- we can win or lose people in our first few words.

IT WON'T COME AS any surprise that we humans make quick judgments about people and situations. You've likely experienced what it's like to be judged too quickly and at times you've no doubt been hasty in your own assessment of others. What might be news is the reason we make these quick judgments.

We do so in order to *classify* our experiences. Rather than engage in time-consuming analysis, we rely on first impressions and gut feelings to quickly classify people, situations and experiences.

Our classifications are binary in nature; they are an *either/or* category. The most common is *good or bad*. Other common classifications are *them and us*, *like me or not like me*. In organisational life some leaders claim to have made the *tough* decisions, and people comment on others being *a team player/not a team player*, *with us/against us* and *strategic or tactical*. All binary language. We don't think and talk about someone being 40 per cent strategic and 60 per cent tactical. We think and describe other people and our experiences in black and white terms. There is little grey in the way we classify.

Why do we do this? How quickly do we make up our minds in order to classify? And how can leaders use this knowledge constructively?

We learned in the previous chapter that organisms are wired to keep out of harm's way. Classifying is part of our survival machinery—to screen information into 'good' and 'bad' and other binary categories and to do so quickly. In the formative years of our hardwiring on the plains of Africa this trait served our ancestors well. It meant the difference between life and death where instant reactions were necessary in an often harsh world. We still act this way—all day, every day.

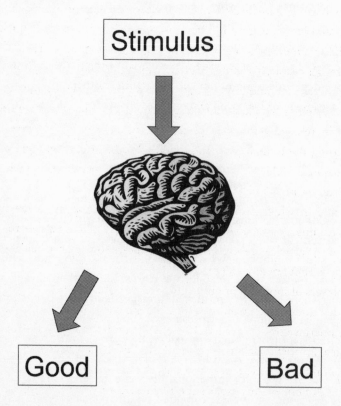

Figure: We instinctively classify into binary options based on our first, instant emotional reaction. We might as well use this instinct thoughtfully.

Partly, the purpose of classifying is to make sense of the world and to do so in a way that allows us to cope with the amount of data and stimuli we are required to handle. We classify the weather into 'fine' or 'poor'. The traffic is 'flowing well' or 'it's a disaster'. When we get on public transport we quickly classify people we're okay sitting next to versus those we're not. The radio announcer classifies to help the audience make sense of what they are hearing—like the announcer recently, after an update from a court reporter explained a case of rape and murder, wrapped up the report with the classifying words 'a *sad* case'.

When we interact with someone, that person is seeking to make sense of what we are saying or doing. The clue to sense-making is that each person is seeking to classify the information shared. Kids know this. A child will say, 'Mummy, Mummy, I have good news!' It's clear to Mummy that what's about to be shared can be classified down the 'good' arc even before hearing the story. As adults and in work-life things tend to be much more subtle. Yet it doesn't have to be so. One way to use the knowledge that people are trying to make sense through classifying is to be explicit in the way we position things. In applying this as a technique, you might find yourself prefacing comments with statements such as, 'I'd like to update you on a good thing that happened just now', or 'There's one item on the project that we need to fix'. The point is that you are using the human processing method to be understood and to allow people to quickly achieve what they need to do when interacting with others; to make sense through classifying.

Any time in which we are unable to classify just delays sense-making. Imagine reading a newspaper without headlines. Headlines provide the classification of the article—a snapshot of what follows so you have classified what the article is about before you read it.

Our powers of intuition or gut feeling are part of *impressions to classify*. Gut feeling, that unexplainable sense of something being good or bad, can be powerful. In one instance it saved a chief executive of a major bank from being caught in a terrorist attack in the foyer of the Taj Mahal Palace hotel in Mumbai, India on the day the terrorists attacked in November 2008. Mike Smith is the CEO of one of Australia's largest banks, ANZ. Checking out of the Taj Mahal Palace hotel to go to the airport, he was early and his host, the local ANZ manager, asked him if he would like to have a drink in the hotel before leaving for the airport. Mr Smith says that he had an uneasy feeling that all was not well. So he declined the offer, explaining to his colleague that he'd be happier just to head to the airport and wait there. He had only just got into the car and driven around the corner when the terrorists attacked the hotel, storming the foyer where he had stood moments before. Mr Smith credits gut feelings with saving his life that day.

Building on what we covered in the previous chapter on emotion, the process of classification is done primarily on the emotion we feel at that screening moment.

Here's an example of a positive classification based on first impressions. A few years ago I was attending a meeting at a Westin Hotel. I arrived by taxi. As I stepped out of the cab the hotel porter handed me a business card which contained a four-digit number, 6641, and he said with a smile, 'Sir, welcome to the Westin. This card contains the number of the taxi you have just arrived in, which you might need just in case you left your mobile phone or wallet in the taxi.'

'Wow!' I exclaimed, 'Thanks very much. I really appreciate that!' What an instant positive impression! I have immediately classified the hotel as *good*. At this point I haven't even entered the hotel and I'm already impressed with the service. The first experience becomes the imprinting experience, and if the second experience is similar to the first then the imprint is consolidated and unlikely to change. I entered the foyer and wasn't sure where to find the meeting room. A hotel staff member offered to help. She was friendly and directed me where to go. This was the second experience, consolidating the imprint or classification. Two things happen from this point. The first is that I will, and indeed I do, associate positive emotion with Westin. A Westin Hotel logo anywhere in the world triggers happy thoughts! Second, I am going to give Westin a fair degree of latitude if they disappoint me sometime in the future. That's the power of first impressions—once we make up our minds we are much less likely to change our opinion (or reclassify). The Westin makes this work for them by creating a positive first impression.

Equally, a first impression can generate a negative classification, like in the case of Lani, a young chimp at Taronga Zoo. Lani is now eight years of age. When she was three she was introduced to turtles for the first time. Alone at the time, she was exploring the edge of the moat that separates the chimps from the public. In her exploration Lani came across an Eastern long-neck turtle. For years the turtles had been laying their eggs in the chimp exhibit. She was playing with this turtle when suddenly it bit her finger. Lani screamed. The turtle hung on as Lani waved her little arm trying to shake the turtle off. Still the turtle hung on. Presumably in Lani's mind, *turtles* were instantly classified as *bad*, as she later made a regular practice of going to the moat to kill them. Amongst the young chimp community the practice of killing turtles soon spread. After Lani's first experience the keepers observed a band of youngsters trailing Lani heading down to the moat with apparent intent on hurting the turtles. The young chimps would catch a turtle, pull the shell apart and throw the wounded turtle to each other, biting into the shell. The routine became part of the culture of the youngsters of the community until the keepers intervened to save the turtles.

We have the benefit of Dr Goodall's observations of wild chimps to know that *classification* occurs naturally. There was one male called Prof who, unusually for a chimp, had a negative classification of monkeys. This originated from a nasty experience when Prof was only two years old. He was attacked by an adult male colobus monkey and had a toe bitten right off. 'That experience left Prof with a deep-rooted fear of monkeys. He did not start hunting monkeys until he was eleven, some six years after some other young chimps. And even then, his hunt was half-hearted. If a large male approached him, he whimpered in fear and hid behind his mother.'

How much time do we need?

It's no surprise that with our powers of intuition we need little time to judge strangers—to *classify* them, generally into a binary alternative of whether we like them or dislike them. How *little* time might surprise.

Two Harvard researchers, Ambady and Rosenthal, turned their minds to this question in a leading study published in 1993. Up until this point studies of strangers assessing each other had focused on five-minute observations. That turns out to be significantly more time than we need.

The setting for Ambady and Rosenthal's study was university teaching. First they took what we'll call the control evaluations. These were assessments made of 13 teachers by students at the end of a semester; by the end of a semester you would know your teacher well. The students rated the teachers on 15 behavioural dimensions: accepting, active, anxious, attentive, competent, confident, dominant, empathetic, enthusiastic, honest, likeable, optimistic, professional, supportive and warm.

Next they took video footage of the teachers giving classes. This footage would be cut into small, or 'thin slice', segments to show subjects who had never met the teachers. How similar would their judgments about the teachers be to those made by real students after a semester with these same teachers?

The strangers viewed 30 seconds of video footage comprising three segments—10 seconds from the beginning, middle and end of the video. Only the teacher appeared in the footage so there was no other information to go on, and the sound was turned down so only nonverbal behaviour was observed. Each teacher segment was shown only once.

Stunningly, the assessments of the 15 attributes made from just 30-second exposures by people who had never met the teachers were substantially similar to the assessments made by students after a whole semester with the very same teachers. The correlations on the 15 attributes ranged from 0.6 for accepting, attentive and honest up to 0.89 for active and enthusiastic (with confident and optimistic also in the high 0.80s).

And then the researchers wondered that maybe people don't need 30 seconds to make up their minds and to do so accurately. How much time do we need? The researchers reduced the 10-second video clips down to five-second and two-second clips. With three clips in the one showing, strangers would look at either 15 seconds or even just six seconds in total.

And still the ratings made by strangers and course evaluations made by students after spending an entire semester with the instructor were strikingly similar. We make surprisingly accurate assessments on thin slices of information. As the researchers concluded, 'Judgments based on 30-second exposures were not significantly more accurate than judgments based on six-second exposures.' The findings work in two directions. Not only are we humans remarkably accurate with the impressions formed from a small amount of information, we also communicate a great deal of information about ourselves.

In a recent study (2007), Dr Dana Carney from Columbia University Business School in New York and her colleagues have added significantly to our understanding of judgments based on thin slices of exposure. They wanted to study when our first impressions are more likely to be right or wrong and how much time people need to increase the likelihood of producing an accurate judgment. The setting for the study was college students getting acquainted with a member of the opposite gender. Five slices of time were examined: 5, 20, 45, 60 and 300 seconds.

The first stage of the study involved around 100 female and male college students coming into the laboratory on five separate occasions for a two hour research session. All participants were videoed while engaging in a five minute paired interaction with a single member of the opposite sex. The pairs were to talk about whatever they liked in order to create an informal situation. From this body of videotaped interactions, 30 (15 female and 15 male) individuals (only one from each pair) were chosen to be the *targets*. The targets were rated by people who knew them well on eight criterion behaviours or constructs (positive affect, negative affect, neuroticism, extraversion, openness, agreeableness, conscientiousness and intelligence). ('Negative affect' is judging the extent to which someone is feeling badly.) To provide a comparison to later thin slice assessments, each construct for each target was measured in different ways to provide a robust index of each dimension.

So having developed comprehensive measures on each of the targets, the next step was to thin slice the video footage. The five minute actual interactions were cut into the five different length slices ranging from five seconds to the full five minutes, with segments taken from the beginning, middle and end of the interaction.

Three hundred and thirty four participants were then recruited to view and judge the tapes. Generally the judges were asked to rate targets on a scale from 1 (not at all like the target person) to a 5 (exactly like the target person) on the eight personal attributes.

The findings add substantially to our understanding of accuracy of first impressions. First of all, 60 seconds is about the time we need to make an accurate first impression across all dimensions studied (longer than Ambady found but consistent with Ambady was that emotional information and extraversion—essentially the dimensions measured by Ambady—were remarkably readable after only a few seconds). Sixty seconds exposure yielded more accurate judgments than smaller slices. But increasing exposure time to five minutes did not increase accuracy obtained from one minute.

In terms of accuracy for significantly thin slices of exposure of around five seconds, the research found that the most accurate judgments made regarding people were negative affect, neuroticism, openness and intelligence. Accuracy was no different at five minutes than at five seconds. The researchers supposed that quick and accurate judgments for negative/threat dimensions and competence might be critical for life-saving or life-promoting outcomes.

So, if we rely on our very first impressions from five seconds, we might be right with respect to some characteristics of a stranger but substantially wrong on others. Yet after a minute we will be substantially right on most dimensions. So we're still talking about a small amount of time in which people will be generally accurate in their judgments of other people!

One possible interpretation of these studies is that people only need seconds to make up their minds and that anything beyond these first seconds or minute is superfluous.

A second possible explanation is that once we make up our minds, any further information about the other person confirms the assessment that we have made. In other words, we look for supporting evidence and we interpret subsequent information to fit our assessment and once we *classify* we are quite unlikely to change our minds. Perhaps the students in the real classes in the Ambady study also made up their minds about their teacher the moment their teacher walked into the classroom for the first time, and then subsequent experiences with the teacher over the semester confirmed their first impression (the psychological principle of 'confirmation bias').

This does indeed appear to be the case.

In another study, one morning 55 college students in a psychology course at the Massachusetts Institute of Technology were told that their regular teacher was not available and there would be a substitute. They were informed that at the end of the class they would be asked to complete a questionnaire about the teacher. Before the teacher arrived the bio of the substitute teacher was distributed to all students. What the students didn't realise was that there were two bios—half the class got one bio and the other half received the second. The bios were the same except for two words. Here are the two bios—can you spot the two words that are different?

Mr X is a graduate student in the Department of Economics and Social Science here at MIT. He has had three semesters of teaching experience in psychology at another college. This is his first semester teaching Ec 70. He is 26 years old, a veteran, and married. People who know him consider him to be a very warm person, industrious, critical, practical and determined.	Mr X is a graduate student in the Department of Economics and Social Science here at MIT. He has had three semesters of teaching experience in psychology at another college. This is his first semester teaching Ec 70. He is 26 years old, a veteran, and married. People who know him consider him to be a rather cold person, industrious, critical, practical and determined.

Yes, in one of the bios the substitute teacher is described as being 'very warm' and in the other as 'rather cold'. *Warm* versus *cold* is another good example of a binary, either/or, classification.

The teacher then appeared and led the class for a 20 minute discussion. During this discussion the experimenter, who had posed as a representative of the course to introduce the teacher, kept a record of how often each student participated in the discussion.

All students had the same experience—the same class given by the same teacher. At the end of the class the questionnaire was distributed for the students to indicate their opinion of the teacher. Answers on the questionnaire were anonymous. The students wrote free descriptions of the teacher and rated him on a set of 15 rating scales.

Sure enough, the influence of first impressions was significant. Those students who received the 'warm' bio were inclined to *like* the teacher. They described him as 'considerate of others, more informal, more sociable, self-assured, more popular, better natured, more humorous and more human'. Those students who received the 'cold' bio tended to *dislike* him and described him as, 'self-centred, formal, unsociable, uncertain of himself, unpopular, irritable, humourless and ruthless'.

The influence of *warm* or *cold* pre-information also influenced the interactions students had with the teacher. Fifty-six percent of warm subjects entered the discussion whereas only 32 percent of the cold students did so. Our first impressions affect our interactions and communications with a person. If we take a dislike to someone we will tend to interact with them less which will restrict our access to data that might change our minds.

Two words were enough to colour the students' opinion and influence their subsequent experience. That's the power of classifying: we go on very little information, rely on hunches and intuition, and once we classify, usually in binary terms, subsequent experiences are interpreted according to—and to align with—our first classification. Once we make up our minds about someone or something, it takes an awful lot to shift our opinion.

While the findings may be disturbing that people can be so judgmental on such shallow information, the more resourceful approach is to use this knowledge to make informed choices in the way we interact with people, especially as a leader. Your mind has probably jumped to the importance of the first impression you make as a manager on a new staff member joining your team or when you are pitching an idea. Yes, you have only a few seconds! Let's add to this concept and then share a specific technique in how you can use this knowledge.

The magical number 7

The significance of the first few seconds and a small amount of data is related to the capacity of our brain. At least in recent history, psychologist George Miller appears to be the first person to identify the significance of seven items of data. In a 1956 paper he outlined a pattern from research that we have the capacity to process seven, plus or minus two, items of information before we start to make mistakes. He called this our capacity for making 'absolute judgments'. As the amount of information increases, a person will begin to make more and more errors.

He reviewed studies involving different stimuli, for example people making judgments about tones, loudness and tastes (different concentrations of salt). There was a consistent theme. For example with respect to sound, most people could identify one out of only five or six pitches before they began to get confused. 'When only two or three tones were used, the listeners never confused them. With four different tones confusions were quite rare, but with five or more tones confusions were frequent. With 14 different ones the listeners made many mistakes.'

Miller states that 'there seems to be some limitation built into us either by learning or by the design of our nervous systems, a limit that keeps our channel capacities in this general range' corresponding to around seven elements with one standard deviation meaning from five to nine categories. He also found that the span of immediate memory is also around seven elements.

Years later, this hypothesis matched the neuroscience discovery that the working memory of the brain has the capacity to handle about seven items of data or, measured by time, about two seconds of data.

If that's the way our brains are wired then we may as well use that design consciously. A key way is in our ability to communicate our meaning and to persuade and influence people.

Persuasion and the first 7 words

There have likely been occasions when you have not been as persuasive as you would like. There may have been times when an idea you had was not accepted by the person you were seeking to convince. A likely cause of your setback was that you failed to use well your first two seconds and the moment when the listener *classified* your idea.

Imagine that you have an hour with your boss, or with the executive team or with a client to pitch an idea. Given the power of first impressions and the capacity of the working memory of the brain, you have two seconds, or seven words, to influence their classification of your idea. Being human, they will classify your idea within two seconds. The question is whether you have used your first seven words to deliberately influence their reaction, or whether you've been careless.

You might have an hour to discuss the idea with your client or your boss or 30 minutes with the executive team, and they might give you a polite hearing, but it will pretty much be all over after two seconds. After your first seven words the listener has, often subconsciously, classified their assessment. It's the same as the students in the laboratory forming their opinion of the teacher on the video. For your listeners, their classification is based on the emotion they experience in those first few seconds, and once they have formed their judgment, they are unlikely to change their minds.

I call this technique *The First 7 Words* (acknowledgement to anyone else who might have independently coined this phrase). To be persuasive, you need to use the window provided by the working memory of the brain. Whatever you say in your first seven words will mainly determine the person's response.

Because we believe it's a rational world, we generally start positioning our idea rationally and tend to overlook the primacy of emotions. The listener and speaker have not realised that *interest* or *disinterest* happens in the first few seconds, both unaware that it all happens based on gut feeling and the emotional processing in the mind of the listener right at the beginning.

Here's an example of how *The First 7 Words* can be applied—to a situation you might already have experience of. You've been away from home for the week. The business meeting you were attending was due to finish late Friday afternoon which unfortunately meant you were going to miss a family function that Friday night. The *good* news is that come Friday, the meeting finished mid-morning. Great, you think to yourself, if I go straight to the airport I might be able to get on the lunch-time flight and be home in time for the family event. The *bad* news is that you're on an inflexible ticket which doesn't allow flight change on the day of travel. But you know that the airline employee at the counter does have discretion to change some tickets by exception but they can't agree to everyone's request, otherwise they will be in trouble with their boss.

So you decide to head to the airport to take your chances. If you gain agreement you'll be on your way in an hour saving yourself a four hour wait at the airport and you'll be home with your family that night.

You know from the powers of persuasion that it's all over in the first seven words. (There is also the impact of body language and face reading that play a part as well, which we'll cover in Instinct 7.) *What are you going to say?*

The following principles guide the choice of the first seven words. Their aim is to subconsciously trigger the desired classification from your listener.

1. Specific—your first few words are not generic and are specific to the situation
2. Plain language—so your point is easily processed by your listener(s)
3. Truthful—so that you are ethical, your words are congruent with your feelings, you are believable and considered trustworthy
4. Single concept—as more than one concept is likely to confuse your listener
5. Emotional—you trigger the appropriate emotion for the moment
6. No jargon—the listener might attach a different meaning to any terminology
7. The narrative—provides a theme for your ongoing discussion or proposition.

You approach the airline employee behind the counter. You know that you have seven words only before the airline employee has decided if they will agree to your request.

A participant in one of our programs shared her recent success in making a flight change while on an inflexible ticket. Her opening words to the airline employee were, '*You probably get this all the time.*' She then politely requested the flight change and added that she understood if he was unable to do so. His response was that he would see what he could do to help her. He made the change and she was on the earlier flight. The *see what I can do* response was made by the airline employee in the first few seconds based on how he felt, or more accurately, how *she* made him feel.

Not so long ago I succeeded in changing flights myself. It was also interesting that the airline staff member shared with me his binary classification, or rule of thumb, that he uses to handle such requests. My first few words were, '*Hi, I'm on an inflexible ticket.* Is there any chance of switching to an earlier flight?' He said quite matter of factly (not knowing he was actually sharing his classification rule of thumb with me), 'You look like a nice guy, I'll see what I can do.' His binary alternative was *nice guy/not a nice guy* (or other words that can be used to describe *not a nice guy*). My first seven words had been chosen to trigger that type of response.

The opportunity to use *The First 7 Words* technique will become available to you every day. You're a manager running a project review meeting. You're a HR manager presenting a proposal to your CEO for investment in leadership education. You're an IT project manager updating a client regarding a project that is at risk. You're a manager commencing a staff member's performance review. You're a senior executive about to talk to a group of staff joining your organisation through an acquisition. You're a manager proposing an idea to your boss. You're a sales executive about to put a proposition to a client. Your success, to a significant degree, depends on what happens, emotionally, in the first few seconds.

Now you are attuned to the concept of the first seven words, you will be amazed by the number of times and places you can see their power. Recently I had the pleasure of holidaying in Prague, the capital of the Czech Republic. My wife was there for work, and one night when she was occupied with her business commitments I attended the Prague opera. My timing was ideal as the opera that night was The Bartered Bride by a local Czech composer, Smetana. Act II opens with the male chorus boisterously drinking beer from their steins, quite appropriate as the Czechs are the largest per capita consumers of beer in the world. For a brief moment a non-Czech speaker like me wonders what they are singing. Then the surtitle provides the translation, capturing the point beautifully in seven words: 'Beer is truly a gift from God'!

Gut feelings

Let's go further into the subject of gut feelings. Humans have keenly developed hunches. It's part of our ability to be able to infer things and to intuit conclusions from the available information.

Gert Gigerenzer is a director at the Max Planck Institute for Human Development in Berlin. He is an expert in gut feelings. His proposition is that gut feelings, including rules of thumb, allow us to make effective decisions without conscious thought. He defines gut feelings as referring to a judgment:

1. that appears quickly in consciousness
2. whose underlying reasons we are not fully aware of and
3. is strong enough to act upon.

CEO Mike Smith's unexplainable hunch that all was not well in the foyer of the Taj Mahal Palace hotel fits these three criteria—he was consciously aware of something that was not fully explainable yet it was strong enough to act upon, deciding that he would leave the hotel and head to the airport.

Gut feelings or rules of thumb allow people to accommodate the most important information and to ignore the rest. Professor Gigerenzer goes so far as to say that 'the mastery of human intelligence is to go beyond the information given'. In other words, we are able to infer information.

Gary Klein studies decision-making, and is particularly interested in decisions made by people in emergency situations such as in the military and firefighting. One story he tells in *Sources of Power, How People Make Decisions* is of a fire chief who, based on a sixth sense, made a decision that saved his team from likely disaster. It was a simple house fire in a one storey house. The lieutenant led his crew in to the house to spray water on the fire, but the fire just roared back at them. That struck the chief as strange because the water should have made an impact. Then the chief 'starts to feel that something is not right. He doesn't have any clues; he just doesn't feel right about being in the house, so he orders his men out of the building—a perfectly standard building with nothing out of the ordinary. As soon as his men leave the building, the floor where they had been standing collapses. Had they still been inside, they would have plunged into the fire below'.

The chief had been guided by gut feeling. The pattern of circumstances did not fit with what he knew. While he couldn't put his finger on key elements at the time, his senses were telling him that the living room was hotter than expected for the size of the fire in the kitchen, and it was very quiet, whereas a fire with that much heat would be expected to make a great deal of noise. While the chief couldn't explain it, he knew enough that he should listen to his gut feelings. They learned later that the source of the fire was the basement directly beneath the floor where the crew was standing and at the time they had no knowledge that the house had a basement.

If people can't classify

The power of the urge to classify explains our uneasy feeling when we are *unable* to accurately classify. In this case, we humans become anxious and tend to infer the worst.

A friend told me the following story. One Friday afternoon a manager and one of his staff were walking to their cars ready to head home for the weekend. As they separated, the manager said to the employee, 'I'd like to see you early Monday morning about your project.' That's all he said.

The poor employee was worried sick all weekend. He tried to infer the reason why his manager wanted to see him, but had next-to-nothing to go on. He didn't have enough clues to know whether the reason his manager wanted to see him was *good* or *bad*. Being unable to classify, he a) gets anxious and b) assumes the worst.

He started to imagine that Monday might be his last day at work. He was distracted and miserable, unable to enjoy his children's sporting activities.

First thing Monday morning he presented himself to his boss's office, standing nervously at the boss's desk. The boss looked up and said, 'Thanks for calling in. I wanted to let you know I've had sensational feedback about your project. I wanted to thank you for doing so well.'

In the next chapter we will cover why we err on the side of bad news.

Them and us

On 20 April 2007 in the Cambodian capital of Phnom Penh two groups of Buddhist monks got into a fist fight. Given that monks are not known for being violent, what is it about the human condition that could possibly explain such an unusual outburst? The answer goes to another form of classifying: *them and us*. The two groups of monks were from rival sects.

In organisational life we can start to see where silos and petty turf wars come from. They reflect whether a group is categorised as *one of them or one of us*.

This behaviour is further emphasised if we add the dimension of territory and border protection. All countries are protective of their borders and seek to control the influx of strangers—especially people 'not like us'. In Australia, Asian refugees arriving in rickety boats is a politically sensitive issue. In the US, the southern border with Mexico generates similar passion and legal responses. In the UK, sub-continent immigrants polarise the 'native' population. The German Chancellor declares that multiculturalism has 'failed, utterly failed'.

Chimps show similar border protection behaviours, irrespective of whether we are talking about wild chimps at Gombe or captive chimps at Taronga. At Gombe, every week or so, mainly the adult males perform a border patrol. They swing through the trees at the edges of their borders on the lookout for strangers, and woe betides a stranger from another community if it gets caught by the border patrol. If the stranger is a *he* and he is captured, he is likely to be brutally killed. If the stranger is a female she will likely be welcomed into the new community, if not taken against her will. She is especially welcome if she is 'good looking', meaning she is at the sexually receptive stage of her monthly cycle and displaying an oestrous swelling around her rear, an alluring sign to a male chimp. Similarly, the Taronga chimps conduct sporadic patrols of the borders of their exhibit. All of a sudden the urge to patrol will cause the males, usually led by Lubutu, to conduct a border inspection. Sometimes the juvenile males tag along but invariably lose interest before the task is done.

The significance of *them and us* explains the lengths people go to in order to belong. Most people in your organisation wear clothes of a similar style. If it's coats and ties for men, it's coats and ties all round. If it's casual on Friday, it will be the same casual look. If it's a social event, people will mysteriously wear similar styles, and of course feel very self-conscious if they are the odd-person out.

With language, while we might laugh about TLAs (three-letter acronyms), using them demonstrates a sense of belonging—only the 'in group' knows the language.

When an organisation grows significantly beyond the 150 natural clan size, often one department might not get on well with another (e.g. HR versus Finance, Sales versus Delivery). Because one group differs from another in their orientation they see the world differently.

IMPLICATIONS OF THIS INSTINCT FOR LEADERS

Here's a snapshot of what we have learned about the instinct of *first impressions to classify*.

1. Humans make their first impressions of people, events and places within a few seconds.
2. In terms of communication, the time frame of first impressions is the first seven words.
3. First impressions are mainly driven by the emotion generated in those first few seconds.
4. Based on the first emotional feelings we classify our meaning.
5. Our classifications are binary in nature (good versus bad, like me versus not like me).
6. Once we have made our instant assessment we are unlikely to change our opinion.

There are significant practical implications of *first impressions to classify* which, if incorporated into your toolkit, will make managing people easier.

Implication 1. Communication and your first 7 words

An important use of the concept of *The First 7 Words* is in our communication—to help the listener or reader classify our meaning within our first few words.

In our various forms of communication—emails, letters, reports, verbal— it's essential to help people make sense of our meaning, and in particular how they should classify our message.

Take for example an email. Have you ever received a lengthy email and had trouble making sense of it? This frustration was most likely caused by your difficulty in classifying the meaning right from the beginning. You had to read too far into it to get to the point.

Here's another example. Imagine you are a team leader about to commence a performance review of one of your team who has performed well this last year. What are your first seven words to begin the meeting? You know the staff member is compelled to classify what this meeting holds for them. The usual binary alternative for an employee about to have their review is *good* (no danger) or *bad* (defensive). What are your first seven words? A group of participants on one of our programs suggested the following: 'I'm looking forward to this good review'. (If I don't comment on the appropriateness of this example you won't know whether I'm suggesting this is a *good* or *bad* approach!) It's a good approach—it lets the employee immediate make sense of the meeting (and not to be anxious for the time sense-making is delayed).

Patricia Clason coaches leaders in emotional intelligence from her base in Milwaukee, USA. Patricia liked the idea of the first seven words and applied the technique in her coaching of a senior executive we'll call Connie. Connie and Patricia were exploring the negative impact that Connie's style was having on her team. Based on the concept that the first few words have a trigger effect on people's emotion, Connie achieved a dramatic adjustment to her style and impact. Patricia shared with me the story of Connie's transformed approach using the first seven words.

'Bill. My office, 10 am,' ordered Connie. Bill froze, his brain hijacked by fear. 'What have I done wrong?' He quickly mentally scrolled through the events of the last few days attempting to figure out what had upset his demanding boss.

This was Connie's style; short, abrupt, direct. Always in a hurry yet always demanding that every little detail be done perfectly. She was, after all, the vice-president of quality in a health care company. Mistakes meant people could die! Driven to get things done quickly, she moved fast, talked fast, and didn't mince words.

In her most recent performance review with her own boss, she was told that her leadership style had to change. Everyone reporting to her was stressed and demoralised. A recent product recall was hard enough on everyone and her style of leadership was only making matters worse. 'Lighten up, energise your team, improve the morale or you and your department will sink,' her boss warned her.

So she turned to her coach, Patricia. 'Help! I don't know how to be anyone other than who I have been all these years.' Together they embarked upon a program of awareness—not to change who she is, but rather to improve her awareness of others and to be more effective in her communication and interactions.

'What are your first seven words when you open a meeting?' Patricia asked. 'Think back. What do you say?'

'Hmmm, I guess I usually start with something like, "Okay, let's get started, we've got some real problems to address". Or, "What the hell happened here?" Now that I stop to think about it, that sounds pretty intimidating.'

The coach explained the concept of *The First 7 Words*—that the meaning people take occurs in the first few words based on the emotion triggered in the first two seconds. Connie and Patricia then brainstormed new first-seven-word openings for conversations with employees. Connie ran with the concept, took a little more time to prepare for her meetings and consciously chose her opening expressions.

Within a month, the downward spiralling morale in her department had turned. People were lighter because they no longer feared Connie or meetings with her. They sought her out to tell her about successes and ask for her input on challenges. She got more smiles as she walked through the plant and she felt more like smiling herself. The lighter mood was indeed contagious. In meetings, people started coming up with creative new ideas, now that their minds weren't preoccupied with the fear of *what have I done wrong now?*

Here's the list of Connie's brainstorm first seven words that she began to use in her interactions with her team:

    I'd like to ask a clarifying question
    Please help me understand
    I'd like to understand more
    Please explain this one point
    I don't quite understand yet
    I'm not clear on
    You are the expert, so please explain
    You know this so well
    I'm curious about something
    I was wondering why
    You're the right person to help me understand
    The reason why I'm asking

This is what I am thinking
My frame of reference is
I suggest we look at
I notice that
This is excellent.

Implication 2. Meeting for the first time

The classifying, or imprinting, event is based on the emotion experienced at the first interaction. We can use this knowledge when we meet people for the first time.

When the CEO of a major finance company was appointed to the top job he sensibly managed his first meetings with key clients. He didn't want to run the risk that a first meeting might be in relation to an issue with negative emotions attached. So in the months prior to the handover, he had a series of meetings with key clients in an effort to get to know them and understand their business. He ensured that each first meeting, each first impression, had positive emotions attached to it. Otherwise, he was leaving the first impressions to chance and running a risk that the first meeting, and hence their relationship, was negative. In this way he laid a sound platform for his key relationships.

Implication 3. First action is a winner

Whenever we are in charge of a project or an assignment we should try to ensure that the first update with our sponsor or client is positive.

From the sponsor's point of view, they are most likely using an unconscious rule of thumb that the project is either *in control* or *needs my attention*. Life will be less stressful and more productive if their first impression is positive. Provided that the update is truthful, we should seek to make the first review a positive one. If the project is going well and classified this way by the sponsor then the sponsor will tend to carry forward that classification most likely for the life of the project, unless of course it dramatically veers out of control justifying an alternative classification and consequential emotional excitement.

The power of the instinct of classifying is that once the executive sponsor or client classifies the project as going well then they will see subsequent events through that lens and it will take a fair amount to alter their classification. Once classified as *good*, you will be given a greater degree of latitude if things do start slipping. Of course if the first impression is *bad* then you'll be forever recovering without perhaps knowing why.

Implication 4. First with the news

The person who speaks first about an issue is believed. To illustrate, imagine the project you are in charge of hits a rough patch. Should you talk to the client? It's useful to know that if you get to the client first, you have the best opportunity of reassuring them about your investigation and recovery of the project. If someone else gets to the client first, say a competitor or rival, then that gives the other person the best opportunity to influence events, probably to your detriment. By getting to the client first, you have the best chance of them classifying the situation as you would want, such as *under control*.

The classification will be made by the client based on the emotion they feel the instant they hear the information. It's easy for a competitor to catastrophise the situation and for the client to instantly feel that sense of dread, knowing a project is careering out of control. If the client does experience that emotion, chances are by the time you get to them there is almost no chance of recovery. The strong negative emotion has been experienced and the classification made.

If you reach the client first you can express the situation in a reassuring way, carefully choosing your first seven words. While there's no set of words to cover all contingencies, one group of leaders workshopping such a scenario developed the following for their particular situation: '*There's an item we are investigating* that I wanted to give you a heads up on'. The focus is to protect against the client jumping to a strong negative classification.

Getting to a client first is not about being untruthful or unethical. It's about being informed about the human condition to enable sensible leadership choices. Knowing what you now know about the speed and implications of how people make up their minds, it would be self-defeating not to choose to be early and first to update a client.

Implication 5. Giving bad news

It's handy to know—or more accurately, to have explained what you always knew—that people intuit bad news quickly and usually accurately. We can also use this knowledge to effectively communicate *bad* news.

Let's say you're a team leader and you've been recruiting to fill a vacancy in your team. You've made the decision and phoned the successful candidate to tell them the good news. That was an easy call to make. Now you must call each of the unsuccessful candidates. How long do you think it will take for the person to intuit that they are unsuccessful? There is something in your tone, your slightly hesitant speech, your slightly less warm greeting than when you last spoke. Given that the human you are talking to has a compelling need to classify—good news or bad news—there is usually enough revealed instantly for them to accurately know what's coming. And of course a dead give-away is that they might not have heard from you for some time. All of this means that they will sense very quickly that they have been unsuccessful and are about to be disappointed.

The point of knowing about impressions to classify is that you can say something right at the beginning that allows the person to classify immediately that they have been unsuccessful. For the listener, being able to accurately classify is actually less anxious than having to wait to classify, and of course if we have to wait more than two seconds we assume the worst.

What is your best approach in dealing with this type of interaction? In particular, what are your first seven words to allow the person to accurately classify your message? One recruiter I know addresses this well. Her approach is to commence the call with words such as, 'I have some news that might disappoint you'. A manager I know says, 'I'm sorry to let you know you've been unsuccessful.' After this first statement, put sensitively because you've put yourself in the other person's shoes and allowed them to get the meaning of your phone call immediately, you can then explain the detail.

Implication 6. Giving negative feedback

Almost every manager finds that one of the most difficult duties they face is to give negative feedback to a staff member. Managers often delay or avoid the task. Giving negative feedback or managing a poor performer is enough to keep you awake at night.

Given the universal nature of this difficulty there must be attributes in human nature that explains this challenge. Indeed there are. The instincts that we have covered so far have a role: emotion, social belonging, the non-family paradox, status within a social group and first impressions. Others will be covered shortly, including the power of loss and potential loss. Similarly, our knowledge of instincts also helps us find a way to overcome the challenges involved in giving negative feedback, and in particular applying the technique of *The First 7 Words*.

First, let's challenge a popular and conventional method of giving negative feedback—the so-called 'feedback sandwich'. This approach suggests starting with a positive, going to the negative and then ending with a positive. The negative element is sandwiched in between the positives. In light of what we've already learned about how humans process information, this approach defies human nature.

The better approach is to be clear in the first seven words. This actually reduces the tension for both the manager and the staff member. The manager finds they are speaking truthfully, the staff member is immediately able to classify and the emotional tension is reduced.

How would you handle the following scenario? You are a manager and Sam is one of your direct reports. Sam has been with your organisation for three months. He is a strong performer on the technical side of his job, but appears not to be respectful of the team and teamwork.

You are just finishing a team meeting. Sam was late for the meeting and during the meeting frequently checked his BlackBerry. Several times he interrupted other people who were speaking. This is Sam's second team meeting since he started and he demonstrated the same behaviour at the previous meeting.

During the meeting you observed people glancing at each other in apparent annoyance at Sam's behaviour. You had similar concerns and felt the mood of the meeting was lower than was the case before Sam joined the team.

As people are leaving the room at the end of the meeting you ask Sam to wait behind. You expressed the request in a neutral tone so that neither Sam nor the departing team members had any sense of the reason.

What are you going to say? Your objective is to communicate with Sam in such a way that he acknowledges your concern and responds with words and tone similar to, 'Yes, I can see what you mean. Thanks for letting me know.' The situation here, while undesirable, is not a major misdemeanour. So you should be approaching the conversation (your own classification) as a *good one to have* rather than *a major issue*. This will affect your emotion, which Sam will intuit, and in turn affect his emotion and response.

Your first seven words are the key. They are key in not only affecting the reaction and discussion that follows but also in easing the emotional tension on you so that you are more confident and capable of having these types of interactions.

There is a range of possible approaches a manager might choose to start such a conversation. Let's go through the most common ones and explain why, based on human nature, only one approach works.

Some managers start with the obscure option: 'Thanks for waiting behind, Sam. How do you think the meeting went?' What is Sam to think and feel in response to this question? He is instantly on guard, will assume the worst and will be most motivated to keep out of harm's way. The response most likely triggered in Sam is, 'Why is my manager asking me this question?' What he says aloud is, 'Yeah, really good. We got through a lot.' The core problem here is that Sam cannot yet classify. He becomes more anxious than he needs to be and you still need to get to the issue.

A variation on the obscure theme, even more pronounced, is for the manager to start with, 'Sam, how do you think you're fitting in with the team?' In Sam's mind a red alarm screams and he immediately assumes the worst. The conversation is all downhill from here, with Sam protecting himself.

The second approach is to go with the 'feedback sandwich'. This is likely to start with, 'Sam, you've been with us for three months now. The technical skills you've brought to the team are greatly appreciated.' Have you got to the point yet? Given the importance of the first seven words, where has Sam's mind gone?

He's gone in one of two directions. Direction one is that he believes that he is indeed receiving positive feedback and might be thinking to himself, 'Gee, I've never worked for a manager who gives positive feedback after just three months.' In other words, he's *misclassified*. When he shortly finds out his error, his misclassification, he swings to a negative reaction because of the surprise and negative emotion he now feels from his error.

A further problem with this approach, in the light of the significance of classifying, is that you have reduced your ability to give positive feedback in the future. For Sam, he has classified that whenever you start with a positive you are heading towards a negative. All this is predictable based on the way humans process and intuit information.

The second direction in how Sam might classify your positive opening in the feedback sandwich is that he instantly smells a *but* coming. When you begin with, 'Sam, you've been here three months. Your technical skills ...' Sam instantly anticipates the *but* and classifies the purpose of the conversation as *negative*. When the *but* comes his suspicion is confirmed. He classifies more broadly the nature of your approach to giving feedback. He feels you tried to mislead him.

Looking at the two responses to the feedback sandwich, the second one is the more likely. Right at the beginning when Sam is seeking to know why he has been asked to wait behind there was something in your tone, something more mechanical, an ever-so-slight stressed look on your face that Sam detected through his powers of intuition and unexplainable gut feeling. His radar was telling him that this was *not good*.

So what's the best approach based on human instincts? The best approach is to state in your first seven words the subject you want to cover.

An ideal opening would be, '*We need to cover our team's protocols*'. Sam immediately knows what the conversation is about, meaning that he can accurately classify the subject. He knows he is being held to account, and he knows the degree of seriousness (not drastic) and that he doesn't have to assume the worst and have a flash that he might be getting fired.

Having facilitated Sam's accurate classification, you can now raise the range of topics you want to cover, and of course ask for Sam's perspective and explanation. You might point out the several behaviours you observed—late to the meeting, interrupting others. You can then go to the principles, such as, 'It's something that I should have covered when you first joined us. Team meetings and respect for each other are very important to me. So it's a good opportunity to cover that now.'

The First 7 Words approach gives you the best chance of achieving your objectives: that Sam acknowledges the feedback, that he agrees to adjust his behaviour, that he appreciates he works for a manager who can cover situations like this with competence and that you have laid a foundation for giving negative feedback as no big deal.

Implication 7. Licence to give feedback

There's one more idea to add to your leadership toolkit when it comes to giving negative feedback.

The fundamental factor that causes managers to experience difficulty giving negative feedback is the weight of the negative emotion on the manager in doing so. The way to best address this weight is to find a way to remove much of the negative emotion. We can do this by gaining a licence early on to give feedback and position the classifying of such an event.

As a manager who found giving negative feedback harder than giving positive feedback, I found a way that helped me to remove much of the negative emotion. Negative feedback is only a problem if it is assessed by the giver and the receiver as negative. I felt responsible for giving the necessary feedback; otherwise I was letting the person down by not pointing out something that might be helpful. If I didn't point out my observations then I might also continue to be frustrated by the other person's behaviour, which was no good for either of us. The way I found, and recommend, is to establish an early classification in the mind of the receiver that the feedback when given is coming from a *helpful* orientation.

One of the early people I tried this approach with was a HR graduate named Gerard Behr who joined our team. I said to Gerard in his first week, 'I'd like to be the sort of manager who helps with your development, so that in years to come you'll look back and say that you were lucky to have worked with Andrew early in your career. Now for me to achieve that, I need to be able to point out things that I observe, good or bad, that might help you. Is that okay?'

Of course, Gerard answered enthusiastically, 'Yes!' What's not to like about such an offer? This approach enabled a positive emotional attachment for giving feedback. In Gerard's mind *feedback* is now classified positively as he knows where I am coming from and will have an opportunity to learn. I have gained a licence to do so and the weight has been moved off my shoulders in the future.

A few months later I overheard Gerard on the phone talking to a manager. Although I heard only one side of the conversation I thought he could have expressed his advice differently. Because I had classified my intention early on, I was easily able to invite him into my office and say, 'I just noticed a coaching opportunity!' 'What's that?' he asked eagerly. 'I just overheard the phone conversation you were having. If I was the person on the other end of the phone, my interpretation might be different to what you perhaps intended.' I explained what I meant and asked, 'What could you have said that might have been clearer?'

Gerard answered, we discussed it momentarily, and then I closed the conversation happily with, 'Very good—head back to work!' The feedback was given easily and received as a learning benefit based on a prior classification set up three months earlier.

A similar licence can be gained at the beginning of a business year, such as at goal-setting time. In this case the manager might say, 'What's the one thing you would most like to achieve this year?' When the person is able to articulate an answer, the manager says, 'Okay, what I'll commit to is that if I see anything—good or bad—that might help I'll let you know. Is that okay?'

Using this method, the classification of feedback being *helpful* is achieved and the emotional burden on the shoulders of the manager is eased.

Implication 8. Recruiting

You might have been advised in the past to leave gut feelings out of the selection process when recruiting to fill vacancies. But to seek to take gut feelings out of human assessments is to both deny reality and also ignore a vital source of information.

The problem with gut feelings is that they are not necessarily accurate. When you and the candidate first look into each other's eyes in those first two seconds (and perhaps even faster with face reading which we will discuss in Instinct 7), the decision by both of you is in danger of being decided there and then. The subsequent hour's interview on your part confirms the decision you made in the first two seconds. You filter the discussion to fit that classification and discount information that does not conform to the classification. The danger is that if you go with that instant gut feeling then you may well hire a poor candidate, or reject a candidate who would have been an excellent hire but for something unexplainable right at the beginning.

With the knowledge of the power of classification, we can seek to suspend judgment. It's difficult to do, but a form of suspension can be achieved. We can accept the first impression the candidate makes as useful information and then consciously 'park' that impression and conduct the interview, seeking to draw an informed assessment gained from the whole interaction. We can make a point of saying to our self at the beginning of the interview, after we have pro-cessed our first impression, *I am going to make my assessment based on the whole of what I am about to learn*. Andria Wyman-Clarke is the Vice President of Human Resources for Thales Australia, the subsidiary of the global engineer-ing and defence firm. She's an advocate of instincts. In taking account of *first impressions to classify* in recruiting, she listens to her gut feelings in the first few seconds and then during the interview tests for the opposite: if when they first meet she feels a pang that the candidate might not be suitable, she uses the hour's interview to find all the reasons why the person would be good for the job. This helps her both to use gut feelings yet not to be blinded by them.

Implication 9. New role for you

Imagine you are soon starting in a new role. You will have a sense that the new people you will be working with will be sizing you up, as you will them. That's not necessarily good or bad; it's just how humans work. To make this work for you, what actions are you going to take to make the first impression positive?

Here are two examples of how two different managers approached the situ-ation. What first impressions are likely to occur in the minds of their new team members?

A good example: The new manager phoned each of his direct reports before day one, just to introduce himself.

A poor example: The first the team knew of their new manager was when her bar fridge arrived some days before she did!

Implication 10. New team member

Similarly, what if you are a team leader and a new person is joining the team tomorrow? What will you do on their first day, and in fact the first moment of the first day, to make a positive first impression? You don't have a choice whether or not you'll make a first impression. The question is whether you take steps to make it a positive one.

You have asked the new team member to start work at 9 am. If you are not in reception on time, what message—what classification—will that send? Once classified, the imprint is quite enduring. So if you are not there at 9 am you are being self-destructive. If you delegate someone else to meet them instead of meeting them yourself, you are likely to be classified as *not interested* and you will weaken your connection with the person. If you leave it to HR to meet the person on their first day, you will sacrifice the primary connection with the person—that first warm welcome in reception. If you pass the person too early to a buddy, then similarly you'll miss opportunities to be the primary connection to the new person. If their work space is not ready—for office workers, their desk, computer, logins—then you will create a negative first impression.

Until reading this book you might have been able to claim ignorance of the significance of these first day's—well, first morning's—events. But now ignorance has been removed! Sorry, it's now a question of what choices you make.

Implication 11: Decision making

Once we are aware of the power of *first impressions to classify*, we can become more considered in our decision making.

Mark Richardson is Managing Director of the Sydney based private equity firm, Wolseley Partners. Mark and his senior staff assess businesses to determine whether to make an investment. An analyst or director might work on an opportunity, and then bring forward a qualified opportunity with a buy or decline decision. On the surface, we would think such assessments by equity fund financial wizards are entirely rational. Not so, says Mark.

After becoming familiar with human instincts, Mark says he has no doubt that over the years his company has rejected investment proposals based solely on an initial poor gut response. The poor emotional response was most often caused by the decision makers forming a negative impression if the proposal was not well researched and presented when first submitted.

Mark and his colleagues now consciously monitor emotional reactions and initial impressions when an opportunity is first brought to the management committee. If an opportunity is brought forward too early in its analysis phase and is heading towards being judged, good or bad, the directors counsel themselves to suspend judgment and to take the proposal off the table until a more comprehensive analysis has been completed. They seek to avoid a classification at that point, to give the opportunity a chance so that a possible good investment is not given the kiss of death by the initial impression, or of course the opposite—that a poor investment doesn't get approved based on an ill-informed positive first impression.

Implication 12. Suspend judgment

Finally, by knowing about *first impressions to classify* we can choose to avoid being too judgmental about other people or situations based merely on thin slices of information. By all means we should accept the information presented in those first few seconds but we can try to avoid jumping to conclusions and racing up 'the ladder of inference' to make broad classifications; suspend judgment pending more information. Otherwise the problem is that once we classify then our mind has been made up.

So the emotional picture we have so far is that we classify, or make sense of people and situations, based on the emotion we feel at that first instant. These feelings are often subconscious. The third of the three elements of the emotional picture goes to what happens if we can't immediately classify? The next instinct explains the default position.

Instinct 5. Loss Aversion

This instinct helps explain why:
- people seem to resist change
- when our boss wants to see us we assume the worst
- performance appraisal systems rarely seem to work
- people dwell on the negatives
- staff get annoyed at losing their free fruit.

WHEN WE CAN MANAGE to do so, my wife and I enjoy walking in the evenings after work and catching up on each other's day. One night in November 2009 Jude told me a story that captures the essence of this next human instinct: *loss aversion*. Jude works for a global pharmaceutical company as head of her department for Australia and New Zealand. Her company was acquiring another company and a few days before our walk the acquisition had been finalised and employment transfers were being considered. Several members of her team had done an exceptional job in their piece of the acquisition and Jude wanted to acknowledge them with a recognition award. Jude prepared a thank-you letter for the team members. Jude's plan was to thank them by presenting their award individually with a quiet discussion and then later acknowledge them publicly. Jude stepped out of her office, envelopes in hand, and saw one of the recipients in the corridor. 'Oh, Victoria, can I see you for a moment, please?' Victoria's mouth dropped in fright, instantly concerned about why her boss, letter in hand, might want to see her. In the absence of any other information, Victoria had involuntarily assumed loss—in a nanosecond! Knowing about *loss aversion*, Jude quickly gave Victoria a quick reclassification. 'It's good news!' she said with a reassuring smile. Of course, Victoria was delighted to receive the recognition and grateful that the letter was not a termination notice and that her fear was misplaced.

Why is it that people err on the side of loss, and what can we do with this insight?

Why loss?

The avoidance of loss is a far greater motivator to humans than the opportunity to gain.

In Instinct 3 we looked at a neuroscientist's explanation as to why people assume the worst. Antonio Damasio says he can't imagine an organism being wired for anything other than first screening for pain and danger. If we were wired for pleasure above pain we could not survive at all, he says.

Assuming the worst, or guarding against loss, is a resourceful place to be. It's the place that will most keep us out of harm's way. This erring to avoid loss would have served our ancestors well. If they saw a shadow move in the bush it was wise to assume the shadow belonged to a predator. It would not always have paid to investigate whether the cause of a rustle in the bush was a man-eating predator or a harmless bird. We had to be on our guard, and those who weren't probably didn't live long enough to become our ancestors.

In their wonderful book, *Sway*, authors Ori and Rom Brafman refer to research on egg prices and consumers' sensitivity if prices rise (price increases representing loss to the consumer). When the price of eggs drops, consumers buy a little more. But when the price of eggs rises, consumers cut their consumption by two and a half times. As the authors put it, 'We experience the pain associated with a loss much more vividly than we do the joy of experiencing a gain.'

Let's look at *loss aversion* research in the workplace. Tanjim Hossain from the University of Toronto and John List from the University of Chicago investigated the impact that incentive payments offered as a gain versus incentives offered as the avoidance of a loss on workers' behaviour and productivity. The research took place in a Chinese high-tech manufacturer of consumer goods. Subjects were engaged in their regular tasks. In one treatment of the bonus offer, subjects received a letter with the bonus framed positively as a gain. This letter was expressed as per the normal bonus practice that most organisations follow:

> 'You will receive an RMB 80 bonus for every week the weekly production average of your team is above or equal to 400 units/hour ...'

In the other treatment to test the power of loss, workers were *provisionally* allocated the bonus to be paid at the end of the pay period. The relevant portion of their letter, with the bonus expressed as the threat of a loss, read:

> 'For every week in which the weekly production average of your team is below 400 units/hour, the salary enhancement will be reduced by RMB 80 ...'

Any difference in behaviour or outputs would be from the language used, not the monetary effect.

The difference in productivity was significant. The magnitude of the effect of an incentive paid as a loss versus a gain was roughly 1 per cent productivity, a significant effect on manufacturing output—all due to the avoidance of loss being a greater motivator than the opportunity to gain.

In workplaces the forms of loss or potential loss are many and varied. There are the obvious ones such as loss of income, loss of benefits, loss of role through redundancy or loss of role through demotion or a restructure. There is potential loss of social standing through being socially embarrassed, if not humiliated. There is the loss of routine or of the familiar. There is the potential loss of no longer being a subject-matter expert if systems and processes change. Loss can even be experienced just by someone else gaining.

Leaders are often surprised when staff rebel against the loss of an apparent minor benefit. *Loss aversion* explains why staff get annoyed. Perhaps you've experienced the withdrawal of fruit or biscuits as a cost-cutting initiative. If people never had free fruit in the first place the absence of fruit would be no big deal. But once the fruit has been provided the loss of that fruit can be downright annoying.

A study by Robert Cialdini resembles the cost-cutting withdrawal of fruit or some other apparently minor benefit. Participants in the study were asked to taste a chocolate chip cookie and rate its quality, desirability and value. Some participants were asked to taste a cookie from a jar containing ten cookies and others from a jar containing just two cookies.

There were various iterations of the study. One iteration generated the highest rating of the cookies. These participants were given a jar of ten cookies, but before they could taste a cookie, another researcher came into the room, apologised that they needed some of the cookies in another room and replaced the jar of ten cookies with a jar of two cookies. The participants then tasted the cookies from a jar now containing only two cookies.

The participants who experienced this withdrawal of cookies rated the cookies as more attractive and more valuable than did any other participants. Losing them made the cookies more desirable. That's loss aversion.

People are not wired to resist change

Knowing about *loss aversion* helps us make sense of what really happens with people's response to change, and how we can better manage change if we know about human instincts.

There is a saying that *people resist change*. While this might be conventional wisdom, it just isn't true. If humans were hardwired to resist change we'd still be living in caves.

Think about change in your own life. No doubt, many have been welcome and highly beneficial that you wouldn't want to be without. Perhaps others have been detrimental and painful, changes that you would rather have avoided. Obviously, it's not change itself that presents the problem, so we can't be hardwired to resist change. There must be something else that explains the observed tendency for people to respond poorly to change. Humans are very happy with change provided the change meets one criterion—that it does not involve loss.

The next layer of understanding how we can use *loss aversion* to manage change is to link it to the speed in which we *classify* information. When we first hear about a change we instantly decide at an individual level, filtered by our immediate emotional response, whether this change for *me* can be classified as gain or loss. If we detect gain, we support the change. If we detect loss, we resist. If we are uncertain—and here's the big swinger—we err on the side of loss as the default if we cannot yet classify. And as we learned in the last chapter, once we have classified the change as loss then we are unlikely to alter our classification, and subsequent events are interpreted according to that classification.

It's no wonder that in organisational life people appear to resist change. Many changes don't involve loss to individuals at all. But people are generally uncertain when they first hear about the change and how it might affect them. They are driven to guard against loss so overwhelmingly the negative possibilities loom largest. Although a restructure might mean actual loss for a few, usually the vast majority of people fear the worst and are anxious about the change. For example, the CEO of an organisation of around 400 staff announced one day via an email, 'I am reviewing the structure of the organisation. The review will take around three weeks. I will then hold a staff meeting to inform you of the changes.' As we would predict, almost everyone was frightened by the possibilities, even though a) they had no other information and b) a restructure would likely only affect a few of the most senior employees as the tasks by most others would continue unaffected by any restructure. Being human though, and in the absence of knowing what the change meant to them, the staff assumed the worst. There is no value in the executive team then proclaiming, 'Our people resist change'.

This of course points to the great opportunity to manage change more effectively—to avoid the instant classification as loss. We will come back to that.

If you've ever been close to a community of chimps experiencing a group panic attack you are left in no doubt that chimps appear, like us, to process uncertainty and screen for loss, and if they are unable to classify then they assume loss, often displayed as abject fear.

One afternoon I took a small group of business leaders to Taronga Zoo for a behind the scenes visit to the chimpanzees' night den. After taking us through the safety drill, the keeper had us in position behind bars and well out of harm's way. The 19 chimps were allowed access to this night area. The chimps excitedly rushed in from their daytime area and grabbed the food laid out for them. Suddenly they froze, and then screamed in terror. Our visit happened to be at the time when preparations were underway for the temporary relocation of the chimps. That day, while the chimps were outside, crates each standing about an average human's height had been placed in the den. The instant the chimps sighted this change to their environment pandemonium erupted. Ear-piercing screams filled the den. Chimps held each other. Two males mounted each other, an act of reassurance. The fear was palpable and deafening. It was as noisy as a night club!

To us observing this chaotic state of affairs it was clear that the chimps were petrified of the mysterious cages. The cages were classified as negative, presumably for no other reason than uncertainty or perhaps because several chimps may also have had a prior negative association (classification) of cages. The emotion of the moment was overwhelming.

One of our visitors compared this response to what might occur at the office if a builder wandered the floors with a note pad and pen. Curiosity would be triggered and pandemonium might well spread as people try to make sense of what the mysterious person is all about.

Once you apply this lens of *loss aversion*, your experiences regarding change will quickly make sense and your capability as a manager to lead change will accelerate. There are several problems caused by the myth that people resist change. First, this belief is self-fulfilling. You and your management colleagues believe that people resist change, so you don't manage the change as diligently as you could, and guess what—people resist the change! Second, you attach negative sentiment to the change and feel a weight attached to implementing the change, which in turn makes the organisation less change-capable. Third, you become apologetic about imposing the change, yet we expect our leaders to lead the response to change in our environment and to lead us to a better place.

Realising that we are not hardwired to resist change opens up breakthrough opportunities for organisations to better manage change. Organisations effec-tively applying instincts to manage change are focusing on, amongst other things, taking great care to influence the emotional reaction to how people feel when they first learn about the change so that they are more inclined to *classify* the change as *okay* and to avoid the default to anxiety about loss.

Here's an example of how one organisation avoided the default to loss when people were uncertain about the impact of a change. The focus of the approach was on influencing the first impression through the trigger of desired emotion in the first two seconds.

In January 2006 a professional services firm was planning to implement a new project management software system. A key business measure in account-ing, legal and consulting firms is billable hours. So a characteristic of working in a professional services firm is the recording of time. This particular firm had a rudimentary system that they planned to upgrade. The system had the potential of being an annoyance to the consultants as it could be interpreted as potentially requiring the consultants to do more data entry thus spending less productive time with clients. Less productive time means less billable hours and less interesting work with clients. That's the loss potential.

If the consultants took a negative view of the system at the outset then they might subtly refuse to use the system which would erode the business benefits of the investment and they would be a resistant group to train in the use of the new system. But we have learned that people are *not* resistant to change, therefore any such resistance would mostly be due to careless management of the change.

Here's how a change like this is normally (poorly) managed. Given that *we need to communicate* and given conventional wisdom that *we need to brief people with the one message at the one time* a meeting is called via email calendar invitation. At this point, predicted by human instincts, the change has immediately gone off the rails.

Following that conventional path, when the consultants read their emails it's downhill from there. They don't have a lot to go on. They can't say for sure that the change is a good thing. They default to the negative classification because the avoidance of loss far outweighs the possibilities of gain. They need to gain more information to know what's really going on. They talk to their colleagues. Everyone has a theory as to what's behind the change. People listen most to the negative views. It's all over before the meeting even takes place. Don't blame *resistant to change* on staff, blame the careless management of the change.

But this project team knew about human instincts. Mindful of *loss aversion* and the speed of classification, the team developed a successful approach.

It was decided that a member of the project team would be allocated to a group of consultants and at an appropriate time, approach each consultant individually. Given that the consultants were coming and going and often busy with clients, it took three days to talk to each person. The conversations went something like this and all ended with the same positive *classification*. We'll call the consultant 'Chris'.

Project team member: Have you got a moment, Chris?

Chris: Sure.

PM: I wanted to let you know about something. You'll soon notice that a meeting is coming up in your calendar for next month. I just wanted to let you know what it's about.

Chris: Thanks.

PM: Most of us consultants aren't very disciplined at quoting fees for a project, tracking its progress along the way or knowing whether we made money at the end.

Chris: Yes, I fall into that category!

PM: We're implementing a system that will help.

Chris nods, interested.

PM: At this stage I just wanted to give you a snapshot and to let you know about the training next month.

Chris (at the end of the one minute conversation): *Sounds good.* Thanks for letting me know.

The project team has successfully generated a positive meaning to the system—a positive classification based on the emotion attached to the feelings staff had when they first heard about it, including the first few words at the beginning of the discussion. The consultants have successfully been steered away from the default aversion of loss. They have classified as *good* based on feeling *okay* the moment they first heard about it. And predictably, because the consultants felt fine when they first heard about it, they didn't gossip on Friday at the pub because it was no big deal. When the time came, the training and implementation went smoothly and the new system was successfully utilised.

Change implications at the individual level

Loss or gain is felt at a personal level—in effect, what does it mean to me and my family? So part of cracking the code in how people respond to change is knowing the effect the change will have at the individual level.

You might think that the collapse of the Berlin Wall in November 1989 was a beneficial change in the lives of East Germans and their personal freedom and one that was universally welcomed. Not so. Back then there was at least one group of East Berliners who complained. This group was the East

German border guards. For them, understandably, they would no doubt have gone home the morning after that eventful night shift, walked in the front door and said to their families, 'The Wall has collapsed. I'm out of a job.'

Given that our assessment of loss or gain from change is experienced at an individual level—for the individual and their immediate family—it's fair enough that at that moment the East German border guards were less concerned about the social benefits of freedom for East Germany and the reunification of their country. For them, it became a question of providing food and shelter for their family.

Likewise, your team members respond to change based on how it affects them personally. Let's look at a simple example where two of your team members react differently when they first hear of the change.

Your organisation has decided to relocate its offices. The organisation is currently in an office block in the centre of the city. You are moving to a suburb 10 kms (six miles) from the city. You communicate this to your team. The team's reaction is fairly equally split. Nicole is typical of the happy group. She's beaming and you know why. She lives close to the new site. For her, it's all gain. She will save time at both ends of the day with more time for the exercise she likes plus saving on transport costs. For her, this change sounds fantastic and not surprisingly is classified as *good*.

Kevin is downcast. For him the news is negative. He loses. He lives on the other side of the city so he'll take more time to get to and from work and will be up for extra travel costs. He will have less time with his young family. For him, the change sounds terrible and is classified as *bad*. He gives the impression of resisting the change which is hardly surprising and not something deserving criticism. It's not the change itself that's the problem. It's a question of whether the change results in personal loss or gain.

With a relocation type of change, the screening for loss and gain happens in an instant because the advantages or disadvantages are generally clear. For a change like a restructure, the loss and gain implications are less certain. If uncertain as to the implications, people assume loss. In a restructure there might be a few winners. For someone who is promoted as part of the restructure, and having a heads-up before the announcement, they are fine with the change. They are keen for the change to be implemented and might even be frustrated with any delay. For someone who is demoted due to the restructure they are losing and they will most likely oppose the change. For the great majority of people the consequences of a restructure are uncertain—do I have a job? Who will I be reporting to? Will our group be disbanded? In the absence of knowing the consequences and being able to classify the meaning of the change, people will err on the side of loss. For the majority of people, a restructure in fact means no change at all, but that doesn't stop them fearing the change with all the potential losses flashing through their minds.

Connecting with individuals is scalable and can be prioritised. My brother Paul works with Accenture in the US and gets involved in major SAP systems implementation projects. These are huge, complex, expensive projects. And for the users of the systems, a change often generates fear about the implications of the systems for them and their role—fertile ground for people's *loss aversion* instinct. At the time Paul was working on an implementation for a large industrial equipment manufacturer and, giving him some free brotherly help, we discussed how he might influence a positive classification in the minds of key individuals and avoid the default to loss aversion. There was indeed a key group—the warranty representative in the client's dealerships and even better, this group was often forgotten about. How would Paul and his team influence them to be positive about the system (not to fool them in any way; just to give the project a fair chance and avoid the negative default)? Knowing about instincts, we know the warranty representatives will form their impression right from the beginning and that those impressions will endure.

The Accenture team scheduled a pilot training session and invited a small group of ten warranty representatives from the largest dealerships to be the pilot participants. Now, here is the finesse. Paul and his team didn't just email an invitation. They *called* the representatives and spoke with each of them, letting them know about the training, what to expect and that the team was looking forward to meeting them. The objective of the strategy is that when the phone call finishes, the warranty representative is thinking *that sounds good*.

When the warranty representatives flew in from around the country they were met at the airport. The Accenture project team hosted a small welcome dinner the first evening and the second night invited a number of senior client executives to dinner with the warranty representatives. Throughout the two days of training Paul and his team were conscious about all the little things that go towards a positive emotional experience.

The initiative was successful in positively influencing a key first group of people about the change, of establishing positive emotion associated with the system and the project, and seeding a key group of opinion leaders into the organisational network.

When change involves actual loss

Sometimes change does involve actual loss, for example when lay-offs occur. A restructure might mean a person is demoted and therefore lose their social standing. Sometimes benefits are reduced. A relocation of an office means a person may incur extra travel expenses or have less time with their family. If you are the manager of individuals losing from a change, then understanding *loss aversion* helps you to acknowledge and manage the loss for the person.

The most resourceful approach is to acknowledge the loss. Help the person classify the change as indeed a loss. This covers the need that people most have in making sense of the change. Acknowledging the loss is much better than concealing or seeking to diminish the loss. When leaders try to spin the explanation of a change it's so much more frustrating to staff and detrimental to the trust they have in you, than if the leader acknowledges that loss and empathetically understands its impact. Significantly, the acknowledgment of loss can diminish the emotional antagonism from staff.

Similarly, a leader can lose the trust and goodwill of their people if they overstate good news or understate bad news. People's trust detectors warn them to be wary. But if leaders treat loss as loss and resist diminishing it by dressing it up as anything other than loss then the leader will more likely earn and retain the trust of their people. People *can* process and accommodate loss. It's often the attempt at concealing loss, as much as the loss itself, that annoys them.

On one occasion the company I worked for was acquiring another business. In this other company there were a small number of people covered by a type of pension or retirement benefit (a 'defined benefit plan') that our company was not prepared to continue. Rather than inheriting the risk of uncertain future obligations to the employer, our plan was to introduce a more predictable ('accumulation') plan. Indeed, if the defined benefit staff had chosen not to convert to the accumulation plan we may well have not gone ahead with the acquisition. The implication of the change for the small number of staff was that their future retirement benefit would most likely be less under the proposed new arrangements. We approached the change as a loss for the affected staff. We did not dress up the change as anything other than loss. We briefed the individuals on the plan and prepared actuarial estimates, comparing the likely outcome of their retirement benefit under their existing plan and under the proposed plan. The actuarial comparison showed that they would most likely be worse off by the change. Of course, there was a greater potential loss as well—they and their colleagues might not have a job if their company folded because the sale fell through. Our purpose in giving the staff the comparisons was so they could discuss the situation with their families and determine whether they supported the change or not. We also reimbursed the cost of them obtaining their own actuarial and legal advice.

Because we called the loss a loss and handled it accordingly, the staff appreciated our honest approach. They trusted us. We did not understate the *bad news*. We were said to be empathetic and definitely didn't begrudge the affected staff seeing the change as a negative for them.

The outcome was that all affected staff agreed to the change and expressed appreciation for our approach, for our candour, and for the information they were able to discuss with their families.

The weight of negative feedback over positive

The predominance of loss aversion helps us see the significance attached to any negative feedback we might receive from our manager—the potential loss being loss of social standing, prestige and self-esteem.

We know it's good practice when we provide feedback, say at annual reviews, to give people many more elements of positive feedback against one item of negative feedback. How many elements of positive feedback are required to outweigh a negative element? There is no conclusive research as far as I am aware that goes *specifically* to this point, but the number might be close to 14 to 1. That number comes from a Dan Ariely study.

Dan Ariely is Professor of Behavioral Economics at Duke University and he makes sense of apparent irrational behaviours. In one study he and a colleague assessed the relative price we attach to avoid losing what we have versus the price to gain what we don't have.

From first-hand experience Ariely knew that basketball tickets at Duke are greatly sought after, hard to come by and hence highly prized. Fans camp out at night to be in the queue just to enter a ballot for tickets. So anyone who even goes into the ballot for tickets has to be keen. Ariely and his colleague wondered a) what people who missed out on tickets would pay to obtain one—to gain, and b) what people who obtained a ticket would need to be paid to give up their ticket—to lose?

The researchers approached fans from the ballot who missed out to find out what they would be prepared to pay for a ticket. And they approached the fans who had been successful in the ballot to see what price would need to be offered for them to forfeit their ticket.

The results give us quantifiable insight into the significance of not losing what we already have. The students who did not own a ticket were willing to pay on average $175 to obtain one. However, the students who owned a ticket demanded about $2,400 to lose it—around 14 times greater.

Given the nature of humans, the answer might well be that no number of positive items of feedback can overcome the weight a person gives to just one item of negative feedback.

If you are a staff member, it's handy to know why you dwell on the negative. If you are a team leader, this is handy for the next time you conduct a performance review. Up until now you might have been surprised and critical of a person's response to your feedback in a review. You might have been careful, following good practice to give many more items of positive feedback to negative. You might have weighted it about seven to one. Having done so, you were then annoyed that the person focused on the one negative! And guess what they talked about that night at home when they described their review. They were highly likely to say, 'And guess what my manager tells me I should improve!' and they relate the negative while overlooking or diminishing the significance of all the positives.

The benefit of knowing about the power of *loss aversion* is that you no longer need to be surprised or derailed by a person's response in this or a similar situation. The further benefit is that you don't avoid pointing out the valid negative. If you did avoid it, the person might miss a learning opportunity. The point is that you are now equipped to know how a person will probably respond. So, next time one of your team attaches significance to the negative, don't be surprised by their apparent irrational behaviour. They are being very human. You would well do the same!

Making sense of appraisals

Loss aversion, along with the other instincts, helps make sense of performance appraisals. To what extent do you look forward to your appraisal and if you are a manager, how much do you look forward to conducting performance reviews? For most staff and managers the answer is a resounding, 'Not at all!'

You probably find that performance review discussions are unlike any other conversations you have between you and your manager (or as a manager, between you and your staff). They tend to be strained and artificial. In many organisations managers only conduct reviews under duress from a cajoling HR team (I've been there). And in many organisations, HR as the custodian of the system is frequently fine-tuning the system just *one more time*.

Human instincts helps makes sense of appraisals, explaining why we invented them and why almost everyone finds them more than challenging. And human instincts gives pointers for leaders to help make them work.

On the one hand we can see through the lens of instincts why we invented appraisals with rating assessments: the allocation of a rating is a power device and one that hierarchical social animals would use; because we love to classify people a rating is a method of doing so; they do provide a way of knowing how we fit in our social group at work; as organisations grow way beyond 150 people designers of the systems begin to treat staff as strangers and it's okay to rate strangers versus family and clan; we are attracted to simple solutions and can deny the deeper effects of those solutions on the system; the appraisal process at least drives a discussion between the manager and their staff so that each person receives individual attention; and we seek to take judgment out of performance assessments.

On the other hand, also because of instincts we can see why they tend to be problematic and always being tweaked to try to make them work. The prospect of being rated triggers loss aversion, not only in terms of possible impact on salary but just as importantly on social standing and personal self-esteem; the rating raises the emotional stakes for both the individual and the manager; most people end up being rated average which is not uplifting for people; because not everyone in a team can be rated high, the team works out that they need to look good compared with their peers so competition is established within the family unit; managers intuit the negative impact ratings have on team harmony; ratings and the degree of fairness of a review triggers gossip;

and while we might wish to, we can't take judgment out of an assessment. (The evidence is that a person is more likely to be rated highly if they were appointed to their role by the appraising manager. If your manager did not appoint you, you are less likely to receive a good rating.)

Shortly we will discuss what a leader can do about these challenges. More details about these pros and cons are covered in a March 2009 newsletter archived on our website: www.hardwiredhumans.com.

IMPLICATIONS OF THIS INSTINCT FOR LEADERS

Here's a snapshot of what we have learned about the instinct of *loss aversion*.

1. As a natural pattern for living organisms humans are attuned to avoid loss.
2. We screen information for loss versus gain.
3. When change is presented, if people detect gain, they support. If they detect loss, they resist. If they are uncertain, the default is to assume loss.
4. The assessment of loss is at the individual level.
5. When being reviewed or receiving feedback, people focus and dwell on the negative as a defence against loss.

There are significant practical implications of *loss aversion* which, if incorporated into your toolkit, will make managing people easier.

Implication 1. People will tend to assume loss at times of change

Understanding that people are not resisting change, just screening for loss, will help make sense of people's response to change. A leader on one of our programs had a light bulb moment. He'd been managing the implementation of a new overtime policy. For him and his team the change meant that overwhelmingly people would be better off under the new policy. Before hearing about instincts and in particular *loss aversion* he just couldn't fathom why he had so much trouble convincing his team that the change would be good for them and that they should sign the new policy. The penny then dropped. He realised that the very first communication, via email, triggered fears of loss. Here's what the employees received (you can see from the first few words where the readers' minds might jump to classify!):

> We would like to introduce the attached new overtime policy. It is proposed that this new policy will replace our current overtime policy and form part of your new terms and conditions of employment. We would like to introduce this policy for the April pay period.
>
> Would you please review the attachment and if you have any questions or concerns please raise them with either me or your manager by 5 March 2010.
>
> If we do not hear from you we will assume you are fine with the new policy and we will introduce effective 1 April 2010.
>
> Thanks
>
> HR Manager

The manager was never able to shift his team's belief that they would be worse off, the team never signed and they missed out on increased overtime payments.

Implication 2. Understanding change in terms of loss aversion empower leaders

The myth that *people resist change* is quite a burden for leaders. If we believe that people resist change then we tend not to lead change as creatively as we should, which then becomes self-fulfilling. The belief that people resist change can lead to leaders being apologetic about imposing change.

Yet the opposite is closer to the truth: we expect our leaders to watch for and respond to changes in the environment and to lead us and our community to a better place.

The breakthrough concept here is that leaders just need to be better at managing the change so that the people involved don't just default to fear of loss due to clumsy leadership. No wonder 70% of change initiatives fail.

Companies applying instincts to managing change are finding that change need not be a big deal.

At the beginning of 2010 Philips Healthcare was about to manage a restructure, going from a design based on business units to a structure based on geography. The Australasian Managing Director Harry Van Dyk and Human Resources Director Jo Hilyard took their management team of thirty managers with us to Taronga Zoo to understand and apply instincts in order to manage the change well. One of the ways the team applied instincts was to be conscious about concerns of loss and to cover those concerns with staff right up front in order to avoid unnecessary fear and uncertainty for the majority.

The management team identified a number of things that people would be most concerned about:

1. Will I have or lose my job?
2. Who will I be reporting to?
3. Will the membership of my team change?

Some roles were unfortunately made redundant and the affected staff would lose their jobs. If the specifics of job loss was not covered explicitly then most people would be anxious about the possibility of losing their job and would be distracted until they knew otherwise.

So Philips did a few things. Before the key announcement they let the affected people know that they would be losing their job. Then when they held the staff meetings all staff could be told that anyone being made redundant had been advised. In other words if you have not been so advised then you are not losing your job—number one loss concern covered. For loss concerns two and three, prior to the meetings organisation charts had been prepared showing the reporting structure. People were invited to view the charts on the wall—there was a stampede! Staff didn't have to make it up for themselves, didn't have to assume the worst and didn't need to gossip to try to make sense of what was happening. The facts were there covering what they most wanted to know.

Now that loss aversion was covered the Philips leaders could then talk about business strategy, client service and the reasons for the new structure.

Three months after the change the thirty managers came together to talk about how they'd managed the change. In hearing their stories and seeing the increased confidence of the managers in leading the change, Harry closed the meeting by stating, 'I hate to think how we would have managed if we hadn't applied human instincts.'

Implication 3. Change is assessed at the individual level

Because people screen for change at the individual level—assessing the implications for themselves and their family—we can expect a range of responses to change. The response will most likely be explained by *loss aversion*. Understanding that people are not resisting change but guarding against loss or potential loss allows leaders to be more empathetic and less critical of their people.

Because each individual is assessing the implications of a change for them it is not sufficient to plan and communicate a change at the group or team level. That's not low enough—it needs to be at the *individual* level.

Implication 4. If change involves actual loss

When change involves actual loss for individuals then the messages from instincts is clear. Leaders are best to explain the change so that affected people can *classify* the effects as loss. People will appreciate your candour and will trust you. They won't need to look anywhere else to make sense of what you are telling them.

One senior executive I was told about was explaining on a global telephone call a change of how services were going to be delivered to clients. Everyone on the call had an expectation that jobs would be lost. But unfortunately the senior leader hosting the call skirted around the issue and tried to conceal this key point—the point of immediate interest to the listeners.

The staff on the call were disgusted. Their anger fuelled their disengagement and attitude that it was 'everybody for themselves'. We humans are quite resilient and would much prefer to receive bad news directly.

It's why the chief executive who fronts up to a manufacturing plant to inform 600 staff that the plant will be closing finds that she is told by the employees, 'We really appreciate *you* came and told us.'

An example of a positive application of explaining a change in terms of loss was the HR manager who had the task of explaining to staff a number of changes to their health insurance scheme. Some of the changes were to the benefit of staff and some would be to their disadvantage. The HR manager commenced the explanation this way, 'There are some changes that will be to your advantage and there are some changes that will most likely be to your disadvantage. What I want to take you through today is the detail of when you are likely to be better off and when you are likely to be worse off.' With this approach, people are being advised about the changes in language that reflects their innate need to classify into gain and loss in order to make sense of the change.

Implication 5. Safe environment

People explore and are curious about the world around them when they feel safe. Effective leaders establish an environment where people feel safe and secure. Humans do amazing things and deliver beyond expectations when they feel confident, and much of that confidence comes from a feeling of being held in high regard by their leader and within their intimate social group.

The elements of a safe environment are straightforward. One, of course, is physical and mental safety—that people are not in harm's way. Second is the context of the team's direction and performance and the standards of behaviour expected. Third is clarity about what is expected from each person, achieved by personal goals linked to the team's goals. Fourth, the leader's behaviour needs to be consistent so that people don't have to guess what mood you are in and how you will decide things.

Implication 6. Performance appraisals

From the discussion earlier as to why performance appraisals tend to be awkward and defensive, there are several key lessons for leaders when conducting performance reviews.

1. Accept that sitting down and discussing a person's performance over the last 12 months is more emotional than rational, usually for both the team member and the manager. If it is approached as

predominantly rational and transactional then the discussion is destined to be ineffective.

2. Appreciate that your team member's bias is to protect against loss. If your organisation uses a performance rating system (numbers or words), then a person being appraised is unlikely to reveal weaknesses as they will be worried that doing so will diminish their rating. There's a lot riding on a rating for a person, and it's not just about pay reviews or job promotions. More fundamentally is the person's social standing, both at work and at home.

3. If you work with a rating system, appreciate that the rating will tend to dominate the conversation because that provides the focus for loss or potential loss. An implication of this, contrary to conventional wisdom, is to cover the rating as soon as possible in your discussion so that it's known and you can move to a more open and learning-oriented dialogue.

4. Use the power in your hands appropriately. How you conduct the review impacts on your relationship with the staff member. This includes your investment in preparation—high-power people are inclined to put less preparation in than they should. It includes the words you use. For giving your feedback on things the person might improve on, the less sensitive manager might say, 'You have weaknesses that need to be addressed'. A more sensitive manager, and one more likely to achieve a receptive response, might be, 'As I think about this past 12 months and what will help you, I've been thinking about anything holding you back. I reckon there is one thing …'

5. Your staff member knows you have opinions of them and most people want feedback to help them grow, so be prepared to provide them with helpful information. Ask them to identify areas that they a) are proud of and b) that they could develop. They might well identify what you want them to, which allows you to be in a position of agreement rather than judgment.

6. Performance reviews—when done well—provide the opportunity to cover topics that people very much want to discuss with their manager. The most important ones are:
   • What did I do well this last year?
   • What did I not do so well and can learn from?

- How did I develop last year and what should my development plans be for this coming year?
- What are my personal growth and career opportunities and how do I best get ready for them?

Finally, as we discussed earlier, don't be derailed, frustrated or critical when the team member dwells on the one negative that you might point out. That's the dominance of loss aversion over gain. A hundred positives might not overcome the focus on one negative.

Implication 7. Understanding the response to feedback

Loss aversion helps explain why we respond the way we do to negative feedback. It's only natural for people to respond emotionally, to be defensive and perhaps, if the feedback is significant, for the person to respond aggressively. The instant defensiveness is to protect against loss, including loss to self-esteem. We'll fight frantically when threatened. Neuroscientist Joseph LeDoux lists aggressively defending oneself as one of four strategies animals call upon in response to fear or being attacked. He refers to a researcher Isaac Marks who lists the four responses as withdrawal (avoiding the danger or escaping from it), immobility (freezing), defensive aggressive (appearing to be dangerous or fighting back) or submission (appeasement).

For a leader, the benefit of knowing that a range of responses is natural helps you avoid being thrown by any emotional reaction appropriate for the moment.

In fact, the appropriate emotional response will reassure you that your intended message has been received. If the appropriate emotional response to the feedback you are providing would be defensiveness, argument or tears and you don't see something close to this response, then you should reassess what you said and how you said it because it probably means your message was missed.

These last three chapters have painted the picture of how we process information to make sense of the world. We do so predominantly through our emotional radars in order to classify information, and if we are uncertain as to whether the information can be classified as either good or bad, we will tend to err on the negative in order to protect ourselves and our families from harm. In this way we follow the natural laws of the universe that serve living things well. One of our capabilities that can well differentiate us from other species is our verbal capability. Yet, if we understand one of the key functions of how we use language we find that its purpose is not so different after all. A key way we use language turns out to be critically linked to our life as social beings.

Instinct 6. Gossip

This instinct helps explain why:
- the informal grapevine is always buzzing
- people talk about others behind their back
- 'communication' is usually an issue in employee surveys
- people gather in small groups during breaks at large meetings
- some people are as thick as thieves and always support each other
- when a new leader is appointed they bring in their key allies and the old guard drifts away.

YOU'RE ON A COFFEE BREAK at a conference. You look around the room and notice a curious thing. The groups in which people are gathered are a consistent size. Hardly anyone is alone, and if they are they feel pretty uncomfortable because as a social animal if we are on our own in such a setting we feel awkward. All the groups are small, made up of two, three or four people. When a fifth person joins a group of four, within seconds the group either breaks into two groups of two and three, or one person wanders off to join another group. You'll notice the same phenomenon at a party or wherever people stand around in informal gatherings. This phenomenon is a result of how we use our vocal capability.

We humans have the most developed vocal capability of any animal. Indeed, Dr Goodall nominates this as one of the two attributes that distinguishes us from chimpanzees (the other being our superior intellectual abilities).

Combine this vocal capability with our instinct for social living and we have powerful ways in which our language capability is used. A major manifestation of this is seen in our natural urge to *gossip*—to engage in social chitchat.

There are two reasons why we gossip. The first is quite obvious—to gather and share information. Thousands of years ago this was a vital survival tool—to gain useful information about where the food sources were and the predators to avoid. The second and less obvious reason for gossip is to form and maintain alliances. For us, gossip is our form of grooming: to lubricate friendships, to create and service relationships, to establish reciprocity, to work out who we can trust, who we need to be careful of and to dance the delicate politics of community living.

Of course, 'gossip' may have negative connotations. That's understandable based on the classification of the word from one's prior experience, but while gossip may indeed be malicious, it need not necessarily be. It's interesting, though, that *communication* wouldn't quite do as the correct description of the instinct. While we have a verbal capability unique amongst animals, it's the way we use that unique communication capability that is significant and of interest in our behaviour and the implications for life in organisations.

The definition of *gossip*, courtesy of Professor Robin Dunbar of Oxford, is 'social chitchat'. These are conversations of a social nature, typically of the guess-what-I-just-heard variety, or you'll-never-guess-what-the-boss-is-up-to-now type. For humans with our advanced vocal capability, gossip is our form of grooming.

Grooming is a characteristic of social animals such as monkeys and apes and the way in which they form bonds and alliances. Robin Dunbar provides an explanation of coalitions and gossip. Humans are social animals. While living in groups has its advantages, particularly as a defence against predators, it also has its tensions. If we upset others we are forced to be with it can be awkward. The mechanism that helps us balance this closeness-and-distance tension is by forming coalitions between small numbers of individuals. This mechanism of managing coalitions in our group seems to be unique to higher primates including humans, apes and monkeys.

Dunbar continues his explanation that with our bigger brains, early humans lived in larger groups than other primates, and to physically groom other members of the community would have occupied too much of the day. So humans needed to find an alternative to physical grooming to relate to others and form coalitions of people they could trust and rely upon. Our alternative was vocal grooming.

Vocal grooming is much more efficient than physical grooming. With physical grooming, chimpanzees for instance are limited to one-on-one connections. With vocal grooming we can reach more individuals at the one time. Dunbar calculates this ratio at 1:3. Hence at those informal gatherings such as outside a conference venue we gather in groups of up to four, being one speaker to three listeners. Our social grooming ability doesn't extend, in the normal course of events, to a group bigger than four because we won't be heard and won't hold attention of a larger group. Dunbar extends this point to say that language, combined with our bigger brain, may have had great significance for human evolution. The capability of language may be the factor that allowed humans to gather in the largest groups of any of the hierarchical social primates. Our natural sized community, covered in Instinct 1, is around 150 people. The natural size of chimp communities is, on average, around 50. This greater ratio of humans to chimps (150:50 equals 3:1) is the same ratio of vocal grooming (3:1) compared to physical grooming (1:1). Given the evolutionary success of humans, living in larger groups appears to have had an advantage.

What proportion of mobile phone conversations are of a social chitchat nature for the purpose of cultivating relationships? Recently I was walking along a city street and overheard a young lady talking on her mobile phone. All I heard as she passed was her earnest reply to perhaps a female friend: 'I wouldn't trust him either!' That's social chatter. Only humans can perform this behaviour. And of course it is an obligation one friend has to another—if they are to remain friends, if they are to be in an alliance and if the favour is to be reciprocated. Imagine if the person I overheard had information that might be important to the other and she withheld that information.

Professor Dunbar has found that 66% of our conversations are of a social chitchat nature. Dunbar makes the point that if a work team goes out for lunch or coffee—provided they don't have a visitor with them which alters the dynamics—66% of the team's conversation will be of a social nature. Some of the conversation might be task related, but quickly the conversation will turn to important social news: who's doing what, the latest information about what's going on in the organisation, what other departments are up to, who's coming and going, the normal social news of the community including sports teams, family activities and the like. In fact, of course, one can't imagine a team being close that doesn't easily engage in social chitchat.

Obviously we don't spend every minute of our day in conversation. If we look at the proportion of our day spent conversing, and knowing that most of those conversations are heavily weighted to social chitchat, it turns out that the average person spends 20% of their day grooming.

Chimpanzees also spend 20% of their day grooming each other. Whereas we groom vocally, chimps groom physically. In the life of chimps, who grooms who is a critical social dynamic.

One night the battle between Lubutu, the alpha male of the Taronga Zoo chimps, and his rival Chimbuka got physical. The fracas occurred during the night when there were no human witnesses. When the keepers arrived in the morning they found Lubutu had lost two of his four canine teeth and Chimbuka had suffered a nasty gash to his face caused by a canine tooth. He almost lost an eye. Shabani, the third male, didn't have a scratch.

As a result of the tooth loss, Lubutu had to visit the dentist. Now, as any business professional knows, taking the alpha out of the group has potential dysfunctional implications. With Lubutu temporarily separated from the group, the keepers managed the social and political implications by separating the beta males and their families. The keepers took this action to make the reintroduction process smoother when Lubutu returned and the chimps were released back together as a group.

Like flies on the wall at an executive meeting, the keepers observed the reintroduction of the chimps, taking special note of the grooming patterns to monitor the social dynamics. Grooming amongst the three males would indicate reconciliation and possible coalitions. On this particular occasion when the three males were reintroduced they kept their distance from each other. There was a standoff. Chimp communities are politically charged. We can only presume that Shabani was in a delicate political situation. By not taking sides, at least not apparent to us humans, he ran the risk of alienating both other males. If Lubutu retained his position, he would remember that Shabani didn't support him when he needed help. If Chimbuka gained the top job, he would remember that he did so without any thanks to Shabani. Then again, maybe Shabani had plans of his own!

The grooming decisions made by the remainder of the chimp community were significant. With the three males back together with the community, as with prior similar occasions the females predominantly groomed Lubutu, showing their support for him as their leader. Chimbuka was given the cold shoulder. One assumes that this sign of moral support encouraged Lubutu to battle on to retain the alpha position, and also presumably weakened Chimbuka's resolve to take on the fight to try to wrestle the top role.

It took three days until finally the males groomed each other, calling a truce to hostilities.

Changing grooming preferences is a sign of shifting friendships. Females Shiba and Sacha had never been particularly close, until they gave birth to infants around the same time. Now as new mothers, with their offspring often playing, they spend much more time together and are now often grooming each other.

Positive gossip

Gossip doesn't have to be negative.

Given that people will gossip, leaders can use this constructively by creating the news themselves. James Strong tells a story of when he became the CEO of Qantas, the major Australian airline. To get to know the business he visited different groups of staff. On this occasion he was visiting a group of baggage handlers and asked them about their work and if there was anything he could do to assist them in their role. The baggage handlers told him about a problem they had with loading luggage on planes. They said that the containers were easy to load up the conveyor belt from the ground into the hold of the plane, but then it was a difficult and slow manual handling exercise to turn the containers and store them in the plane. With frustration they added that they didn't expect him to do anything about it as it had been a problem for years and plenty of people before him had listened but not cared enough to fix it. James did facilitate a fix. He talked with the manager of engineering who then had a couple of enthusiastic young engineers work with the baggage handlers. They found a fix to a long-term problem. James tells that this story spread like wildfire through the organisation. For the next month, wherever he went around the world, Qantas staff had heard this story and the fix. The story had spread around 30,000 people entirely on the grapevine. No formal method of communication—no company email, no staff newsletter, no executive video clip, and no Intranet news—could have spread the word as far, as efficiently and as convincingly as the story spread by word of mouth. That's social chitchat about important organisational news. Of course it's also a story about what sort of boss the new chief was, which was important news to know. For the staff, the story is the evidence of the type of leader now in charge. The channel is the gossip grapevine.

What do you want people to talk about?

Another positive use of *gossip* is to influence what people talk about and what spreads through the informal channels.

Here's an example of how *gossip* can be used positively by a leader. Early in my career I was a HR manager with IBM for around ten years. At one point I had the good fortune of working for a terrific executive called Tony Bowra. Tony had just returned to Sydney from an international assignment in Tokyo. At one of my first meetings with him Tony talked about his focus on staff engagement and retention and that he wanted his managers to treat staff morale as a priority. At that time in IBM, staff engagement was high and we did not lose many people, but Tony still wanted to ensure his managers were leading teams of high morale. I brought along to my next meeting with Tony the monthly staff attrition report. An employee had just resigned at our Wangaratta manufacturing facility in country Victoria. We'll call her Mary Smith. Tony asked whether Mary had been a good employee and I said she had. Her manager was Barry Sullivan, at that time a young production manager. While I was in his office, Tony picked up the phone and called Barry, having skipped the level of Barry's boss. Fortunately for the sake of the story this was in the days when people actually answered their phones! Barry answered. I imagined his surprise to find it was his divisional leader two levels above him who was calling. I listened to the conversation from Tony's side. 'Hi, Barry this is Tony Bowra. We haven't met yet and I look forward to doing so soon. I'm going through the staff attrition report with Andrew and I notice Mary Smith left recently. I understand that Mary was a good employee we were sorry to lose. I just wanted you to know that if anytime you need my help to avoid a person like Mary resigning, *please let me know.*' There was nothing intimidating in

Tony's tone, although of course his hierarchy and status were significant and would have had Barry's attention.

Now, in terms of gossip, what is Barry compelled to do? What does he do the moment he hangs up the phone? Yes, he has to tell his management colleagues about this phone call. Imagine if he did not! He'd be denying them critical information. If he did not share this conversation with them he might be allowing them to head into harm's way. And this is exactly what he did. He left his office and let the other managers know, 'I just had a call from Tony Bowra. I'll tell you what, he's hot on attrition.'

I visited Wangaratta a week later. The managers were still talking about 'Barry's phone call from Tony'.

Tony Bowra did not need to do anything apart from the sixty-second phone call to spread the word that he was focused on staff retention, and have a management team share his focus. Tony called only one of the managers at the plant. Gossip did the rest.

Stories convey meaning

Writing systems were invented around 3,000 BCE. That's a pretty recent invention, although a very clever one it was. But long before we could read and write, we told stories. Mark Schenk is the co-founder of Anecdote, a company specialising in equipping leaders in the somewhat lost skill of using stories to convey meaning.

I asked Mark to explain three aspects of stories: why they work, what the principles of a good story are and to give a good example of a story told by a leader.

Why do they work? The first reason, he tells me, is that they are fundamental to the way we learn and the way we convey information. It's a natural process. Our brain is wired with the ability for us to listen and to talk. Prehistoric humans passed information from generation to generation through stories. The second is that they are memorable and they achieve that outcome because they contain emotion. We remember a story better than mere facts because we remember how we felt when we heard the story. The third reason why stories work is that they are concrete. When we face ambiguity we are compelled to make sense of the situation (to *classify* it). We make sense of uncertainty by telling ourselves or each other a story.

When he was telling me this we were sitting in a cafe outside an office building. He said to me, 'Imagine we work in that office and we see the CEO of a major competitor walk into the building. We take an immediate interest as to why she's here and engage in conjecture to explain why she's mysteriously appeared at our office. I might say, "Oh, I know why she's here. Her company is on the acquisition trail right now—looks like we might be her next target." It sounds plausible, and in the absence of you having a better explanation that rationale takes hold. But then someone else joins us at the table. When we share with our friend what might be happening, he laughs and says, "They're both on the board of a not-for-profit. They're probably working on a charity initiative." Now this new story sounds, in fact, more plausible, and that becomes the explanation of the ambiguous visit.'

The fourth reason that stories work is that they reveal what's really happening. A statement of opinion has little meaning, but then when a story is told explaining the speaker's opinion the listener gets the meaning because it's now concrete. Mark explains that a staff member might make a statement of opinion that, 'Communication around here is lousy'. But that has little meaning, and little emotion, until the person provides the evidence by sharing a story. I laughed and shared with him a story an employee once told me about the proof that communication is really bad in his workplace: 'We found out who was invited to the Christmas party when one of my mates found an email left on the photocopier'.

He adds a fifth reason why stories are so important and natural. Stories form part of our identity (a subject we'll come to in Instinct 7). If you don't know the organisation's stories, it's hard to identify with the group, but once you know the stories then they and the organisation form part of your identity.

Mark explains why we have tended to lose the knack of incorporating anecdotes into the way leaders communicate. He says that in modern organisations there is a widely held view that we should be dealing with facts in a rational way, and we diminish, ignore or reject the value of stories to convey meaning. He adds that part of the barrier to anecdote is the imprint or meaning associated with 'story'—that it is associated with 'a fairytale' or 'fabrication'.

What are the principles of a good story? Mark lists five. A good story:

1. has a time and place marker ('Last week...')

2. is specific—the story explains an event that allows the listener to picture the event in their mind
3. involves characters—we can picture the people involved
4. resonates and the emotion of the story helps us remember it
5. is plausible and if the story purports to be true it must be true.

The third subject I asked Mark about was to share an example of a good story—to provide an example of how a leader might use an anecdote to convey their meaning to staff. He shared with me a story based on true events involving the Kwik Kopy printing company and its franchise store in Coburg, Melbourne. Imagine that the CEO of Kwik Kopy is talking to a group of franchisees about the company's value of excelling at customer service (a worthy aspiration but with an uncertain meaning without the evidence of a story).

> Kelvin runs our Coburg store. On Wednesday two weeks ago he demonstrated what customer service means to us at Kwik Kopy. At 4:30 pm that day a client collected a box of workbooks that he would use the next day for a workshop. When the client got home about 6 pm he opened the box to find that the workbooks were in a shoddy state. Unusually for Kelvin and his store, some of the pages were in the wrong order and all the workbooks had untrimmed edges. They were unusable.
>
> The anxious client called Kelvin and explained that he needed the workbooks for 7:15 the next morning. Kelvin swung into action. He immediately drove to the client's house, apologised and reassuringly said that he would set it straight. He went back to the store, reprinted the workbooks and at 10 pm dropped off to the client a perfect set.

The gossip test

With our insatiable appetite for talk and social chatter, the challenge is how to use this instinct thoughtfully and deliberately. I recommend using what I call the 'gossip test'. The gossip test is a simple question: *What do you want people to say afterwards?* 'Afterwards' is the situation at hand. You can use this question when you hold a meeting, when you give a project update, when you meet a candidate for a job or as a candidate when you meet a prospective employer, when someone joins your team on their first day, when you conduct a performance review, when you visit a client or when you manage a change. What do you want the person to say to their colleagues at the coffee shop or to their family when they go home that night? Here's the point: What you do and what you say will significantly influence what the person says, which is a reflection of how they feel.

I first used the gossip test in September 1999. I was employed in Australia's number two telco, Cable & Wireless Optus, and we had just won the privatisation contract to outsource the telecommunications services of the Northern Territory government. My colleague Cathy Wilks and I were on the bid team and taking the lead on the people dimensions of the change.

Well, we thought, if people are going to gossip how do we use that to our advantage in crystallising our actions and influencing outcomes?

We asked ourselves what we wanted the staff to say about us the night they went home after first meeting us. We decided that when the staff walked in the front door and reported in, 'Hi, darling, I met Optus today,' we would then want them to say five things: 'They seem like a friendly company (we care). They're straight (as in, no bullshit). They seem competent (we look like we know what we're doing). They seem fair (in the treatment of staff). I think I'll stay (we wanted to retain all staff).'

The power of the gossip test is that if that's what we wanted the staff to say, then we would need to act in ways that generated that outcome—in who we first introduced from our company, in our approach to employment benefits, in how and what we said, in our communication process and how we planned the transition of employment.

The approach was successful. Notwithstanding that staff had a choice to decline our job offer and stay employed by the government, all staff except one chose to join Optus or our consortium partners. The one person who declined the offer had previously declared his intention to retire. Significantly, the government as the client was delighted with the way we managed the people dimensions—they heard nothing but good things about Optus (the gossip test at work, again).

Applying the gossip test can assist leaders make an intelligent choice in their interactions with people. Take for example the scenario of a new person joining your team. The gossip test question you might set for yourself might be, *what do I want the person to say about their first day when they get home?* There aren't many managers who would say, *I hope the person says it was terrible. No one cared about me. I was left waiting in reception. I saw my manager sail past me late morning and it was obvious I wasn't expected because nothing was ready for me. I was thrown a bunch of manuals to read. I think I've made a terrible mistake joining this crowd.* Yet that may well be the way many managers handle a new person's first day.

More likely you would want the gossip to go something like this: The person gets home, walks in the front door and says, *It was a wonderful day. My manager met me in reception right on the dot of 9 o'clock. My desk and all the computer logons were ready for me. Would you believe my business cards were already on my desk! They even put on a morning tea for me. I had some quality time with my manager and then I got straight into some chunky work. I reckon I've made a great decision to join this team.* Obviously, your actions as manager will have influenced this desired gossip—indeed your actions will have predominantly influenced the person's experience and subsequent remarks.

Team dynamics and the gossip map

Who's talking to who is a proxy for the dynamics of your team. Mapping the connections between team members provides a clear picture of the degree of harmony or level of cliques and factions in your team. I call this the 'gossip map'.

Consider the following gossip map of Ally and her team. Ally is the team manager. The lines show the connectedness between each person and every other person on the team. The degree of connectedness is defined as the extent to which two people on the team interact. For instance, they go out for a coffee and easily engage in social chitchat about the organisation. The thick line means the two individuals (say Ally and Fred or Cindy and Erika) are 'thick as thieves'. The thin line means the two connect to a reasonable extent, like Bob and Fred, and the absence of a line means they don't really get on at all. In our example Bob and Cindy have no meaningful relationship, which could mean they don't trust each other or they have little in common, or perhaps one of them has just joined the team. The lines are not defined by how often people interact or how much time they spend together. Two people can spend time together on work tasks but not be part of each other's alliances. The point of the gossip map is that it reveals the extent to which people are open or constrained in their social chitchat and grooming.

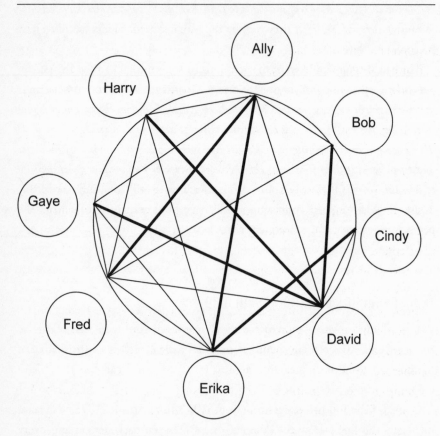

Figure: Ally's team gossip map. There appears to be two cliques and an isolated individual.

Looking at Ally's team, what insight can we gain about the social dynamics of her team? Who appears to get on with whom? Are there any apparent cliques? What are the signs that tell us who is close to Ally? What are the implications for Ally and her team if nothing changes? What actions should Ally take?

Here are some key observations about the dynamics of Ally's team. Ally is closely connected to Erika and Fred. David is close to a few people (Bob, Gaye and Harry) yet not that close to Ally. We don't have enough information to know if that is a good or a bad thing (how to *classify* it), but we suspect it means there is a clique around Ally and a separate clique around David because David and Ally are not close. Cindy is quite isolated. Cindy is closely connected to Erika who in turn is closely aligned to Ally. Apart from a moderate connection to David, Cindy is not incorporated into the team. Of course this could be for a range of reasons. Perhaps she is new to the team, or it could be that people keep their distance from her. The gossip map will assist Ally to make sense of the likely dynamics in the team so that she can make decisions and take action to improve the dynamic. From this map of their level of connectedness, we suspect that this is a divided team.

The most frequent cause of division is that the manager has favourites. One can imagine in this team that Erika and Fred are Ally's favourites. What are the likely signs that show Ally is closer to these two? Perhaps Ally with Erika and/or Fred often have coffee together; they are in and out of each other's offices or meeting rooms; Erika and Fred seem to get more air time and a better reception to their ideas in team meetings; they seem to be more in the loop with the latest information compared to others; and they are the ones Ally calls from her mobile after hours.

Given our powers of intuition, people don't need lots of information to make a usually accurate assessment of a leader's relationships. To the extent that a manager has favourites, it causes others not in the 'in-group' to rally together for support.

Chimps too seem sensitive about alliances and cliques. Frodo became alpha male of the Gombe chimpanzee community in 1997 at age 21. Being sensitive to the alliance implications of grooming, one of Frodo's leadership techniques was to disrupt grooming syndicates of other males. If he saw the males grooming each other, Frodo would charge the group and break up the bonding session because, unlike Julius Caesar, he appeared unwilling to risk that the males might be in coalition plotting his downfall. Although he is still alive, he is no longer the alpha male. He was alpha several times but never held on to the top job for long.

IMPLICATIONS OF THIS INSTINCT FOR LEADERS

Here's a snapshot of what we have learned about the instinct of *gossip*.

1. Gossip is the human form of grooming.
2. Social chitchat is part of normal, healthy group interaction.
3. We gossip to form and maintain alliances as well as to gain and share information.
4. Factions or cliques in a team are first and foremost caused by a manager showing favouritism to one or a few team members.
5. Gossip-sized groups explain the dynamic of people gathering in small groups.
6. Telling stories is the natural way to communicate and for a message to be memorable.
7. The gossip test can be used to both influence the narrative and to design the implementation of change.

There are significant practical implications of *gossip* which, if incorporated into your toolkit, will make managing people easier.

Implication 1. Don't stop the gossip

Some leaders try to stop the gossip—good luck! Gossip is the social chitchat of group living and is a critical dimension of life as a human. Sharing stories and opinions is part of the natural order. One cannot imagine a group of humans being closely bonded without social grooming, and rather than try to resist it the better focus is to use gossip effectively.

Implication 2. Monitor team dynamics to avoid favouritism

Ideally our family-size team will be free of factions or cliques. When your team goes out for a meal together, how sensitive are they about who sits next to whom? In a harmonious team it's no big deal and people will be relaxed no matter who they happen to sit next to. In a cliquey team people will strategise their seating arrangements so they can spend the time with their alliances.

They might even travel to the restaurant together so their seating plan won't be disturbed and they won't have to sit with people they don't like or don't connect with.

In a fractious team there will be a significant amount of whispering in sub-groups and closed-door conversations. There will be segregation of who goes for coffee with whom and who is excluded from sub-groups. It will be like a school playground.

Prior to his current role, Glen Thompson was a new first-level manager with Meat and Livestock Australia in Sydney. To give him a fast start to leadership I was coaching him in human instincts. In one session he drew the gossip map of his team. He was initially concerned that there was not a single thick line (strongly connected in a social chitchat sense), only thin lines (somewhat connected) between all six people in his team, including himself. But when we discussed this and he reflected on the positive, professional dynamic of his team, he realised that the evenness of the connections meant that there were no cliques in the group. Everyone was friendly and equally connected. The team got on well and worked collaboratively without being strongly connected. And one of the key positive elements about his map was the even lines that branched from Glen to all his team members. There were no favourites.

We know from basic manager school that *thou shalt not have favourites*. Here's why. When managers are closer to some team members than to others, cliques are likely to form. Team members easily intuit who has the most attention from the manager, who's most in the loop and who seems to have the latest information. If some of the team members are close to the manager (the in-group) then those who aren't are the out-group who initially might vie for recognition and social acceptance, but if that is not successful, bond as the out-group. Factions have formed as a consequence of favouritism by the manager. Like family, we do not appreciate being loved less than others.

Implication 3. Healthy reciprocity

For primates, one of the functions of grooming is reciprocity. If I'm a chimpanzee and I spend an hour or two grooming you, then when the chips are down for me and I'm being picked on by dominant individuals some time later, then I expect that you'll come to my aid. Of course if you don't, the grooming sessions might dry up. I know that I'm expected to return the favour as well. And besides, grooming is enjoyable. In chimps, grooming stimulates the production of endorphins, natural opiates—similar to opium—that create an overall sense of pleasure and wellbeing.

You've likely noticed a similar dynamic at your own workplace. In meetings there will be a consistent pattern of who supports whom with allies always endorsing each other's ideas and suggestions.

If this is a normal human pattern then we should use it consciously. We should reflect on who we are connected to and, as a leader, whether we are investing in the relationships with people who report to us so that loyalty is developed. At the extreme, a leader who does not invest in connecting with their people is denying nature and likely has little loyalty from their troops.

This dynamic of bonding and reciprocity is another reason for regular one-on-ones between leaders and their people. As well as task catch-ups, the one-on-ones become a time of chitchat where an individual and their boss can talk about what's going on around the place. This doesn't mean maliciously talking about other people or passing on negative news. It means that without social discourse two humans cannot be close.

Implication 4. Who do you groom, want to groom and try to groom?

Are you connected to the right people? Networking is an important activity for any human group and organisations are no different, especially if you want to get on.

Of course it might initially be tricky to break into to an established group, especially if you are seen as a lower level person in the pecking order. One day at Taronga the beta male Chimbuka started his display, wailing at the top of his lungs and swinging a heavy climbing rope in the exhibit. Keeper Allan Schmidt says the thing that most stirs Chimbuka is if no one pays him attention. Alpha male Lubutu, sitting alone at the time, ignored Chimbuka, a not unusual choice of an alpha to refuse to concede respect for a lower ranked individual. As Chimbuka's display gained in intensity, the third adult male Shabani moved to sit with Lubutu, clearly signalling his political support. At the height of his awesome display Chimbuka launched himself at the other two males. But as soon as he hit the ground he meekly joined the other two in a friendly huddle. The three of them commenced an intense grooming session. Nine-year-old Samaki tried to be one of the big boys and join the adults in their grooming. But the three adults refused to permit him to do so and Lubutu lashed out at the youngster to make it perfectly clear that he wasn't welcome and he was not yet 'one of them'. Of course, when Samaki is accepted his status will rise.

In organisations, managers tend to have more gossip connections than individual contributors. An average manager has, surprise surprise, 7.4 people who they trade gossip with. Individual contributors trade gossip on average with 3.9 people.

An observation Dr Goodall made is that there are benefits to a chimp who aligns themselves with a powerful male who happens to progress in the hierarchy. If chimp B supports A and A secures the top job, then B's position is elevated in the hierarchy. Of course, if A doesn't make it then there will be consequences for B.

In one organisation where I worked there was a beta male who, with the patronage of the chief executive, was groomed for the top job. This aspirant male had emerged from the succession planning process and was given all the experiences and development to equip him for the CEO role. But the fateful day came when the beta male could no longer contain his ambition and refused to bide his time pending the CEO's retirement. In a bloody coup the younger male turned on his patron. The older male conceded defeat, licked his wounds and quietly slipped away.

A matching scenario was played out in the forests of Africa. According to Dr Goodall, Figan was the most powerful alpha male in her 50 years at Gombe. Goblin was a young aspirant when Figan was in his prime and Figan supported Goblin as his protégé. Goblin clearly had that inner drive to rise through the ranks—he left his mother at the young age of seven to spend time with the adult males and began challenging the lower ranked males at a younger age than normal. The young upstart benefited from Figan's support, the alpha signalling to others that Goblin had his support and that others should leave Goblin alone. Goblin thus rose through the ranks, dominating each male in turn. 'Eventually,' Dr Goodall tells the story, 'the inevitable

happened. Finally, there was only one male left and Goblin turned on Figan.'
For about a year Figan and Goblin, erstwhile patron and protégé, battled it out
until finally Goblin wounded Figan and took over.

Implication 5. Social settings to allow chitchat

We covered earlier that 66% of our conversations are of a social chitchat
nature. This is normal and healthy. One cannot imagine a bonded group of
humans who don't engage in social chitchat. Therefore a leader conscious of
this need will organise gatherings where team members can freely engage in
such social discourse. The settings can be simple: team lunches, morning teas,
dinners and social gatherings.

And when you do gather in such settings, expect people to talk about what's
going on in the organisation—who's moving where, what so-and-so might be
up to and what the other department is planning. All this does not need to be
malicious. It's just the wheels of social dynamics being greased.

Implication 6. Use of gossip-sized groups

A specific way to create social discourse is to serve drinks at the end of the
work day! In December 2009 Metro Trains became the operator of Melbourne's trains. Part of the contract involved Metro taking over the functions
of three companies that operated different parts of the network so that staff
transferred from one of three companies into Metro. After a few months of
urgent initiatives, then HR Director Bill Armstrong and his team decided
that they needed to do more to connect people now working together in the
HR team.

Bill and his head of Learning and Development, Nicole Sullivan, organised a
team planning session to discuss future priorities. I was invited to facilitate the
session. The knowledge of gossip groups was applied at the end of the day when
at about 5 pm drinks and hors d'oeuvres were served. Earlier in this chapter
we saw that when humans stand around to chat they will predictably do so in
groups of between two and four. What also happens in these settings is that
people tend to talk about things they've probably not talked about during the

busy hours at the office—social and family topics. In one of the groups I was chatting with, one person asked her colleague, 'So Scott, how many children do you have?' What an important topic to Scott. You could not know Scott without knowing the answer to that question. A team can only be close if you know that type of information about each other and without this informal setting a question like that is often not asked. The social discussion will be as significant to the functioning of the team as the formal planning session that preceded it.

Implication 7. Ask the gossip question to find the truth

The grapevine is a reliable source that reveals how people are thinking and feeling. It's worth monitoring and tapping into. This can be done informally if people are prepared to share with you what's being talked about. And it can be done formally by asking someone to tap into what people are talking about.

A manufacturing company asked for my assistance to review their low staff engagement to identify barriers to performance. In a series of individual meetings with generally trades and production people, I asked, amongst other things, a direct gossip question: 'In your lunch and coffee breaks, what do you spend most time talking about?' The answer revealed the number one issue holding the organisation back. Almost everyone said, with obvious disgust, 'We talk about the foreman!' 'What do you say?' I asked. 'We say he's a (various swear words).' The kindest description was, 'He's a little Hitler.' With a little more prodding they often added, 'We don't know why management puts up with him. This tyrant is causing so much anxiety and division, destroying morale and causing people to leave.'

The management subsequently fired the foreman. Six months later I was asked to check in with the staff. I asked a similar gossip question: 'Six months ago I asked what you spent most time talking about in your breaks. What's the situation now?' Unanimously they looked at me and with a smile exclaimed, 'You know, that's all changed! We don't talk about work stuff. There are no issues now. We talk about personal stuff and things in the news. Management no longer features!'

Another situation when asking the gossip question is useful is when you are considering a new role. Imagine you are a candidate for a role with another organisation. You are keen to know what it will be like working in this new organisation. You're interested in the culture and interested in the style of boss you'd be working for. The problem is that you'll tend to be told information that, even if not done so deliberately, biases towards the positive to ensure you are kept interested as a candidate. But then you might get a rude shock soon after you join—information that comes to light within a few days that would have influenced your decision if only you knew!

To get over this problem you can ask the gossip question, *If I join you, what will I find that people say when they talk about the boss I'll be working for? What are the positives and negatives people say about the culture?*

The questions rely on the fact that not many people lie. Your potential colleagues interviewing you, while they have been representing the best side of the organisation, won't lie to questions like these—partly because a week into your employment they don't want to be found out as having misrepresented the truth.

When you ask your question, you'll also pick up their instant response, written on their face. Are they embarrassed by the questions and grasping at ways to express their answer diplomatically? Or is there an unequivocal positive joy in their response?

Implication 8. Seed the grapevine to influence the narrative

Sometimes it pays to feed information into the informal grapevine to influence what people talk about and the opinions people form.

Nick Evdokimov is a manager in the Queensland office of Philips Healthcare. When he and his colleagues acquired the knowledge of instincts to use in the management of an organisation restructure, one of Nick's takeaways was that gossip can be used constructively—it doesn't have to be negative. So he set about using gossip as an aid to successfully manage the restructure.

A challenge Nick faced was that in the Brisbane office the leadership position, District Manager, was vacant, so there was an absence of the normal high-power person. Yet Nick still wanted to get some momentum for the change. He decided he would have to do so in an informal way as he didn't have the formal leadership position to rely upon.

Part of his thinking was that with the amount of change that had happened in the past, like in many organisations, the long-term employees had got pretty cynical regarding changes which were often announced with fanfare but then slow to be implemented. He wanted to avoid the 'we've-seen-all-this-before' response that drives people to ignore the change.

So, in thinking about how to use gossip constructively, Nick identified three people in the Queensland district. He would have a chat with each of them, separately, to let them know about the restructure. Nick wanted to be 'up-front' with them and to avoid the perception that the information was a management secret. One of the three people was an account manager who is upbeat and who interacts with other account managers. There was an enthusiastic young engineer. And he talked with one of the old hands—a senior engineer who can be a bit cynical but is also an opinion leader.

Individually, Nick confided in them as to what he had learned in Sydney when the managers had met to talk about the restructure. He shared his insight that the plan to structure around geographical districts was a good one, especially as it allows local offices to make their own decisions to control their destiny and where Sydney head office would be there for support, not control. The three individuals were enthused by the discussion. They could see how the structure fixed issues for them personally.

Ten days after those conversations Nick had a regular team meeting of his group of engineers. The restructure was not on the agenda. But people started to ask, 'What's all this about the new model?' There was high engagement. The tone was one of enquiring, exploring and positive energy. Nick tells me, 'It wasn't me shoving it down their throats. It definitely wasn't cynical. They'd heard interesting things about the restructure on the grapevine.' Nick answered the questions that he could and said that there would be an official meeting when the district leader took up their position.

Nick concludes, 'Using gossip really demonstrated to me how I could better influence things as a manager. It helped the change go smoothly and to gain strong acceptance.'

Implication 9. The gossip test and influencing the narrative

Given that we humans talk and share stories and opinions, it's not surprising that the words people use reflect the leadership style of their manager and the emotion associated with the leader. The question therefore arises: What do you want the story of your leadership to be?

I recently coached a new manager, Robert, who needed a fast start to people management. In addition to Robert being new to his role, the members of his team were quite new to the company. I introduced him to the 'gossip test' and suggested there were two questions he should reflect on (similar to the 5 word test outlined in Instinct 3. Emotions Before Reason):

1. What five things do you want your people to say when their friends and family ask them, 'What's it like working for Robert?'
2. What five things do you want them to say when they are asked, 'What's the team like that you work in?'

After he'd had time to reflect, Robert emailed me with his desired answers to the two questions. In relation to what he would want his people to say about him, his aspiration is that people would say that working for Robert is:

- personally and professionally rewarding
- stimulating and we're always learning
- fun
- fair (Robert won't ask you to do something he wouldn't do himself)
- predictable (Robert does what he says he will do).

In relation to the second question as to what people would say about the nature of the team, he would like the answer to be that it's:

- cohesive
- collaborative
- winning (we over-achieve targets)
- unselfish
- fun.

Having used the gossip test to clarify his aspiration on these two subjects, a major part of what he now needs to do is a) live those sentiments himself and b) insist on those behaviours of his team by managing any exceptions. If you're a leader, what would you want the answers to be in relation to yourself?

Brad Newton leads a sales team at the IT firm Symantec in Australia. He used the gossip test to crystallise the desired culture of his team. When Brad took over the team he knew how the team was talked about—by other teams and by his executive. It was not all favourable.

Brad put to his Northern Enterprise team, 'How do we want to be known?

What few words do we want other people in the company to say about us? And then we'll live those values.'

The team decided on the following words:

- engaged
- successful
- supportive
- motivated.

Brad then began to reinforce those values at weekly team meetings. As a result the team soon started to work differently. They helped each other and they related more positively with other sections of the firm. After a few months Brad checked in with the senior executives. What words were they using now when they talked about the Northern Enterprise team? The words matched the aspiration of the team. Brad had successfully applied the gossip test to change his team's culture and the regard in which they were held. Over that year during the difficult climate post the Global Financial Crisis, sales increased by 14% year-on-year, one of the strongest performances in the company.

Implication 10. Using stories to convey meaning

Given our preference to hear and tell stories, our communication is enhanced if we incorporate stories into how we explain our opinions and requests. As discussed earlier in this chapter, stories provide meaning that's not available if we communicate by fact alone. In writing this book, I've sought of course to follow my own advice by providing anecdotes to illustrate points. They're sure to be one of the most memorable parts of the book and the facet talked about by readers to their friends and colleagues.

Implication 11. Change management and the gossip test

Managing change is a good time to think about the gossip test. Anticipating what people will say, and what you want them to say, will help you manage the change effectively.

The gossip test made a difference to a company planning an office reloca-tion. The location executive and his team used instincts to plan the people dimension of the move to manage the change as smoothly as possible, to reduce any distractions to productive work and for staff to attach positive emotions to the new building. Part of the challenge was that the layout of the new premises was open plan which meant a number of people would lose their offices. Understandably, given *loss aversion* and *hierarchy and status*, these folks were not going to be delighted by the change. In planning the project, the gossip question was asked, *Given that the staff affected are not likely to be happy, what's the best we can hope they will say when they go home the night they first hear they'll be losing their office?* The answer was, *Guess what, darling. We learned about the new office layout today. I'm about to lose my office. But I sort of knew that it was just a matter of time. Paul* (the top leader) *is also losing his and he was nice enough to come by and let me know.* How would the project team achieve that sentiment?

Paul decided to see each of the affected managers individually before others knew about the open plan. So just before the announcement, Paul called on each affected person and spent a few minutes with them letting them know, 'Those of us with an office will be losing our office when we move into the new building. I wanted to let you know personally before any announcement is made.' The response from all the affected people was, 'Yeah, I reckoned that this would happen. I understand, and thanks for letting me know.'

While we're discussing this change case, the project team also developed the first seven words that Paul would say when he gathered the staff together to inform them of the relocation. The move was necessary because the business unit had just won a significant contract and space was getting tight. The project team brainstormed what Paul should say. Monday morning the staff filed into the room to hear the announcement of the relocation. They were well aware of course that space was getting tight and that a relocation was on the cards. So it was not a surprise but nevertheless a change that most people would prefer not to have to worry about. Paul opens the meeting, conscious about the speed to emotionally classify based on their instant emotional reaction, 'Our success means it's time to move.'

Implication 12. Change management and gossip groups

An ideal time to use the natural gathering of people in small groups is when managing change.

Earlier in this chapter I mentioned the case of Optus winning the telecommunications outsourcing contract from the Northern Territory Government in Australia. As well as using the gossip test, we also used the natural dynamic of people to gather in small groups of between two and four people. The time had come when we were presenting to the in-scope staff about the planned employment transfer approach. We could predict from our knowledge of instincts that in a large meeting there will be very few questions—*loss aversion* predicts that there is a fair bit to lose by asking questions of your new employer in front of your colleagues (for starters, you're concerned that you might look silly if you ask what turns out to be a 'dumb' question).

Aware of this, we knew there was still a way where we could quickly and effortlessly tap into people's questions and concerns. At the end of the formal session, as the head HR person I closed the meeting by saying, 'If there are no more questions,' looking at my watch, 'that's good timing as it's now time for morning tea which will be served outside. Please enjoy morning tea.'

Predictably, people outside the room stood around chatting in groups of between two and four. Our project team members, cups of coffee in hand, could now easily move from group to group, introducing ourselves and asking whether there were any questions about the transition and the presentation just made. Not only were staff now in small groups, but they were also most likely to be with their friends. So on both counts people now felt more comfortable to ask questions. The benefit of tapping into these small groups was soon evident when in a group of three people I joined one employee said she had a question. Now, based on what we've learnt about *loss aversion* we can predict that this person's question will almost certainly be about possible loss (therefore the loss concern can be raised and covered within a few minutes of the formal meeting). 'I'm pregnant,' she said, and it was clear that she was. 'I have a question about my maternity leave. In our organisation we get paid twelve weeks' maternity leave and I've just heard in the presentation that you pay six weeks. I'm worried about what's going to happen to my extra six weeks?' There it is, the loss aversion question!

I was able to respond immediately, 'Clearly you're pregnant. You will be covered for your twelve weeks' maternity leave with no loss of benefit.' I handed over my business card and said, 'If you run into any problems about this, please let me know.'

From a gossip perspective two things have now happened. First, the person goes home that night, walks in the front door and says, 'Hi, darling. I met Optus today. And guess what? My maternity leave is covered.' Positive gossip has been generated.

Second, her two colleagues at the morning tea conversation overheard the response to the maternity leave question, which sounded to them like a fair approach. This then affects their views about Optus and will influence how they think and speak about the company afterwards.

From a loss aversion perspective, the pregnant employee has had her loss concern question covered right from the start. Without covering her question facilitated by this small group design, she may have gone weeks without an answer, and given the dominant fear of loss, she would most likely have convinced herself that she would lose six weeks' pay. If we had not tapped into her concern early on, she would have unnecessarily but understandably assumed loss before gaining her answer. She would likely have had negative feelings about the new company based on her assumption of loss.

If all of what we have covered so far isn't enough—gossiping, emotional processing, pecking orders and politics—we are about to add a further complicating dimension. Well, on the one hand it's complicating, but on the other we can't hope to make sense of leadership and working in organisations unless we accommodate this dimension. In leading humans we are dealing with individuals.

Instinct 7. Empathy and Mind Reading

This instinct helps explain why:
- it's great to put a face to a name
- body language is trusted more than people's words
- people get really annoyed if they feel like just a number
- being interviewed over the phone doesn't really work—we need to meet
- emails are used to be more direct with another person than we would be face-to-face.

LUDDE INGVALL IS A renowned ocean sailor. As a kid growing up on a Finnish-Swedish island, his dream was to sail and win open-water races. He's pretty much achieved that dream, twice winning the world championship of maxi racing, he's won the Fastnet race, and has twice won what he rates as the toughest offshore race in the world, Australia's Sydney to Hobart. You might well remember seeing him and his crew on the news in 2001 when his boat got caught in a twister, a giant water spout, while racing in the Sydney to Hobart.

To succeed at the level Ludde Ingvall has you'd need to know a thing or two about leading people as a highly cohesive team. He says that his key to building high performance teams is to know and appreciate each person as an individual. This takes us to the instinct of *empathy*—a theory of mind—and its associated dimension of *mind reading*.

I met Ludde at the yacht club where his boat is berthed—all glistening 30 metres (100 feet) of her—with a mast the height of a 14 storey building. I asked him about his approach of managing at the individual level.

'In my world,' he began, 'I have no alternative. I must engage my people as individuals.'

'How do you do that?' I asked.

'In Sweden we have a philosophy called *lyhord* which is about being attuned to other people's needs. It means that I need to listen to and respect what a person wants and needs—their desires and dreams. I need to care for you as a person.'

'If I were to work or sail for you,' I asked, 'what would you do to fulfil that philosophy?'

'I let people know that *I know* they have dreams. You'd get to know that I'm interested in you as a whole individual—if you have kids, if you have a mortgage. When someone joins our team I don't just ask them what their dreams are. They might not know themselves at that point or they might not be ready to share their dreams with me. I tell them that I am going to help—no matter what their ambition is. I tell them that I am a stepping stone for their career and life journey. For some people their dream is to be an America's Cup sailor. I tell them that I'll teach them what I can, that I'll coach and prepare them and then when the time comes, when they're ready for the next step, I'll make the call. I'll call Russell Coutts if you want to sail in the America's Cup.'

'Then when they leave I want to remain a part of their lives. I love to get a card from an ex-employee letting me know they've had a child or had some sailing success or success in another area of business. I want them to remember me and my team as being a valuable stepping stone.'

He repeats the key, 'I let *you know* that *I know* that you have dreams and aspirations.'

Empathy

Humans are one of the few animals that appear to have a sense of 'self', or 'theory of mind'. We are also a facial animal, meaning that we read others based on what's written on their face. It's only through a sense of self or 'me' that we can have a sense of other 'selves'.

The way scientists test for theory of mind is to have an animal, such as a chimp, a gorilla or a monkey, get used to handling a mirror. Then with the animal under light sedation the scientist puts a dab of blue makeup on the forehead of the animal. As the animal regains consciousness it will at some point pick up the mirror. A chimpanzee is the only animal that will look into the mirror and try to wipe the blue spot off *their* forehead. In other words, *that's me in the mirror and somehow I now have a blue spot on my forehead.* Monkeys tend to drop the mirror and scream in fright at the 'other' monkey in the mirror. Dog owners tell me that a dog barks at the dog in the mirror, and cat owners say that cats hunch in the ready-to-attack position. The head of primates at Milwaukee Zoo in the US tells me there may soon be research testing this phenomenon on bonobos (another of the great apes and most closely related to chimpanzees). Bonobos may well be added to the list, but so far it's only chimps that demonstrate this theory of mind and sense of self.

Understanding self and seeing other individuals as separate selves is connected to acts of altruism or selfless service to unrelated others. Gombe chimp Mel was a little over three years old when he lost his mum. He had no elder brother or sister to care for him. Like a human baby, Mel would not have survived on his own. An unrelated adolescent male, 12-year-old Spindle, 'adopted' Mel. Spindle would wait for Mel during travel, allow the infant to ride on his back or cling ventrally (under Spindle's body) when Mel was cold or frightened. Spindle would draw Mel into his nest at night and share food with him in response to Mel's begging. Spindle would even put himself in harm's way by rushing in to rescue Mel if the infant got too close to adult males displaying. Spindle's caring behaviours were the same as a mother's, even to the point of taking hits from socially aroused males as he protected Mel. The curious thing about selfless acts towards non-family is that there is no genetic advantage in doing so. Something else is at play in those species that demonstrate altruism. Dr Goodall can only speculate why Spindle adopted Mel. It might not be a coincidence, she wonders, that Spindle lost his mother in the same epidemic that killed Mel's mother.

Individual expectations and self-fulfilling prophecies

The significance of our sense of self is that leaders are not just managing teams—you are managing individuals. Managing at the individual level provides a clue to being an effective leader.

One way to demonstrate this critical dimension of managing at the individual level is to consider the impact your belief about individuals has on their confidence and performance. If we weren't individual souls then issues associated with our view about another person wouldn't come into play.

Like all good lines of research, investigation into the impact of a leader's expectations on performance started with rats in a laboratory. In an early study back in 1964, one group of unsuspecting laboratory students was told that the rats they were studying were bred for maze-brightness, and thus this group of participants had high expectations. A second group of students was led to believe their rats were bred for maze-dullness, and hence they had low expectations. In actual fact the rats were assigned randomly to the students. In a sobering result for sophisticated talent planning, in the groups where expectations were high, the rats ran faster than in groups where expectations were low!

From the rat laboratory it was time to take the research to school classrooms. Students in 18 elementary (infants) classrooms were tested using a nonverbal IQ test. Twenty percent of the students in each class were then randomly labelled as 'intellectual bloomers', the workplace equivalent of 'high performers'. Teachers were told that students with this classification were expected to improve markedly in comparison to other students. Eight months later the tests were re-administered. Those students who were labelled as intellectual bloomers improved significantly more than the students who were not given this label.

The next step on the path of studying the impact of expectations on performance was to study adults in the real world. The setting was an Israeli Defence Force training camp. The course was an intensive one involving an average of 16 hours instructor-trainee contact daily for 15 weeks.

Before the 115 soldiers entered the camp they were tested by the researchers on a range of capabilities. The soldiers were then randomly assigned to one of three 'command potential' categories—*high*, *medium* and *unclassified*. The researchers created this third category to add credibility to the process in the minds of the instructors and to give an impression that there was not yet enough information about these trainees compared to the other two groups.

Four days before the trainees arrived at the training camp the instructors (leaders) were provided (mis)information about the trainees. The leaders were advised of the trainees' command potential, hence creating a performance expectation in the minds of the instructors. The instructors didn't know that the classification was entirely random. Would the expectation become self-fulfilling?

The potential impact of the expectation on trainee performance was measured in three ways. The first was *learning performance* including knowledge of combat tactics, topography, standard operating procedures and practical skills like navigation and accuracy of weapon firing. The second was *attitudinal*: how much the trainee desired to go on the next course, the extent to which the trainee would recommend the course to friends and their overall satisfaction. The third dimension was the *leadership perceptions* trainees had of their instructors.

What impact did the setting of expectations have over the 15 weeks? The results showed a substantial effect on all three dimensions. The expectancy on trainees explained 73% of the variance in performance, 66% in attitudes and 28% in leadership. Trainees whose instructors were led to expect more did indeed learn more. Trainees of whom more was expected responded with more favourable attitudes towards the course. And trainees expected to do well by the instructors had a more positive impression of the leaders' behaviour. *High command potential* trainees did better than the *unclassified* group who in turn did better than the *medium potential* trainees.

After the course the instructors were debriefed on the study. 'The expectancy induction was so effective that it was difficult to convince the instructors that it had been random,' noted the researchers and concluded that 'managers get the performance they expect'.

There are sobering lessons in all this for managers and the way in which leaders relate to their people as individuals. If a leader has high expectations of their people, then team members will:

1. perform higher (and vice versa if the leader has low expectations)
2. enjoy work more
3. think more highly of the leader—independent of the leader's actual leadership ability!

While in a practical sense leaders might relate better and have a greater regard for some team members than others, this inclination should be contained. Showing a greater regard for some might lift the performance of those few, but it will likely diminish the performance of others. So for managers the tip is to have and show confidence in each and every team member. People will surprise themselves by doing things that they never thought possible.

A person's individual identity

Given that connecting with individuals is critical, we need to go a little deeper to see what this means in practice. What does it mean to relate on an individual level? In a nutshell, it means that we need to know the other person's identity. There are certain things we need to know about someone to know them well (and that they would need to know about us). These are the parts that make up the canvas of our personal being. What are these key things?

We'll assume that, if you are a leader, you know the names of the people who work for you—their name being the foundation element of someone's identity. To a village-level leader this foundation point might be overlooked. Andrew Marks is a leader in a fast moving consumer goods company. When he was about to commence a new appointment as production manager in control of a factory of 80 employees, he got the list of his staff and learned everyone's name before his first day. He said at the time, 'I now just need to put a face to a name and learn something about each of them.' His view was that he couldn't lead them if he didn't know them. 'Why would they allow me to be their leader if I didn't know them as people?'

To know someone well we would need to know about their family or personal relationships. Are they married? Do they have a partner or are they single? If the person is a parent, you'd have to know that and you'd have to know the number of children they have and you'd need to know the basic things about their kids—names, ages and gender. We know from Instinct 1 the central role of family for us humans, so we can't know a person if we don't know about their family. As Ludde Ingvall might put it, *you know* that *I know* about your family. Connected to family, you'd know roughly where the person lives.

You'd know where the person spent their early years of life as those roots form a core of a person's identity. For someone to know me you'd have to know that I was born and raised in Broken Hill, a mining town in the Australian outback. It's part of who I am. You could rationally be my manager, but without this sort of knowledge about me then we would not be emotionally connected.

It would be helpful to know the person's proudest life or career achievements. You would know, as Ludde Ingvall explains, their dreams and aspirations. You'd know what they want to achieve in their career, and whether they are motivated by progression or by professional expertise. To know someone well you would know the experiences that have most shaped the person's character.

Finally, you'd need to know their interests outside of work. If someone is involved in a volunteer or charity group you'd need to know that to know the person. If a person is into golf then you'd know this.

Who are the people at work you relate well to? Who are the people who you like working with and are energised by? There's a good chance you know each other well. Of course the extent to which your values are similar will be a major factor. But beyond values the extent to which we know the factors that make up their identity is critical. Without appreciating each person's uniqueness and identity your influence as a leader will be inhibited.

Every now and then a leader will debate with me about the need to know a work colleague or direct report in the way I have described. The argument put is that this transgresses into people's personal lives and is not work related. I seek to encourage them to shift their point of view by offering that without understanding the basics of a person's identity we will be inhibited as a leader. I add that getting to know someone well doesn't mean completing a template in an interview. Rather, what will happen if we are genuinely interested in finding out what makes the other person tick is that the information will emerge naturally.

Steve Jones is a senior manager with Metro Trains. His job includes responsibility for 200 station staff. He's a straight talking sort of person and his people find him highly motivating to work for. I was impressed by results he received for a leadership profiling tool and asked him what he does to create such a constructive connection with his people. Crediting a piece of advice he received from a prior managing director, he said, 'You need to know three things about people who work for you.' So he sets out, because he is genuinely interested in doing so, to know three key things unique to that person. 'What three things?' I ask. He says, 'Things like their family, where they live and their footy team' (which if you know Melbourne and the tribal passion in which people identify with their football team this dimension is not surprising). It's a given to Steve that he would know the name of the 200 people in his department. Why their location? 'Because with our work having a connection with the local community is important.' I ask him how he gets to know this information about people. He tells me, simply, 'I ask them when they first join.' He adds that it's easy to ask people these questions the first time you meet (and his personable approach means that he would do so in an easy, conversational way). He says that, 'The key thing is that you remember for the next time you see them.' He makes a brief note as a memory jogger after the conversation. He says enthusiastically, 'The benefit is that people know I care about them.'

Steve says that it really impresses the partners and family members of his staff when he runs into them at a shopping centre on a weekend and knows the names of the family members. If you work for Steve you're working for a boss who knows you. And you feel good about that—because your identity is valued and you know you're working for a boss who cares about you as a person, not just as a proverbial number.

Steve's approach is similar to Ludde Ingvall's. When I was sitting at the yacht club with Ludde I asked him what he would say to a manager who doesn't want to know personal information about people—their dreams or personal situation. He answers with two points. First, he says, understanding some managers' caution, 'I agree that the individual needs to tell you on their own terms and in their time, to the extent that they want to share.' His eyes brighten when he makes his second point: 'But, if you don't *want* to know, that's a lousy way to manage. You'd be giving up tremendous potential of people.'

Self interest

This dimension of *self* also helps to see self-interest in a fresh light. We can expect people to seek what they want—even manipulate a situation. Chimpanzees do the same.

Dr Goodall tells a story about Figan who we've met before. Years before he would become the alpha male at Gombe, Dr Goodall was observing him as a youngster trying to get a share of food. He was missing out. 'Commonly when a chimp gets up from a resting group and walks away without hesitation, the others get up and follow. It does not need to be a high-ranking individual—often a female or a youngster may start such a move. One day when Figan was part of a large group and, in consequence had not managed to get more than a couple of bananas for himself, he suddenly got up and walked away. The others trailed after him. Ten minutes later he returned by himself, and naturally got his share of bananas. We thought this was a coincidence, but the same thing happened over and over: Figan led the group away and returned for his bananas. Unquestionably, he was doing it deliberately. One morning, after such a manoeuvre, he returned with his jaunty walk only to find that a high-ranking male had in the meantime arrived in camp and was sitting eating bananas. Figan stared at him for a few minutes and then flew into a tantrum of screaming and hitting at the ground. Eventually he rushed off after the group he had led away earlier, his screams gradually receding in the distance.'

Leaders can expect a fair degree of self-interest in the behaviour and decisions of others, and of course their own. So we shouldn't be thrown when people look after 'number one'. What's critical is that this behaviour is contained so that individual self-interest does not diminish the group's interests.

Altruism

The counterforce of self-interest is altruism—of putting ourselves in the position of others. The classic experiments demonstrating fairness to others is the ultimatum game. Jonah Lehrer in *The Decision Moment* provides a summary of these experiments. Two people are paired together and one of the two receives $10. This person gets to decide how to divide the money. The second person can either accept the offer, in which case both players pocket that share, or reject the offer in which case both players leave empty handed.

If we were rational beings one might expect the proposer to give a minimal amount to the receiver—say a single dollar. We would also expect the receiver to take the dollar, given that this still leaves them better off than before any offer was made. But that's not what happens. People offered an unfair deal consistently reject the offer. People don't appreciate being treated unfairly. Anticipating this outcome, and putting themselves in the other person's position, proposers allocating the money overwhelming make an offer of around $5.

The keepers at Taronga regularly observe acts of empathy. Two-year-old Sule is often harassed by the nine-year-old male, Samaki. As the schoolyard play begins to get rough, Sule tries to escape. Sule's mother Sacha is a bit of an absent mum, never there when the kid needs her. Samaki's peers, Lani (female, 8) and Furahi (male, 7), come to Sule's rescue. Furahi will launch into an altercation with the slightly older Samaki and Lani picks up Sule to reassure him. Neither Lani nor Furahi are family of Sule. Sule is a fun, happy youngster and Lani and Furahi just seem to be watching out for him.

Another common observation is when the 34-year-old female Koko gets into a fight. Sule often scurries over and gives her a hug which calms her down. Again, Koko and Sule are non-family. And when Chimbuka at the age of six lost his mum, Shona, then 14 years of age, stepped in and filled the role of mother.

Apologising

Another way to put the argument for the importance of *self* and acknowledging others is by looking at how we are expected to act if we transgress another. There's power in an apology.

Professor Dan Ariely has turned his attention to this quirk of human nature and the effect of an apology. In an experiment, participants in a coffee shop were given sheets of paper covered with letters. They were asked to find matching pairs and were promised $5 for completing the task. Upon completion, they were given a stack of $1 bills and asked to sign a receipt. Participants were 'mistakenly' overpaid $2, $3 or $4. What percentage of people kept the extra money? The study involved three different conditions.

Group 1 were the control group. Participants in this group were set the task and allowed to complete it with no annoying distraction. In this group, 45% of people returned the cash (as Ariely says, a somewhat disturbingly low number but that's not the point of the study).

Group 2 were characterised by participants who were annoyed but experienced no apology. In this group the participants were set the task and then the researcher pretended to answer his mobile phone. He spoke to his imaginary friend for 15 seconds about a pizza, hung up the phone, then continued to give the instructions without acknowledging or apologising for taking the call. What effect did this annoying interruption and lack of apology have on the inclination of participants to return the money? The answer is that people sought revenge! Only 14% of people returned the cash. It's costly to annoy people.

Group 3 we might call the empathy group. What impact would an apology have for redressing the interruption? In this group participants experienced the same interrupting phone call as for Group 2. Except this time, after the researcher was interrupted he apologised (said, 'Sorry') before resuming the instructions. In this 'apology condition' harmony was restored and 45% of participants returned the money, the same number as for the 'no annoyance condition'. As Ariely says, 'The show of regret was the perfect remedy.' That makes sense for an empathetic animal. The importance of an apology is the respect shown for the other's identity.

IMPLICATIONS OF THIS INSTINCT FOR LEADERS

Here's a snapshot of what we have learned about the instinct of *empathy*.

1. Humans are almost unique in having a sense of 'self', and it is only through a sense of ourselves that we can see other people as separate selves.
2. Our belief about another person affects that person's performance.
3. To connect with people we need to understand and acknowledge the other person's identity.
4. We humans will balance self-interest with altruism.

There are significant practical implications of *empathy* and personal identity which, if incorporated into your toolkit, will make managing people easier.

Implication 1. Adjust your approach for each person

The proverbial penny dropped for one manager on one of our programs. 'Ah!' he exclaimed, 'Given that I have seven people working for me I need to have seven slight variations in how I deal with things.'

One way to manage individuals is to manage to their strengths and accommodate their weaknesses (or more accurately expressed, tasks in which they

have little interest). A breakthrough for me as a young manager was working to the strengths of my team, rather than forcing each person to do the
package of tasks that might have made rational sense, but just was not going
to work. I was with IBM at the time and in charge of a HR team managing staff integrations associated with mergers and IT outsourcing contracts.
One member of the team, Rod Bezer, was terrific at the first stage of the deal
which involved relating to the HR team and the staff of the firm transition-
ing to IBM and in dealing with unions. He was not so good however (as he
acknowledged) in managing the minutia of detail when we got to the stage
of spreadsheets, remuneration calculations, preparing letters of offer and the
like.

What a breakthrough when Rod and I agreed that he should do the parts
he was good at and not be forced to cover the bits he wasn't interested in, nor
good at. And of course we found another member of the team who loved the
detailed spreadsheet work and was not confident in or attracted to the client,
staff and union relationship work that Rod so liked and excelled at.

This event is particularly memorable as I vividly recall defending my decision to another member of the team who complained that I shouldn't be letting Rod get away with doing the stuff he likes and leaving the other stuff for
someone else to pick up. We shaped each person's role around their individual
interests, with a positive impact on performance and morale for individuals
and the team.

Implication 2. Value each person's identity

Earlier in this chapter we covered the importance for a leader to know each
person who works for them, and that in the absence of knowing certain things
about a person there is no meaningful relationship. Let's capture the essence
of this as a checklist.

At the extreme, if a leader thinks about the list of elements that forms a
person's identity and thinks *I have no idea about my people* then the proposition
is that it's not possible to be relating effectively to another person and there is
no platform to be the leader of that person. Imagine this picture: *I have no idea
if Kim is married, single or in a relationship. I've got no clue where she grew up. I
don't know what her early jobs and career experiences were. Gee, I don't know what*

her interests are. In fact, the only thing I know about her is the job she does. I don't think Kim will give you the licence to be her leader.

Would you be able to talk for five minutes about each of the people who report directly to you? That's five minutes on each person! Here's the list of things you need to know about a person to know what makes that person who they are.

1. Their family or kin situation (partner or not, children, parents, siblings).
2. Where they were born and where they spent their formative years.
3. The key life experiences that shaped their sense of self.
4. Their personal and work achievements they are most proud of.
5. Their dreams and aspirations.
6. Their interests outside of work.

Does your boss know these things about you? How well do you get on with your boss?

The sense people have if they work for a non-empathetic manager is that the boss doesn't really need *us*—the boss might need workers, but it doesn't have to be *you and me*. It could be anyone. We're *just a number*. That's a demoralising environment for a human with our sense of individuality.

Implication 3. Create situations for people to know each other

The smoothest, indeed most natural, way to get to know others is to create situations where you can talk freely about a range of topics and get to know each other. Getting to know a person isn't about going through a checklist at an interview. It's about a relaxed dialogue that happens naturally in certain circumstances.

Graham McGibbon is a senior technical manager at Philips Healthcare. He was finding conversations with his team members at their desks pretty stifling so he started to take people out for a coffee. At first his people were a bit intimidated by the suggestion of going for a coffee. It was out of the norm and they didn't know what to expect. 'Why are we going for a coffee?' they'd ask, trying to get the information they'd need in order to *classify*. We know from *loss aversion* that their concern is natural. For Graham, having a chat over a coffee helps the conversation to flow better and he and his colleague cover a richer set of topics, including personal subjects. He does counsel other managers that it needs to be two-way. A manager must be open on topics that might come up.

And Graham goes a step further. He encourages team members to go for a coffee with a colleague and charge it to his account. Graham's thinking is that this facilitates people knowing each other. 'I know that they'll get into conversations that they would not get into back at the office—the type of conversations that bond people.'

Implication 4. When you hire

The ideal time to get to know someone is when they join your team. There are certain topics that are not appropriate to ask during the selection stage, but after a person is hired there is a short window of time where you can get to know each other and talk about each other's backgrounds, including the topics in the list above if they haven't already been covered.

It's also a time to demonstrate that you are attending to them as an individual. Have you made time for them on their first day? Were things organised for them? Have you got them settled and introduced them to others they'll be working with? Have you got them working on something useful?

Even at the interview stage you can show your genuine interest in the person as an individual and not as a number. A friend who recently went for an interview emailed me shortly afterwards and said, 'I'm happy to say I had a good meeting with the global head of HR last week. She spent a long time exploring my motivations which made it feel very personal.'

Implication 5. Individual catch-ups

If I was limited to just one piece of advice to managers on the subject of people-leadership, it is to have scheduled regular individual meetings with your direct reports (regular team meetings are a given). Some people call these reviews 'catch-ups'; others call them 'one-on-ones'. Fundamentally, they provide a platform for respecting and connecting with individuals and for effective delegation. These meetings should go for one hour and be held at least every two weeks.

I've mentioned previously that early in my career I had the pleasure of working for a terrific executive at IBM called Tony Bowra. I'd catch up with Tony every second week for a dedicated review. He rarely cancelled or deferred these reviews. As I walked into Tony's office, he'd swing his chair around and reach into his filing cabinet for my file, a simple buff manila folder. He had scratchy notes from our last meeting and slips of paper with memory jogger ideas that had crossed his mind since last time. We'd work through the list. 'How are you going with the morale review of Operations?' 'Last time you were going away to think about leadership education.' Some things were more operational but important to be addressed. 'Chris asked me about his job level—can you review his level, see if we're being fair and let me know?' That scratchy piece of paper would stay in the file for next time. And it wasn't all one-way of course. I had ideas to share or subjects to check. An hour with Tony was productive and energising. He sought for ways he might help, we bounced ideas around to advance a task and he checked progress on activities so that I knew he was interested.

Some managers think that holding regular reviews might be perceived as micro-managing. I don't see it that way at all. Tony didn't tell me how to do things nor watched over my shoulder. Rather, he showed interest in my work and didn't delegate and then forget. If as a manager you give one of your team a task and never follow them up, that person gets to wonder if it was important at all. Tony always closed the loop.

In conducting individual reviews you'll notice a few things. You'll notice that each person uses the time in their own way. Some use it to go through their task list. Some use it to talk concepts. Some go into more personal things. That's a good thing—the individual variance and accommodating different personalities. You'll notice that the meetings provide a setting for people to raise sensitive topics that might not otherwise have been raised. Often the person might raise a topic by saying, 'Oh, there's one other thing I'd like to talk about.' And they then share the subject on their mind.

These reviews also provide a vehicle for the leader to give feedback in a way that diminishes the potentially negative emotion attached to giving feedback. Earlier we discussed the emotional weight on the shoulders of managers when giving negative feedback as a major reason why they avoid it. If the leader has a coaching point to pass onto someone—a point that isn't a big deal and that to call a special meeting would overstate its importance—jot a note to take it up at that person's next one-on-one.

Over the years I've found that the reason managers often resist the idea of a regular catch-up with their people is that they are unsure of what subjects should be covered to make the meeting productive. Here are some suggestions.

1. Look at the progress of tasks since last meeting.
2. Identify and remove any roadblocks.
3. Discuss ideas of new tasks and initiatives to respond to emerging opportunities/problems.
4. Share any development/feedback observations.
5. Check if the person needs any support or assistance from you.
6. Note the action points for next meeting.

Regular reviews also easily accommodate remote relationships where you have direct reports working in a location other than your location. Individual reviews over the phone are effective enough and indeed critical in keeping connected with those who are in a different geography.

Now, we can predict if you give people a choice as to whether they want regular reviews or not, most will decline! First, they don't know what such a review means so *loss aversion* says it's best not to go there, and second, *contest and display* (which we are soon to come to) says that people don't want to look as though they need a review with their manager. So my advice is not to give people a choice. Then when the first review goes well—classified as *good*—you are up and away. And you might be surprised by the responses you trigger when towards the end of the meeting you ask, 'Is there anything else you wanted to cover today?'

A key measure of the effectiveness of your reviews is the extent to which you and your staff members look forward to your catch-ups.

Implication 6. Self-esteem and confidence

David Campling is another Philips manager. He leads a team of technical staff who are new to Philips. He wanted to show the team members that although they were new to the company they had unique and valuable knowledge because of their prior experience in the healthcare industry. David began by talking individually to each team member, either in person or by phone. One of the team had come from a public health background and was uncertain and lacking confidence that she was successfully making the transition from the public sector to Philips. Aware of this, David deliberately asked her for her point of view on a particular matter he'd been thinking about. By doing this he showed her that she had a current view on an aspect of the business that was both critical and unique, which helped to increase her sense of self-worth.

By asking each person their opinion about a topic within their expertise David hoped to demonstrate he can learn from them and that they have worth because of their unique experiences.

He explained to me, 'I'm giving them permission to ask questions, to challenge things and to express opinions. Everyone's opinion is out there on the table. It allows us to talk about our strengths and weaknesses, which as a package is what makes me, me.'

He's noticed team members now willingly engage each other in conversations to bounce ideas off each other. People are improving their ideas and no one needs to think they have all the answers. People feel valued for their unique expertise.

Implication 7. The birthday lesson about what turns each person on (and off)

I've had the good fortune over the years of working with some wonderful people. One of them taught me a great lesson. Cathy Wilks and I worked together at Optus (the same Cathy who I worked with on the NT Government outsourcing contract I mentioned in the previous chapter). Cathy transferred to report to me and in one of our early discussions when we were getting to know each other she made it crystal clear what she valued. She said, 'There is one thing you need to know that's important to me and that you should not forget.' I lifted my pen and waited with baited breath. 'Don't forget my birthday!' Although she said it with her characteristic short giggle, I could tell by the look on her face that she was serious. This was important to her. How simple for the manager!

Everyone has their idiosyncrasies. Having my birthday recognised might not be important to me, but if her birthday was important to Cathy then that's fine. It's not a complicated or difficult thing to deliver on. A birthday is very personal.

I also took the learning that for the boss to recognise people's birthdays was an easy thing to do. From them on I chose not to delegate the 'birthday thing'. I chose to be the one who sent around the happy email (to a team dispersed in various locations) congratulating the birthday person on their special day. This of course set the tone and others followed and added their good wishes.

Implication 8. Saying 'hello' in the morning

I hesitate adding this final implication regarding acknowledging others as individuals because it is terribly basic, and yet it needs to be included for completeness.

With the people we work with we need to say 'hello' each morning (or at the beginning of each shift) and as leaders expect others to say 'hello' to each other.

I once worked for a business where staff didn't greet each other of a morning. They would come to work, make a bee-line for their desk and slip into their chair with no acknowledgement to their colleagues, including the person sitting at the desk next to them. This is not natural behaviour.

Chimpanzees greet each other of a morning—both in the wild and at Taronga. In the wild if they meet a friend they haven't seen for a while, having perhaps been to different parts of their territory, they will greet each other. Often this involves a touch similar to a handshake, or perhaps holding each other or patting each other on the back. If there's a reason that chimps do this there is probably a reason for us to do so at work as well. There is! And that reason is from our sense of self and individuality.

What about senior executives connecting with front-line staff? It might surprise you to learn that front-line staff often *classify* senior executives according to who says 'hello' versus those who 'don't even say hello'.

Of course, the 'hello' isn't just a verbal greeting. The facial expression that goes with it is critical. Let's now turn to this dimension of *mind reading*— reading people by what's written on their face.

Mind Reading

At one level, *face* for humans is significant because it's our distinguishing characteristic and the way we recognise each other. I hadn't seen my sister for a couple of years as we live in different cities. I met her at Sydney airport recently. Unsurprisingly, amongst thousands of people we had no trouble recognising each other—and that recognition was obviously by the face. If we were penguins, the recognition would be by our chirp. My wife and I have visited Antarctica, and on one particular rocky beach the size of about five football fields were 600,000 penguins busily raising their chicks before the long winter returned. It's a natural wonder that the parents could identify each other and their chicks. They do so not by the face but by sound. Apart from being rather smelly, penguin rookeries are noisy places with parents and chicks squawking to identify each other. The returning parent with a belly full of krill to regurgitate for their chick will not open up the food channel until it's satisfied that the pestering chick is indeed its own.

At another level, *face* is important as it's the window to how we are thinking and feeling. The face is the way we 'read' others.

In *The Hidden Brain*, Shankar Vedantam refers to research that found it only takes five hours of face-to-face contact for a newborn baby to develop a preferential attachment to their mother's face over that of a stranger. He adds that scientists have found an area in the brain—the fusiform face area—that specialises in recognising human faces. It is activated both when we see a face and when we remember a face.

Our skill of reading faces emerges at an early age. Researcher Gert Gigerenzer writes that from birth children seem to know when someone is looking at them. When infants are about one year old, they begin to use adults' gaze to learn language (where is the adult looking when they refer to an object). At about the age of two, children begin to read others' gazes to figure out their mental state such as their desire. And three-year-olds begin to use gaze as a cue to uncover deception.

It's no wonder, given the significance of face and facial clues, that when the baby grows up and joins the workforce they will use visual and facial clues for fitting into the hierarchy. Gert Gigerenzer says, 'In human societies as well as in hierarchically organised social primate ones, a newcomer can quickly figure out the social status of individual group members by tracking who is looking at whom. Careful tracking allows a new group member to know whom to respect, avoiding conflicts that would upset the existing hierarchy.'

Chimpanzees are also facial animals and reading what others are thinking appears to help provide pattern and order in their societies. An incident involving a group of chimps on a border patrol at Gombe matches beautifully an office meeting—specifically that time when you get the signal from the boss that tells you, *oops, I'd better shut up*. The anthropologist Christopher Boehm spent some years at Gombe. From a description he provides of a border patrol party we can see the power of facial expressions and signals that lower ranked individuals use to read the desires of high ranked individuals. The patrol party is scouting their border and silently scanning the forest with the senior males taking turns in leading. They approach the no-man's land between their territory and that of their neighbours to the south. Their neighbours happen to be patrolling at the same time. The neighbours begin vocalising at the group Boehm is describing. One of the males in Boehm's group, Evered, begins to return the vocalisation, but he quickly chokes it off when he looks around at the alpha male, Goblin. The three senior males silently scan the valley and look at one another quickly. 'After nearly 60 seconds Goblin suddenly makes his decision and begins to vocalise and display' and the whole group immediately follows his lead.

The significance of eye movement can also help a young chimp get a fair share of food. Figan, this time as a youngster, features again. At the time a group of chimps were feeding on bananas. The young Figan spotted a banana that had been missed by the adults. The only problem was that the banana was resting in a tree just above the adult Goliath's head. If Figan had gone for the banana then Goliath would have got to it first. But also, if Figan sat and waited then he would likely have repeatedly glanced at the banana. 'Chimps are very quick to notice and interpret eye movements of their fellows, so Goliath would possibly, therefore, have seen the fruit himself,' writes Dr Goodall. So, the smart youngster moved away and sat so that he could no longer see the fruit. 'Fifteen minutes later, when Goliath got up and left, Figan without a moment's hesitation went over and collected the banana.' Dr Goodall concluded that, 'Figan had not only refrained from instantly gratifying his desire but he had also gone away so that he would not "give the game away" by looking at the banana.'

Universal facial expressions

Part of reading faces is to read the emotional state of people—what the other person is thinking and feeling. Paul Ekman has spent a lifetime of research exploring this dimension. His work has been popularised in the television series *Lie to Me*.

The great discovery of Ekman and his collaborator Wallace Friesen is that facial expressions displaying the key emotions of humans are the same all around the world. That's a remarkable discovery. Ekman's six basic emotions are surprise, fear, disgust, anger, happiness and sadness. Expressions associated with these emotions are constant irrespective of culture. When I met Dr Ekman in late 2009 he told me that he first travelled to remote places such as New Guinea in the 1960s to find people who had had no exposure to American movies and 'John Wayne' expressions. The local people 'correctly' identified photographs of faces expressing these core emotions. When we experience emotions we can't help but reveal them on our face—even if just for a microsecond.

Ekman and Friesen compiled a register of human facial expressions. They discovered that there are 43 muscle movements of the face and that those muscle movements can make up to 3,000 meaningful facial expressions. These were subsequently catalogued into a 1,000 page document called the *Facial Action Coding System*!

Inferences from people's faces

Faces are a major source of information about other people. When we look at someone's face we can read all sorts of information. And reading other people's emotions is a fundamental aspect of social living. But we are not necessarily rational in what we read into other people and we often attribute all types of competence in what we see. Attribution of competence from faces can even decide political elections.

Alexander Todorov and his colleagues showed that inference of competence based solely on facial appearance predicted the outcomes of US congressional elections and were also related to the margin of victory.

The researchers asked naive participants to evaluate candidates for the US

Senate (2000, 2002 and 2004) and House (2002 and 2004) on competence. Participants were presented with pairs of black and white head-shot photographs of the winners and runners-up. The participants did not know who won or lost. If participants recognised any of the faces the data for this pair of candidates were not used in the analysis. There was a strong correlation between perceptions of competence and the result. The candidate who was perceived as more competent won in 71.6% of the Senate races and 66.8% of the House races.

They then conducted an experiment where exposure to the faces was only about one second. This was enough time to achieve a similar assessment of competence and an accurate prediction of the winner. To assess that the participants were not evaluating the whole spectrum of traits, the researchers assessed if there was any difference on a range of attributes. In analysing the trait judgments, the judgments clustered around three factors: competence (competence, intelligent, leadership), trust (honesty, trustworthiness) and likeability (charisma, likeability). Only the judgments forming the *competence* factor predicted the outcomes of elections. And competence was also rated as the most important attribute for a person running for public office. 'Looking competent' helps get elected. And that assessment is made from a thin slice (one second) of information at that.

Todorov and his colleague, Janine Willis, went a step further in studying the inferences people draw from the facial appearance of others. They conducted a series of studies to determine the minimum exposure time people need to make inferences from other people's faces. They conducted five experiments focusing on different traits: attractiveness, likeability, competence, trustworthiness and aggressiveness. In each experiment, faces unfamiliar to the participants were presented for 100 milliseconds (1/10th of a second), 500 milliseconds (half a second) and 1,000 milliseconds (1 second). For each face, participants were asked to make a trait judgment and then to express their confidence in that judgment. To provide a comparison between time-constrained assessments and assessments without a time constraint, a separate group of 128 people made the five trait judgments with as much time as they felt they needed to make up their minds.

In the time-constrained part of the study 117 undergraduates participated. Participants were told that the study was about first impressions and so the faces would be shown for only a brief period. Each participant was shown 22 faces for 1/10th of a second, 22 faces for half a second and 22 faces for one second. Each face was shown only once. The only difference for each group of participants was the trait they were asked to judge (for example, *Is this person competent?*). Participants responded with a *yes* or *no* judgment and having made their judgments were asked to rate how confident they were in their assessment, from 1 (least confident) to 7 (most confident).

From what you now know about human instincts you won't be surprised that people make their assessments quickly and confidently. The results affirm the importance we place on reading people when we look at each other's face for the first time. An exposure time as short as 1/10th of a second is enough for a person to make a trait inference. For all five traits, judgments made after 1/10th of a second were highly correlated with exposures of half and one second. And they were significantly correlated with judgments made that were unconstrained by time. Giving people slightly more time from 1/10th to half a second increased confidence to a greater extent than when exposure time was increased from half to one second. The researchers concluded that 'these findings suggest that minimal exposure time to faces is sufficient for people to form trait impressions, and that additional exposure time can simply boost confidence in these impressions. That is, additional encounters with a person may serve to justify quick, initial … judgments' (which is what we would expect from *first impressions to classify*).

The researchers expected the highest correlations between rapid judgments made after 1/10th of a second and judgments made in the absence of time constraints would be for judgments of *attractiveness*. Yet judgments of *trustworthiness* showed the highest correlation. In hindsight, say the researchers, this finding is not surprising. From an evolutionary perspective, detecting trustworthiness may have been essential for human survival (and still a critical dimension of life even today). The researchers refer to other studies that show that detecting trustworthiness of another person may be a spontaneous automatic process linked to activity in the amygdala used in the detection of dangerous stimuli similar to what we covered in Instinct 3. Another possible evolutionary survival finding was that although confidence generally increased when exposure time was increased from 1/10th to half a second, there was one attribute where this increase in exposure time was not significant: *aggressiveness*. For a social animal, assessing aggressiveness quickly and confidently might be a handy survival skill.

Stereotyping from physical attractiveness

We can go one step further in painting the picture of the significance of *face* for us humans. From assessments we make from a person's face we then tend to attribute a range of other characteristics—in other words, stereotyping. It's handy to know this unconscious tendency so that we can contain our inclination to do so.

One study looked at the impact of stereotyping associated with attractiveness. Fifty-one male and 51 female undergraduates participated in a conversation with a member of the opposite gender. The pairs had not met before and even during the study they never saw each other. A researcher informed each participant that the experiment was about studying conversations where there is an absence of nonverbal communication. The participants would thus engage in a telephone conversation. Biographical details were provided to each participant on the other member of their pair. Unbeknown to the females, the males were provided with a photograph of their female counterpart, but the female did not receive a photo of her male partner. With the folder that the male received, the biographical information was real but the photo was not. The photo was one of eight photographs that had been prepared in advance— four of the photos were of 'attractive' females and four were of 'unattractive' females (assessed in a preparatory step by men not involved in this part of the study). The photo that the men received was randomly assigned. What impact would the perception of the person, through the attractiveness of their face, have on the interaction between the two people?

Before engaging in the conversation, each male perceiver rated his initial impressions of his partner on a questionnaire listing 34 trait adjectives (for example, friendliness, enthusiasm, social adeptness). Each pair then engaged in a 10-minute conversation. After the conversation males recorded their impressions. Each female also completed a questionnaire on how much she enjoyed the conversation, how comfortable she felt talking to her partner, how accurate a picture of themselves she felt her partner would have formed, how typical her partner's behaviour had been compared with the way men normally treat her and her own estimate of her partner's perception of her physical attractiveness.

The key purpose of the study at this point was to identify the personality attributes that the males stereotypically associated with attractiveness. Those attributes clustered under a broad spectrum of social skills. Men who expected to interact with an attractive female expected to interact with someone who was sociable, poised, humorous and socially adept. By contrast, males who expected to interact with an unattractive female expected to have a conversation with someone who was unsociable, awkward, serious and socially inept.

So, at this stage we have a predictable confirmation of stereotyping. The next stage is really interesting and rather disturbing. How would the expectations of sociability be translated to the female's part of the interaction?

Another group of eight men and four females ('observer judges') listened to taped recordings of the conversations. They only listened to the female. They listened to two 4-minute segments of the conversations and then rated each woman on a range of behavioural impressions. How did the initial male judgments in the getting-acquainted conversations affect the female's behaviour in that conversation? The researchers expected to find that the female's behaviour was impacted by the male's bias for those traits that had been affected by the male's stereotyping. Because the males expected attractive and unattractive partners to differ in sociability the researchers expected that observer judges would detect differences in sociability when listening to the female's contributions to the conversations.

Indeed, that was the result. In listening to just the female, the observer judges perceived the women in the two conditions differently. 'Attractive' females were assessed to be more confident, to have greater animation, greater enjoyment of the conversation and a greater liking for their partner than those women who interacted with men who perceived them to be physically unattractive. Perceptions based on randomly assigned levels of attractiveness had been transmitted into actual behaviour by the females themselves.

As well as demonstrating the significance of face for us humans, the study shows how we judge people affects the way we interact with them, which in turn affects that person's behaviour. If we replace from the conclusion of the study the words 'men' and 'women' with 'leader' and 'staff' respectively the point is made: 'What had initially been reality in the minds of the leader had now become reality in the behaviour of the staff with whom they had interacted'.

IMPLICATIONS OF THIS INSTINCT FOR LEADERS

Here's a snapshot of what we have learned about the instinct of *mind reading*.

1. We're dealing with master mind readers.
2. We read other people by the feelings that are written on their faces.
3. We have the capability to read 3,000 facial expressions.
4. We are quick and confident in reading people from thin slices of exposure.
5. We attribute personality characteristics from facial expressions.

There are significant practical implications of *mind reading* and the significance of *face* which, if incorporated into your toolkit, will make managing people easier.

Implication 1. You can't fake it

It's good to know that you can't really fake how you are feeling. This is because how you're feeling is written on your face, if only for a microsecond. Although we are not always accurate in what we intuit we are pretty good at the craft of reading another person.

If there is any inconsistency between what's written on your face (your body language) and what you're saying, people will rely on what they read on your face. People are quick to detect any inconsistency between words and expressions, and if they do detect incongruence their intuitive radars scream out warning them not to trust this person and their message.

Imagine that a team member comes into your office seeking your advice on something puzzling them. They're interrupting you from an urgent task you are concentrating on. When they ask, 'Have you got a moment?' and you instantly think, *Gee, I could do without this*, then that response is written all over your face. You might try to conceal your emotion and you might nod and sit there and let the person talk. But it's clear to your team member that *this is a waste of time and the boss doesn't care about me*. In such a situation you've really got one of two choices. If you can genuinely switch from the task you're doing to concentrate on the employee then do so. If you are under pressure with your own task and you'll be anxious to leave it then have that conversation and make another time to meet if the employee's task can wait a bit.

The thing is that our expressions are often involuntary. What we think and feel is displayed on our face if only for a microsecond. My wife doesn't like having her photo taken. She's concerned that her 'put-on' smile is not genuine. She can't fake it! Antonio Damasio explains why. Jude's problem is due to how our brain is wired. The problem is that the part of the brain that controls the facial muscles in a 'true' smile associated with a happy emotional situation (involuntarily controlled from limbic cortices probably using the basal ganglia, he says) is different from the facial machinery we use for voluntarily offering a smile (using the motor cortex and the pyramidal tract). Even actors have trouble faking a genuine smile because of the difficulty in mimicking the genuine expression associated with an emotion they are not feeling. If professional actors can't fake an emotion, leaders have no chance. It's better to be congruent.

Implication 2. Facial expressions linked to high power

A leader has high power relative to their team members. In Instinct 2 we listed the behaviours often exhibited by people with relatively more power. Many of these behaviours are negative. Adding now the dimension of facial expressions, it's handy for leaders to know that the emotions associated with those behaviours are likely to be displayed on your face.

- High-power people are less concerned about what low-power people are thinking—and that glazed look of boredom is easily detected.
- High-power people are less interested in listening to low-power people—when you don't listen it's easily detected and annoying to people.
- High-power people are inclined to talk more and ignore what others say—which means leaders are likely to be less interested in reading people than the staff are in reading the leader's face.

The implication here is that it's imperative that leaders are interested in others, that you do listen and that you do care. All that, too, will be written on a leader's face.

Implication 3. Reveal information

We often seek to conceal our emotions by controlling our expressions. This is particularly the case for high-power people who try to hide their vulnerability from low-power people.

The problem in seeking to hide our emotions is that we deny people useful information as to how we are feeling. Others will have to work harder to know what we're thinking. We will serve people better, generally, if we reveal our emotions. If we are happy it's good to show it. If we are annoyed then it can be productive to show this as people will have their suspicions anyway from our micro-expressions. If people are uncertain they have to work harder at reading us and will have ambiguous information they are struggling to make sense of.

At one extreme, if a leader is an emotional iceberg then their people will often be challenged with how to read their leader. At the other extreme, being too quick to show your emotion (such as quick to display anger) is rarely appropriate. While it might be appropriate to get angry if someone attacks a family member, it's not appropriate to 'hit the roof' at work. The point is that it's generally desirable for a leader to show enough emotion to enable another person to read the leader accurately and for the person to have enough information to know where they stand.

Implication 4. Avoid stereotyping

Once we are conscious of instincts we can make more informed leadership choices. If we know that we are naturally inclined to stereotype people merely from thin slices of information, we can resist the temptation to do so. We referred above to research that described conversations where a male partner treated a female differently based on whether the female was attractive or unattractive, and how that affected the way the female then behaved. We also learned from a study that elections may well be decided by how competent a politician *looks*—an attribute hardly associated with competence as a policy maker.

So, on the next occasion when you're about to jump to conclusions about someone or infer attributes to that person from one piece of unrelated information, listen to the little voice in your head that is counselling you not to do so.

Implication 5. Managing remote staff

We can see from the significance of *face* that being a manager of people located in another location is challenging. It's an unnatural obstacle for facial animals like us humans. What this means is that we need to work even harder and do extra things to overcome that inhibitor. We need to invest in getting people together so we can fill this human need. We need to call remote staff just to say 'hi', like John Loechel's manager does. John is a manager with the Australian finance sector company, The Guild Group. He's based in Brisbane and his manager is some 1,700 kms (over 1,000 miles) away in Melbourne. John tells me that when he joined the company, 'My manager would call out of the blue just to say 'hello'. The first couple of times he did this I couldn't work out why. Then I realised that that was the sole purpose—to say "hello", to keep in touch, to see how I was going. I really appreciated that.'

Now we'll turn to the final two instincts. Both have a dual purpose. Purpose one was and is to help make us attractive to a member of the opposite sex as a potential mate, and purpose two is a tactic to enhance our position in our social group.

Instinct 8. Confidence Before Realism

This instinct helps explain why:
- we set grand strategies but overlook the follow-through
- fads roll through organisations
- we end up with disasters that everyone saw coming
- people have an inflated view of their own ability
- inexperienced people, including managers, can be blissfully ignorant of their own incompetence!

WHEN A US AIRWAYS passenger plane flew into a flock of Canadian geese 95 seconds into its flight and lost both engines, Captain Sullenberger knew almost instantly what he needed to do. He would land the plane in the Hudson River. He assessed this to be the best option because he knew about the human instinct of *confidence before realism*.

On 15 January 2009 flight 1549 left New York's LaGuardia airport bound for Charlotte, North Carolina. Soon after take-off while still under full thrust the plane hit the flock of geese. In his wonderful book, *Highest Duty*, Captain Sullenberger describes the sound of the birds hitting the window as 'the worst thunderstorm I'd ever heard … like being pelted by heavy rain or hail'. Then came the pungent odour of burnt birds. Immediately, both engines failed and with the plane now gliding, one of the flight attendants described the cabin as being 'as quiet as a library'.

Captain Sullenberger had only seconds to make a good decision. He advised air traffic control at LaGuardia of the bird strike. The airport was immediately cleared for an emergency landing. But the captain decided that LaGuardia was not a good option, and neither was another airport, Teterboro. He famously announced, 'We're gonna be in the Hudson'. His decision to choose an icy river over two airports turned out to be an inspired call.

Captain Sullenberger had a long and distinguished career. His early training was as a military pilot and along the way he was a student of aircraft disasters. He sat on safety panels reviewing plane crashes. One theme he consistently observed was that pilots err on the side of confidence and optimism and tend to discount or ignore reality. Beyond the point of no return, pilots tend to hold on to the hope that they can avoid a crash and save the plane. Invariably this proves to be a disastrous and fatal decision.

Within seconds of the bird strike, the captain decided that to try to return to LaGuardia or go for Teterboro would be pushing the boundaries of what was realistic. If he made the decision to turn back he had to be sure that he would make it. 'Once I turned back to LaGuardia, it would be an irrevocable choice.' Within seconds he determined that there was not a good chance of making it back. If they miss the airstrip by just a metre, well, they've missed the airstrip and they suffer a crash landing. He also took into account that if the plane ditched into the river near LaGuardia there would be little maritime traffic to rescue the survivors. And if they didn't make the airport at all, they would crash over Manhattan.

The Hudson River looked like the most reasonable option. Although the river would be almost freezing in the middle of winter, he decided it was wide enough, long enough and smooth enough that he might land and keep the plane intact. He also knew that if they landed at around West 56th Street there would be plenty of ferry traffic to come and pick up the survivors. The plane hit the water smoothly enough, although with a bit of a jolt at the back. From the time of the bird strike to coming to a stop in the water it was all over in three minutes and eight seconds. All 155 passengers and crew survived.

Flight 1549 stands out as an inspiring story because it's exceptional. Similar accidents often end with regretful cries of what should have been. Early reports of the Polish air crash in April 2010 suggest that the pilot was under pressure (with high-power people on board) to land despite heavy fog. Also in April that same year the BP Gulf of Mexico rig exploded killing 11 people and causing the worst environmental disaster in US history. The early reports suggest that the root cause might be confidence over realism and pushing safety beyond the odds. Running over budget with delays costing $1 million a day, an email from a BP engineer reveals the hope above realism to secure the well. On April 16, just four days before the explosion an engineer emailed a colleague, 'Who cares. It's done, end of story, *will probably be fine* and we'll get a good cement job.' (Italics mine)

In a similar it-will-probably-be-fine confidence by a person in charge, in March 2007 a Garuda Airlines plane flying into Yogyakarta, Indonesia crashed killing 21 people. The pilots survived and in late July 2008 appeared in court for the first time. The court heard the sorry sequence of events. The plane was 19 kms from the airport when Captain Komar had the first indication that he should have gone around to restart his landing. Despite fifteen automatic cockpit warnings, a blaring 'whoop whoop' siren and a screaming co-pilot sitting next to him pleading for him to go around, Captain Komar allegedly went on regardless, landing his plane at almost twice the appropriate speed with catastrophic consequences.

In leadership roles in the corporate world, while the consequences of bad decisions are not normally fatal, we often see the same blind confidence where people blissfully deny the signs and go on regardless.

Humans are wired to radiate confidence in order to move forward in the world. We often allow confidence to conquer realism to get what we want. So strong can this be that we often deny what is realistic. There is an evolutionary benefit in doing so. In mate selection, individuals who demonstrate an ability to succeed in the world and provide for their offspring appear to be a good bet as a mate. They appear to have good genes and worthy to be a mate for having and raising offspring, particularly given the investment we humans make in child rearing.

Inflated self-view

In the workplace an individual will often have a higher opinion of their ability than what others around them give them credit for. The scientific term for this inflated self-view is 'illusory superiority'.

Illusory superiority is why 87% of MBA students at a university rated their performance as above average—when really only half can be above average.

We wouldn't have as many motor vehicle accidents if people were as good at driving as they think they are. Drivers in Sweden and the US were asked to compare their driving skill and safety with that of other people. For driving skill, 93% of the US sample and 69% of the Swedish sample put themselves in the top 50%. For safety, 88% of the US group and 77% of the Swedish sample put themselves in the top half.

In every field of endeavour it appears that people overestimate their own abilities. Lawyers often have an inflated belief that they will win a landmark case which leads to a large number of lawsuits going to trial. Gamblers, unfortunately for themselves, overestimate the probability of success. High school students tend to see themselves as having more ability in leadership, getting along better with others and being more skilled in written expression than their peers. Footballers see themselves as being more football savvy than their teammates. Managers view themselves as being more able than the typical manager.

In a managerial study, two researchers investigated the views of business leaders and managerial students to business planning and competitive performance. Having found that management students have an overly optimistic view of what's possible and of their ability to achieve, the findings were then tested on actual business executives. Presidents of 48 different New York state manufacturing firms were randomly chosen from a chamber of commerce directory and interviewed. Similar to the students, the executives over-predicted their firm's performance relative to their competition and over-predicted the increase in total size of their respective industries. Despite different levels of caution introduced by the researchers, the executives continued to feel confident that their own market share would grow. One of the few moderators was whether executives had personally experienced a setback in their business's performance—these people were less likely than others to predict that their company would outperform the average.

The double bind of an inflated self-view

There's a double-whammy in our overconfidence. Not only are we inclined to hold overly optimistic views about our own ability, but we are more inclined to do so if we lack competence. Indeed the less competent we are the more we overestimate our abilities.

Justin Kruger and David Dunning from Cornell University set out to assess the extent to which people overestimate their abilities and the effect of incompetence. They conducted four studies to paint a comprehensive picture of inflated self-views and ways to moderate it. What they found is extremely helpful to leaders in making sense of why people at work behave the way they do and what leaders can do about it. The key finding is that it's futile being frustrated with incompetent people because they might not know that they are incompetent.

The first study related to the social skill of *humour* where participants were presented with a series of jokes and asked to rate the humour in each one. The researchers then compared the ratings with those provided by a panel of professional comedians. Would those who did poorly recognise the low quality of their performance (a handy workplace question)?

The main focus of the study was the bottom quartile of performers. As expected from our inclination to be overly confident in our abilities, those bottom performers grossly overestimated their ability relative to the peers. Whereas their actual performance fell in the 12th percentile (0 = *I'm at the very bottom*, 50 = *I'm exactly average* and 99 = *I'm at the very top*), they put themselves in the 58th percentile. They felt that they were better than average. So while 'everyone tended to overestimate their ability relative to their peers ... those who performed particularly poorly were utterly unaware of this fact'.

Study number two looked at *logical reasoning*. Participants completed a 20-item logical reasoning test. Afterwards, participants were asked to make three estimates about their ability and their test performance—how their general abilities compared with their peers, how their score on the test itself compared, and how many test questions they answered correctly. As expected, participants overestimated their ability compared to their peers. On average, participants placed themselves at the 66th percentile (when mathematically the mean is 50). Again, participants in the lower quartile were the ones who overestimated their logical reasoning ability and test scores to the greatest extent. Although these people scored at the 12th percentile on average, they believed their ability would reach the 68th percentile and their test score at the 62nd percentile. Similarly, they thought they'd answered on average 14.2 problems correctly, whereas they actually answered just 9.6 problems correctly.

Let's add another element to the picture. Do incompetent people learn from competent people? To answer this, the third study looked at the skill of *grammar*. After demonstrating a similar result as above, the researchers wanted to know if incompetent individuals fail to gain insight into their own incompetence by observing the behaviour of others. Several weeks after participants had been tested on their grammar ability they came back into the laboratory. They were then given the tests of five of their peers and asked to assess how competently each person had completed the test. After grading each test they were then shown their own original test and asked to re-rate their own ability and performance relative to their peers. Again, the incompetent individuals overstated their ability and failed to gain insight into their own incompetence. 'Despite seeing the superior performance of their peers, bottom quartile participants continued to hold the mistaken impression that they had performed just fine.'

There's a final piece to the jigsaw. Would training help? Would a dose of skilling help incompetent people be more realistic in their assessments and in their own incompetence? As the researchers point out, if the answer is yes, then there is a paradox in the result: 'the way to make incompetent individuals realise their own incompetence is to make them competent, after which point they are no longer incompetent'.

Study four involved participants taking a test of logic reasoning where they were asked to assess themselves in a similar manner to the prior studies. After that step, half the participants were given a short 10-minute training session designed to improve their logic reasoning skills. The other half were given a filler task, not skills related, for the same amount of time. Then all participants were given the task of going through their own tests and indicating which problems they thought had been answered correctly. Again, they were asked to compare themselves to their peers in terms of general logical reasoning ability and test performance. Finally good news! As a consequence of the training, the incompetent people now assessed their own work as accurately as those who had originally scored in the top quartile. They were more calibrated in every way. Before receiving the skills training, participants in the bottom quartile believed their ability fell in the 55th percentile and that their test scores were in the 51st percentile and that they answered 5.3 problems correctly. After training, those same participants thought their ability fell in the 44th percentile, their test in the 32nd percentile and that they had answered 1.0 problem correctly. While they still overestimated their ability and test score, they were significantly more calibrated after just 10 minutes of training. They could now recognise their incompetence. No such increase in calibration was found for the bottom-quartile participants in the untrained group.

In summary, the researchers paint the picture of overconfidence and what do to about it. First, people generally overestimate their ability compared with their peers. This is particularly pronounced for people who are incompetent and who tend to think of themselves as above average. Second, low performers are unable to discern what is incorrect or correct in relation to their own performance. They don't pick it up by even observing competent people. Third, improving skill levels through training improves the accuracy of self-assessments. We'll come back to these points when we talk about the implications of *confidence before realism*.

Denial in business

A fundamental aspect of *confidence before realism* is the tendency to deny reality when reality does not suit us.

Professor Richard Tedlow from Harvard Business School studies the implications of denial for business. He studies the implications for individual leaders and for industries. One of the individual leaders he has studied is Henry Ford who, for all his brilliance, 'failed to look facts in the face'. In his compelling book, *Denial*, Tedlow describes the implications of Ford denying the reality of the declining sales figures of the Model T. In the end, Ford had to close his factories to retool for another model which allowed General Motors to seize market share from which Ford never recovered. Tedlow writes that the evidence of declining sales was 'everywhere apparent at the time'. But Ford dismissed the sales figures as a conspiracy by his competitors and when one of his top executives warned him of the dire situation in a detailed memo, Ford fired him.

Tedlow explains the reason and elements of denial. 'Sometimes we divert information from awareness because it is too painful or stressful ... more commonly we do so because the offending information contradicts assumptions with which we are comfortable, and it is easier to reject the information than to change our assumptions.' Sometimes it is caused by 'groupthink' where there is a conspiracy of silence or a conspiracy of concurrence and shared illusions, rationalisations and denial. Indeed, denial can make us feel better. Tedlow's key theme is that the denial he concerns himself with is 'the unwillingness to see or admit a truth that ought to be apparent and is in fact apparent to many others. Sometimes, the denial is literal, the assertion that the reality in question simply is not true or did not happen … In other instances, the denial is interpretative. One accepts the facts but denies the implications.' He says that if something is too terrible to be true we can deny it: 'It can't be true, because if it were, things would be too terrible.'

He describes that the dramatic decline of the US automotive tyre industry was due to its denial of the technology change to radial tyres emerging out of Europe and later Japan. Up until the 1970s, five local tyre companies dominated the US market: Goodyear, Firestone, Uniroyal, BF Goodrich and GenCorp. In 1970 these top five firms accounted for 80% of US domestic tyre sales. Foreign firms accounted for less than four percent of sales.

Then came the radial revolution through the 1970s and 1980s. The five companies met the new technology with denial. 'Their denial of the impact of this new technology took place in two distinct phases. At first, they refused to believe that radial tyres would succeed in the American market the way they had in Europe. Second, after it became clear that radials would indeed make it in America, the tyre manufacturers denied that their world would change forever. Denial, however, does not change reality. It simply makes reality tougher to deal with.'

How did this state of denial reveal itself? The firms stuck with the old technology, 'bias-ply' which they'd obviously invested in heavily. They 'trash-talked' the competition. They tooled up to make a better bias-ply tyre. They relied on their long, often family, relationships with General Motors and Ford. They depended on their price advantage of cheaper bias-ply over the more expensive radials. A few of the companies took tentative but timid steps to introduce a radial tyre but there were some serious safety issues. For some, when the opportunity to form a joint venture with a European firm came, they declined to do so, refusing to become the junior partner (we'll come to *contest and display* in the next chapter). By the end of the 1980s, four of the five firms had disappeared with only Goodyear surviving, 'just barely'.

Sometimes in business you don't need to look beyond the daily newspaper to find the facts. It then depends on whether you are inclined to believe the information and motivated to do anything about it. The largest corporate collapse in Australia occurred in 2001 when insurer HIH went bankrupt. In the lead-up to that event the national broadsheet *The Australian* was writing of the company's financial difficulties months before it declared bankruptcy. The eventual failure of the company seemed to take the regulatory body by surprise. Yet the information was there to be seen all along—in the daily newspaper. People who ought to have known denied the facts, let alone the HIH leaders, still hosting award-winning staff parties while the ship was going down. Presumably the reality was too daunting to face.

In business, it's not just in the big decisions where denial occurs. It's also in the response to the regular comings and goings of everyday work events. The HR team of a particular business was receiving a lot of complaints from employees about the head of IT. Frightened people were quietly telling HR that the department head was a tyrant—intimidating people both inside the business (his staff) and outside the business (the suppliers). The head of HR took the complaints to the IT manager's boss, a member of the executive team. The boss didn't want to know. Every point of complaint received a deflecting comment: 'All IT people are a bit unusual' and, 'If we replaced him we would find the same thing' or, 'Surely he can't be that bad' and of course the common, 'I just don't see this behaviour at all in my interactions with him'. For this senior manager, it seemed that he was in a happier place denying the evidence and not taking action. Often in these situations the offending person finally leaves, which happened in this case, and there's a collective sigh of relief with everyone seeming to ask why it took so long to act.

Another example of denial is in senior leaders' responses to high-stress projects. A company had interests in different parts of the world including Europe where a small team was trying to deliver a project but was under-resourced for the requirements of the job. Against the odds the team continued to deliver enough to keep the project staggering along. The team seemed to hang on by their finger nails on the promise of a visit by two senior executives from headquarters half a world away. Surely, the team believed, that when the executives visited and saw firsthand the pressure they were under and their lack of resources, relief would be provided. But the team would be sourly disappointed. When the two executives arrived they spent only half a day with the team and when they asked, 'How's it going?' it was clear to the team that the executives didn't want to know. Even worse, the two visitors spent most of their time engaged in personal interests, abandoning the team altogether. As soon as the executives left, many of the team suffered nervous breakdowns. In one case, one of the employees huddled in bed, curled in the fetal position. Days later he struggled into his car to drive to work, only to shake so uncontrollably at the wheel that he had to go back inside. Most of the team had to be replaced. The signs were there for all to see if only a) the executive looked and b) dealt with what they found.

IMPLICATIONS OF THIS INSTINCT FOR LEADERS

Here's a snapshot of what we have learned about the instinct of *confidence before realism*.

1. We radiate confidence in order to get what we want.
2. We tend to have an inflated view of ourselves.
3. Overconfidence can be so strong that we deny reality.

There are significant practical implications of *confidence before realism* which, if incorporated into your toolkit, will make managing people easier.

Implication 1. Self confidence is good

A bias towards self confidence has to be a good thing. It allows us to have a positive outlook and optimism about what's possible. It means that personally we are in a better place than if we were inclined to the opposite.

It also means, however, that we are relating to others who will tend to be more confident in their ability than what others are likely to credit them with. At performance reviews, for example, a person will tend to have overly optimistic memories of their contribution and hardly ever assess their own capability as just average (a real tension if the performance system expects leaders to rate most people as *average*!). When leaders conduct pay reviews they are dealing with members of a species who believe they are high achievers and who just don't agree with a modest pay increase. Along the same vein, team members will tend to believe they are ready for promotion way before their boss agrees with them.

While this dimension of human nature might be a good thing, it also helps make sense of the tension that a leader has to manage in their role, and for staff to know that their manager will tend to be less positive about their ability than they are about themselves. It might just give each person a better understanding of each other.

Implication 2. For humans to flourish

The science gives specific advice for the environment required by a positively inclined species like us. We require certain conditions in order to flourish. 'Flourishing' is associated with goodness, growth and resilience. In order to flourish we need a greater dose of positive feelings directed at us than negative, and the science is precise as to how much more.

Barbara Fredrickson and Marcial Losada study the impact of *positive affect* (feeling grateful, upbeat; expressing appreciation, liking) and *negative affect* (feeling contemptuous, irritable; expressing disdain, disliking). The key concept that Fredrickson and Losada explore is what they call the positivity ratio—the ratio of pleasant feelings and sentiments to unpleasant ones over time.

The researchers make the point that as part of our survival strategy as a species, humans do better when we experience positive emotions. Back on the savannah, positive emotions would have increased our ancestors' odds of survival, to reproduce, of being more inclined to explore and to develop social connections. Negative emotions narrow people's behaviour to life-preserving responses, of being defensive and being asocial.

Fredrickson and Losada have conducted and reviewed a number of studies covering the impact of positive and negative affect on psychological health, marriages and work teams.

In one study on work teams, the interactions of 60 teams were observed. Behind two-way mirrors, the researchers coded all utterances as *positive* if speakers showed support, encouragement or appreciation and as *negative* if speakers showed disapproval, sarcasm or cynicism. Later, it was identified that 15 of the teams were high-performing teams on measures of profitability, customer satisfaction and performance evaluations. Twenty six of the teams were identified as moderate performance teams and 19 were assessed as low performing.

From this and other research a precise mathematical model predicts that humans and groups of people will flourish at a positivity ratio of 2.9 (let's round it up to '3')—that for every one negative affect there are at least **three** positive affects. (Marriages need a higher ratio to prosper and survive: around 5:1 which stands to reason because of the closeness of marriage and the importance of the opinions of our life partner.)

For teams that are not functioning well—'those that might be identified as languishing'—positivity ratios fall below 2.9; positive interactions might still outweigh negative interactions but not by enough. For example, twice the number of positive behaviours to negative behaviours is not enough to flourish. We need at least three times as many. Is there an upper limit? Yes, but it's a large number. Flourishing drops off after a positive affect of 11.6. The researchers say that there appears to be a role for *appropriate negativity*, such as constructive feedback connected to specific circumstances.

A leader interested in ensuring a healthy dose of positivity in which their team and team members will flourish will do at least two things:

1. Ensure that your personal interactions and language is in the range of between 3:1 and 11:1 and
2. That interactions between team members is in the same range.

You might monitor the incidence of people expressing feelings of appreciation, encouragement, liking and being upbeat. We do our best work and the team is most successful when we can meet our instinctive needs of being in an environment of optimism and positivity over pessimism and negativity.

Implication 3. Guard against denial by being open to the truth

Knowing about the innate ability for humans to deny reality will allow leaders to be attuned to the signs. Tedlow shares the statements expressed in organisations that are likely to indicate a state of denial:

- it doesn't apply to us
- it's not a big deal
- it's not our problem
- it's never happened in the past
- it can't happen here

- there's nothing we can do about it.

And as a consequence we:
- shoot the messenger
- discount the source
- denigrate the competition
- blissfully carry on regardless.

Tedlow makes the point, aligned to the theme of this book, that if we are aware of our natural inclination then we can make alternative choices. While 'denial is a powerful impulse, we are not entirely powerless to resist it. Through self knowledge, openness to criticism and receptiveness to facts and perspectives that challenge our own, we can arm ourselves against denial'.

Implication 4. A balance of confidence and realism

The aim for leaders should be to keep a balance between confidence and realism—to be optimistic about what's possible while maintaining a healthy dose of what's practical. Optimism plays a key role in strategic planning. And then a hefty dose of realism is required with the implementation regarding the time, resources and capability required to deliver the strategic plans.

At an executive level, the business strategy might be to expand the business to a new market. This is the sexy, exciting decision. But the decision falls foul of *confidence before realism* if there is insufficient investment in the unsexy services to make this happen in a controlled, sustainable way—investing in governance, quality, audit, reporting, human resource systems and IT capability.

At a manager level, *confidence before realism* shows up in expecting or demanding the impossible from people. Do they really have the skills to deliver on what you are asking of them? Is too much asked of them with too little time? Again, we need confidence *and* reality—confidence in the team to stretch for achievements *and* the support and time to do the job.

Here's a team-leader's checklist to help retain a healthy level of realism so that our tendency to over-confidence doesn't become a blind spot. To what extent am I overly confident and unrealistic about:

1. The plans for our department and what's possible?

2. What our clients want and our capacity to deliver?
3. Financial performance and risk management?
4. Key projects and timelines (including overloading people)?
5. What I expect with the resources I provide or are available?
6. Our systems and processes—do I think they're better than they really are?
7. Each person's ability and attitude?
8. My ability?
9. Relationships within my team?
10. Relationships with other teams that affect my team's performance?

A handy guide is for leaders to listen to people who disagree with them or have information contrary to what the leader would prefer to hear. The people with the contrary view are not necessarily being pessimistic or detractors. They might be the realists. I experienced this directly with one boss I worked for who got so angry at the messengers of bad news that the flow of market information to his office dried up. The business was subsequently taken by surprise by a sudden decline in revenues. While the information had been available, the professionals with the information had been abused and humiliated by the bully once too often and were now too frightened to say.

Implication 5. Focus on the vital few

An implication of *confidence before realism* is that leaders become overly optimistic about their ability to be across their role and to deliver on a range of responsibilities. This can result in a skating across the surface where the leader forgets to focus on the most critical accountabilities.

In each leader's role there will be only a few, perhaps even just one, dimension that is most critical to their performance and what they and their team deliver to the organisation. Leaders should ask themselves, *what would constitute a disaster in my role?* or *what would cause me to be moved out of my role?* Then ensure focus on those one or two priorities. One manager's answer might be losing that one key customer. For another it might be shoddy product quality or failure to get a product licence. For someone else it might be a safety accident. For a finance manager it might involve a financial scandal caused by criminal activities of others. For an IT manager it might be a project implementation mess-up or systems failure.

With that clarity, when you are forced to make trade-offs in time, resource or capability you can ensure that you don't trade off *that* one.

Implication 6. Simplistic solutions

Our instinctive inclination to radiate confidence and move forward in the world means that leaders are inclined to favour simplistic solutions over time-consuming and complex ones. An element of the attraction to simple solutions is that we often *have to do something*, and it's often appealing to do the simple thing while convincing ourselves that it is the right thing to do. For example, a chief executive might decide to restructure the organisation when the real problem is declining revenues. A restructure is a straightforward decision that the CEO alone can make and which can be readily implemented. But if the problem is a decline in revenue and pipeline of products then the restructure will have little effect. Given that the CEO had to do *something*, this action will make them feel better—it looks like the CEO is in control and on top of things. In taking the simple solution, however, it's likely that time will show that the restructure was no fix at all and only served to mask the problem.

Fads roll through organisations. Fads rely on hope and optimism, rather than effort and reality. Generally the source of a fad is sound: an idea worked for one organisation, given its unique culture, history and capability. The problem arises when leaders in other organisations adopt the idea for their own organisation without assessing the characteristics of why the idea worked in the other organisation (GE, IBM, Motorola) and the differences between the source organisation and their own. Staff, of course, know if the idea is divorced from reality. I've seen my fair share of HR fads. Organisations might roll out the latest HR idea, but so often it's a substitute for the *real* challenge of lifting the capability of leaders; are our managers effective people-leaders, do they have the right skills and training and have we implemented systems so that managers feel accountable for staff engagement? This is a harder challenge that takes significantly more time and effort than rolling out the next borrowed initiative. But the lift in organisation capability is enduring.

On the subject of simplistic solutions, a similar situation can occur when a manager decides to appoint an external person to fill a vacancy in preference to an internal candidate. On the face of it, the external candidate appeared the perfect choice. They seemed so much more capable than the imperfect internal person. But soon after appointment, the outsider proves not quite the perfect person they'd been pegged to be. Perhaps the internal person's shortcomings weren't such a huge inhibitor after all.

Implication 7. Denying information about people

Managers at every level can be inclined to disregard the signs of people not delivering. We've all been there, where a manager fails to see or acknowledge the evidence that an individual is not performing or is having a negative impact on the group. The leader tends to hope that it's not as bad as they might be hearing from others or hoping that it will all get better.

The implication of this human trait is that a leader *needs to know*. The leader needs to have access to information and to know the reality. A challenge for leaders is sometimes that we hear things from team members but people don't want to be identified to the alleged culprit. One HR leader uses an approach that allows her to raise things she hears on the grapevine with a staff member (when she's satisfied there's truth in what she's hearing). For example, she will say to the person, 'I am hearing that you are creating tension with your colleagues. What I am hearing is that you speak down about people to others, including in meetings. Why do you think I am hearing this?' The HR director doesn't answer the predictable question, 'Who do you hear this from?' She deflects that as not the point. The point is, she corrects, why she is hearing it from various people at all. She invariably concludes the discussion with the staff member agreeing that there is substance in what is being said and with a plan of action to correct the situation.

Implication 8. The inflated self-view

The research discussed earlier into people's inflated self-view provides helpful clues to managers. The insight provides a call to action for the role of feedback and training, particularly for the less competent people on a leader's team.

First, it's futile to be tough, critical or frustrated at someone's incompetence. The person isn't competent enough to know they are incompetent! The person can't calibrate their performance and they'll be blissfully ignorant of their overestimation of their own capability. So, to quietly seethe, pull your hair out or talk critically about them to others is pointless.

Second, they need your feedback. They can't work it out by themselves and they can't work it out by merely observing competent people. Let them know how they are performing, their skill gaps and show them what competent performance looks like. We know humans might be sensitive to receiving feedback, but you also know that to hold back on them will leave *them* in a state of ignorance and continue *your* likely frustration.

Third, provide the necessary skills training to enable them to become competent. As they increase their competence they'll be better able to spot their own incompetence, better able to calibrate their capability and less likely to overestimate their ability.

Implication 9. In managing a poor performer you don't need agreement

Throughout this book, and especially in Instinct 4, we've looked at the challenge of giving negative feedback and managing poor performers. We've seen why most managers understandably find this so difficult it's enough to keep the manager awake at night. We've looked at what can be done to make it easier on a manager. With an understanding of people's inclination to hold an inflated self-view, we can now add a further element to the management of poor performers.

A consequence of an inflated self-view is that people generally won't agree with their manager's negative observations. This is generally a good thing for the person for their life journey. It may well be better for their self esteem and their view of *self* that they don't accept the assessment the manager is seeking to impose on them.

In managing a poor performer, managers overwhelmingly work on an unstated assumption that they want to gain the employee's agreement; they want the employee they are counselling to agree to what the manager is saying.

Well, there's often little chance of that. The fact that the manager is unlikely to get their agreement can be a huge release of pressure for the manager.

Let's say you have a situation where one of your team has been creating issues in their interaction with colleagues. Despite your counselling and assistance they're just not seeing it, and certainly not improving. As you escalate your warnings and become more direct in your language, the implication of what you are saying to the person is that they are a difficult person to get along with and that they have interpersonal issues. Quite possibly, they might not agree with you! They are not about to attribute those characteristic to themselves. So they resist your assessment and argue back. From their life journey and sense of *self*, it may well be a good thing that they might resist your assessment. If they accepted your view it might mean they have to alter their sense of who they are. Better in many cases that they go home that night and say to their partner, 'Can you believe what my darn boss thinks about me!' Of course, the ramification of their resistance might be that they don't work with you for much longer.

Fundamentally, all this means that in managing poor performers *you don't need their agreement*. We often want people to say, 'Gee, boss, I agree with you. I can see I'm a difficult so-and-so to work with and I'll remedy that immediately.' It's rarely going to happen quite like this. Seeking agreement is ideal, but often not realistic.

In such situations, the most resourceful approach from the manager is to present the person with a choice. The choice is for the employee to hopefully amend their behaviour so that team interactions are positive. If the person doesn't make that choice, or they say they'll make that choice but their subsequent actions show they really haven't, then the manager retains their right to make a choice themselves. The manager might choose that the person is no longer part of the team.

In summary, if as a leader you share feedback with someone who is not agreeing with you, the tip is to silently accept that as being fine. The person is sticking with their self belief. You can choose to say to yourself that you are not requiring them to alter their self belief and they might never agree with me. But I also don't need their agreement. I'm entitled to make my assessment, share my view and manage the situation.

Implication 10. Leader competence

There is a sobering implication for leaders in the Kruger and Dunning study regarding incompetence and unawareness. Leaders will also tend to be blissfully ignorant of their own incompetence! Leaders will overestimate their abilities and rate themselves highly compared to other leaders. The remedy is to take assessments comparing your abilities, run surveys to assess the level of engagement of your direct reports, gain feedback from competent leaders and take training to increase your competence. Reading books like this helps—hopefully written by competent authors (but then again, if an author is not competent they'll have trouble coming to that conclusion …).

We could give the last word on confidence over reality to Garuda Captain Komar. Appearing in court facing charges of murdering 21 passengers and crew, in denial of the harsh reality of the moment, he said that he 'hopes to fly again'. But let's give it to Captain Sullenberger, an extremely competent professional: 'In so many areas of life, you need to be a long-term optimist but a short-term realist.'

Instinct 9. Contest and Display

This instinct helps explain why:
- people are very sensitive about job titles and pay equity
- plenty of people put their hands up if something goes well
- a new person sometimes denigrates the person before them
- 'pilot' programs are usually successful
- some departments are treated as second-class citizens
- people 'copy all' in an email that makes themselves look good.

ONE OF THE GREAT mysteries of organisational life is how some people, who don't seem so capable to their peers, just keep getting promoted. A colleague once told me of a conversation she overheard where two staff members were sharing their frustration about their boss. One colleague said to the other, 'Sooner or later, in a moment of madness, someone will promote him.' And they did.

Like other social animals, humans are acutely aware of our position in the pecking order and the implications of our position. The key method we use to enhance our position in the hierarchy—to get ahead in our social group—is through contest and display, or looking good.

Chimps are the same. For a male chimp, his rise through the ranks is not necessarily related to merit. Partly it happens through family support and connections but mostly it's by display of power. Take Mike, for example, who was briefly mentioned in Instinct 2. Back in 1963, soon after she started her research, Dr Goodall watched Mike use a unique power display to rise to the alpha position of the Gombe chimp community. Initially Mike was ranked almost bottom of the adult male hierarchy, meaning he was one of the last to eat and was attacked by almost every other male. Yet within four months he rose to the position of alpha. His meteoric promotion through the ranks was achieved through a unique display of power that intimidated all the other males. Dr Goodall used kerosene as fuel for lights and stoves. The kerosene came in four-gallon cans and the empty cans were stacked at the side of the camp. These empty cans became attractive to the male chimps and they would use them as props in their power displays. All the adult males tried the empty cans, but only Mike mastered the skill and learned to keep three cans in his grasp or kicked along ahead of him. The cans made a terrible din, impressive as a display of power. The males would scatter when Mike charged through the forest with his noisy cans banging ahead of him. Soon all the males had submitted to Mike with the then alpha, Goliath, the last to do so. Suddenly Mike found himself in the number one role. Initially he was nervous as leader, particularly when Dr Goodall secured the cans so they were no longer available to the chimps. But Mike did settle into the alpha role and he ruled for around six years.

Life and death

Social standing is a matter of life and death—literally. Our standing in our pecking order and how we look in the eyes of others is correlated to how long we live and our quality of life along the way.

Professor Robert Wilkinson has solved an interesting puzzle. Wilkinson is professor of medical research at Surrey University and the University College London. He and his colleagues were bewildered by the fact that in developed countries differences in chronic disease and life expectancy could not be explained by a country's wealth: there is no correlation between a country's wealth (average income) and life expectancy. Likewise, there is no correlation to the level of expenditure on medical care. Nor could an explanation be found in the incidence of smoking.

Then, Eureka! The researchers discovered a startling link in the data. For developed countries, the incidence of chronic disease and life expectancy is strongly correlated to income *relativity*. That is, countries with narrow income differences between rich and poor are healthier and their citizens live longer than those in countries with higher income inequity.

The correlation is almost linear ($r = -0.86$) between life expectancy and income inequity—the greater the income disparity between rich and poor in a society, the lower the life expectancy. Japan and Sweden are the healthiest countries and the most egalitarian in terms of income. People are healthier and live longer in Greece than in the US, even though the US is a significantly richer nation. Despite its wealth and spending more per person on medical care than any other country, the US stands a surprising 25th in the international rankings of life expectancy.

The correlation doesn't stop at the country level. Researchers looked at comparisons between the 50 US states and found the same result. In those states where income differences are *relatively* narrow, people live longer and suffer less chronic disease such as high blood pressure, high cholesterol, cancer, diabetes and arthritis.

The researchers then went to the next level of society and looked at cities. Even at this level there is the same clear connection. Out of the 282 US cities studied, those with narrower income differences have significantly better health outcomes. The same applies in Australia; Melbourne is a healthier (and more egalitarian) city than Sydney.

The significance of income relativity between the rich and poor of a society goes beyond chronic disease and life expectancy. Trust is an element also found to have strong links to income differences. In the more egalitarian societies, people's trust in each other is greater ($r = 0.7$). In the most equal US states (like North Dakota and Iowa) only 10 to 15% of people feel they cannot trust each other, while in the most unequal states (like Louisiana and Massachusetts) the proportion rises to around 40%.

The same situation exists between income inequity and the incidence of violence and homicide. And finally, income equity is also correlated to social affiliation. In more equal societies, people are more likely to be involved in volunteer and community clubs.

Why does income equity have such a significant effect on social outcomes? The reason has to do with the stress that is associated with our social standing.

Looking good in the eyes of others is key in the life of a social animal. Individuals high up in the hierarchy experience less stress than individuals below them, and the degree of stress increases at each descending step of the hierarchy. People at the bottom of the hierarchy suffer the most stress, and in the most unequal societies stress is greater than in egalitarian societies.

Stress levels are caused by the fight/flight response (see Instinct 3). Wilkinson explains that on the one hand this response serves us well. It readies the body for immediate muscular activity, which works well where the fight or flight situation is over in minutes. On the other hand, the effect of the fight or flight response is that it puts on hold longer-term functions that relate to tissue repair, immunity, digestion and reproduction. Where we sustain stress over months or years, negative effects accumulate.

In a study of 10,000 office workers (the Whitehall study in London) death rates from heart disease were four times higher among the junior (lower status) staff than among the most senior (higher status) staff. The data was controlled for age.

To change a monkey's social standing will significantly affect its health. In a fascinating study of captive monkeys, social status was manipulated by moving animals between troops. High ranking individuals were taken from different groups and placed together in a compound so that some would become low ranking in their new group. Likewise, low ranking individuals were taken from different groups and put into the one compound so that some of those would become high ranking and some would remain low. Diet was controlled. Any physiological change in the individuals could only be attributed to change in status. Observed changes in the physiology associated with low status in monkeys is the same as for humans. These included a more rapid hardening of the arteries, a worse ratio of high- to low-density blood fats and a tendency towards both central obesity and insulin resistance. The animals that moved down the social scale suffered a fivefold increase in cholesterol blockage during the 21 months they lived in their new social group.

In societies with greater income differences there are abundant and persistent symbols of being *relatively* poor and diminished in the eyes of others. A Rolex doesn't buy the owner more time or tell any different time to a Seiko, but it's the image or social differentiation associated with the better brand that makes it desirable. If you are a labourer or car wash attendant in a country or town where income differences are narrow then you are not relatively disadvantaged. But if you fill these roles in a society where there are wide disparities in income, your low status is much more apparent, much more in your face, much more real and much more stressful. Displays of affluence and superiority by some can produce feelings of shame and inferiority for others.

Strategies to elevate our social position

What are the strategies we use to look good and enhance our social standing? This is where different gender strategies come in. Nigel Nicholson succinctly tells me that for men the focus is on politics of dominance and for women it's the politics of inclusion. Contesting and displaying is not just a male thing. Both genders are acutely aware of the implications of looking good—we just show it differently.

Males are preoccupied with dominating the hierarchy and focus on those displays that support status progression. In a classic example, a friend told me of a senior executive who on his first day with his new company counted the ceiling squares to make sure his office was at least as big as others at his level. Men are the ones more inclined to argue and win higher salaries (a proxy for social ranking) and title inflation, and it seems to be working for them. In Europe only nine of the top 500 companies are led by a female CEO (1.8%). In Australia only four (2%) of ASX200 companies are led by a woman. In the US, 13 (2.6%) of the *Fortune* 500 companies have a female CEO. In *Blink*, Malcolm Gladwell refers to the over-representation of tall white males in CEO roles. In the general American population only 3.9% of adult men are six feet two or taller, but among CEOs of the *Fortune* 500 companies almost 33% are six feet two or taller.

With women, social standing is more related to inclusion. I imagine any husband can associate with the daily question I'm asked by my wife, 'What will I wear today?' Or the time we spend before holidays or a business trip when Jude talks me through what clothes she plans to take. Mostly, I just need to agree. A study in the UK found that women, on average, spend 287 days over their lifetime deciding what to wear for work, nights out, holidays and the gym. The average woman spends 16 minutes every weekday morning choosing her clothes and around 14 minutes on a Saturday or Sunday. If she is heading out for the night, she'll take 20 minutes to decide on an outfit. Before leaving for holidays she'll spend 52 minutes deciding what to pack. And once at the destination, she'll take 10 minutes each day deciding what to wear. Even selecting an outfit for the gym or other sporting activities will account for 14 minutes each visit.

This is a book about instincts, so let's talk about sex and the role of sexual symbols in looking good to get ahead. Female chimps have a distinctive calling card that is compellingly attractive to male chimps. When a female chimp is in oestrous—that period of her monthly cycle when she is ovulating and sexually receptive—she shows a swelling around her backside. For the three males at Taronga, a female's sexual swelling becomes a preoccupation, and food, for example, no longer has the appeal that it normally has. And when one of the females displays an oestrous swelling, the males stay close to each other, keeping an eye on what their rivals are up to.

Twenty-three-year-old Shona is the lowest ranking female and for most of the month she gets picked on by the younger males. But because she has a prominent sexual swelling things change for Shona once a month when she has her alluring display. Her social position dramatically improves. For most of the month, if Shona retaliates to being picked on by the young males trying to assert their dominance, the mothers step in to defend their sons. But come her monthly swelling, the whole dynamic shifts. At this point she now attracts the adult males like bees to a honey pot. Now if the young boys pick on her, the females won't step in to protect their sons because to do so will incur the wrath of the adult males who are now taking a great interest in Shona. It takes the young males a long time to work out what's happening—why every now and then they can't get away with intimidating her.

Keeper Louise Grossfeldt says, 'A smart female will use her display. You can see they use it to their advantage.' Louise adds that the female chimps seem to have some control of their swelling. In times of stress, for instance, they seem to be able to retain their swelling, so they get lots of attention and support from the males. It's the primal equivalent to the women's magazine cover I spotted recently where a female TV star revealed, 'How you can have a body like mine for summer.'

While we're on the subject of sex, the alpha male does not have exclusive rights to mating, though he might think he does. Thirty-year-old Sacha doesn't much like Lubutu. When she is in oestrous Sacha goes through the ritual of mating with him but just before the critical moment she'll jump off, turn and groom Lubutu to complete the ritual. Then, when the opportunity presents itself, she'll have a brief escapade with her preferred male, Shabani, behind the shrubs, out of Lubutu's sight.

On the male side, showing off your biceps provides an impressive means of display (yes, we're still talking about chimps). Snowy was the alpha male when Lubutu was young, and Snowy had a distinctive display. In the night den a tractor tyre hangs suspended from a rope. The tyre is enormous and must weigh a ton. Back then, Snowy would take the tyre in his arms and fling it about eight metres up to the ceiling, as though it was a frisbee. It was an awesome display, at least to the human observers, and presumably to the chimps. No other individual adopted this display and no one has thrown the tyre since Snowy died. Not until now. Lubutu was around six when Snowy died. But just last year, at age 16, Lubutu started repeating Snowy's performance, flinging the tyre to the ceiling. Keeper Allan Schmidt presumes that Lubutu remembers the display as a youngster, thinking to himself, 'Man, that's impressive.' He hadn't the strength to fling the tyre before, but now, almost in his prime, he's got the ability to replicate Snowy's display and incorporate it into his own repertoire.

Lubutu's other personal favourite is to take a run and jump at a metal door at the rear of the exhibit. For no apparent reason other than to remind the community that he's there and that he's the boss, he'll launch himself at the door, creating a thunderous bang with his hands and feet.

At one year younger than Lubutu, Shabani has more expensive tastes. No doubt it's not politically smart to do exactly what the boss does, so instead of the door he launches himself at the windows of the exhibit. Although the glass is 30 millimetres (over one inch) thick and won't break, it will shatter, and at $3,000 a panel it's an expensive habit. One particular day a TV show had set up a barbeque near one of the windows to tape a cooking segment. Perhaps the flames of the barbeque spooked Shabani. He sprinted 50 metres on all fours and hurled himself 10 metres through the air, thumping against the glass with stunning results—sending the panicked crew scrambling for their lives. While the security-rated glass won't crack, with the recent refurbishment of the exhibit the opportunity was taken to upgrade the thickness to 60 mm (over two inches)!

Attention-seeking is not beyond the kids either. Shikamoo is a young male, now seven years of age. When he was four years of age he developed a limp that was curiously pronounced when he was around the adults. One minute he might be running around playing with his mates unimpeded by his 'injury' when suddenly, in the presence of adults, he would change his gait and begin to limp. Once out of sight, the limp would strangely disappear. He has just grown out of that behaviour. Allan Schmidt comments wryly, 'They go through this phase!'

As a footnote to the relationship between Lubutu and Shona, the low ranking female he mercilessly menaced as a youngster, they've now grown quite close. These days he spends hours grooming her. She has no family and no social significance, and politically there is little for Lubutu to gain from spending time with her, but he just seems to like her. They spend hours together (although he does allow the current band of juveniles to pick on her, except of course when she has her sexual display). Despite Lubutu's friendship, Shona still suffers by being at the bottom of the hierarchy. When the chimps come into the night den each evening, they are greeted with food and bedding of shredded newspaper spread out on the floor. Being the lowest in the social order, Shona chooses to gather her bedding while she can, before the others finish eating, otherwise she would stand little chance of a comfortable bed. But every night the same routine unfolds. When the high ranking individuals have eaten and start to prepare their beds, they raid the pile that Shona has appropriated.

Power poses for humans

Given the games people play within organisations, it's helpful to know the subtlety associated with power and dominance displays for humans. Dr Dana Carney from Columbia University Business School and her colleagues tested whether adopting powerful body postures actually *causes* people to feel more powerful. Do people feel stronger and do they experience behavioural changes if they deliberately use powerful body postures? And do low-power postures reduce feelings of power?

Power is expressed through specific body language. Expansive, open postures project high power whereas constricted, closed postures project low power.

Participants in the study were asked to hold high-power poses or low-power poses and were tested for four indicators of power: whether individuals felt more powerful, whether they focused on rewards as opposed to risks, whether they experienced increases in testosterone and whether they experienced decreases in cortisol.

Increased testosterone levels in humans and other animals reflect status and dominance and are associated with competitive behaviours. Cortisol, on the other hand, is a stress hormone and has a higher incidence in low-status individuals who tend to suffer more stress-related illnesses as described earlier in this chapter (high blood pressure, high cholesterol, cancer, diabetes and arthritis).

Forty-two participants (26 females and 16 males) were randomly assigned to either the high- or the low-power pose conditions. Participants didn't know the real reason for posing.

The high-power pose participants held two poses for just one minute each. One pose displayed expansiveness so the person took up more rather than less space. The second high-power pose displayed openness so that limbs were open. Both poses were rather exaggerated. For example, the first involved the person sitting with legs stretched out and feet on a desk with hands behind the head.

The low-power participants held two poses. One was constricted so they took up less space with shoulders and arms collapsed inward. The second pose was closed with limbs locked around their torso. These poses were also both held for just one minute each and were rather exaggerated.

Changes in testosterone and cortisol were measured by saliva tests. Saliva samples were taken before the poses and again 17 minutes afterwards. To measure feelings of being powerful and in charge participants self-reported by answering questions on a scale from 1 (not at all) to 4 (a lot). To measure preparedness towards risk-taking, participants (following their poses) were given $2 and told to keep it (the safe bet) or roll the dice to make $4, yet risk losing the $2. The odds of winning were 50/50.

After holding such poses for just two minutes the results were significant and were the same for both genders. The high-power posers felt significantly more powerful and in charge compared to the low-power posers. High-power poses caused an increase in testosterone while low-power poses caused a decrease. High-power poses caused a decrease in cortisol while low-power poses caused an increase. High-power posers were more likely to focus on rewards and take the gamble (86.36%) while only 60% of the low-power posers took the risk.

In summarising the results, Carney and her colleagues concluded, 'Posing in high-power (versus low-power) displays causes physiological, psychological and behavioural changes … of power … elevation of the dominance hormone testosterone, reduction in the stress hormone cortisol and increases in behaviourally demonstrated risk tolerance and feelings of power.' We'll return to this study when we look at the implications of *contest and display*.

BlackBerrys, iPhones and iPads

We don't signal power and position to others by physical postures alone. Fashionable objects and devices are commonly used. At work a favourite fashion item is the latest technology. It's not a coincidence that high-power people are often the ones who first get allocated, or arrange to have, the latest whiz-bang tools. In recent times BlackBerrys have made us look good and then along came iPhones and now iPads. Display rights (bragging) exist for those who are first to get the latest gadget and others gather to be impressed and indicate their desire to own one.

Once acquired, we then use our hand-held devices to, among other things, show the world that we are in demand. The ultimate is to be sitting in a meeting and be called out by a high ranking boss. I was once in a meeting with a senior executive who brought with her only two items: a BlackBerry and a mobile phone. She had no pen or paper, leaving note-taking to a subordinate. This executive announced that she *had* to leave both devices on in case the chief executive needed her. Her frequent glances at the devices throughout the meeting demonstrated that the most important person on her mind wasn't in the room!

Of course, there are a number of instinctive reasons that make hand-held devices compulsive to humans. By now you'll be expert at spotting the reasons. *Contest and display* is just one. There's also *gossip*, so we always have the latest information and can engage in electronic chitchat. There's *loss aversion*, as we'd hate to 'miss out'. There's *social belonging*, which ensures we're never out of contact, like when we get that anxious unloved feeling when our plane lands and there are no messages for us. Indeed, the 'message received' tone sets off a chemical reaction in the brain and a shot of the pleasure chemical, dopamine, is released. Dopamine is one of the neurotransmitters whose function is to carry impulses between nerve cells. When something rewarding happens to us, including pleasurable social interactions, we experience a release of dopamine which triggers a feeling similar to a charge of adrenalin.

We will seek to repeat that experience. It is indeed a pleasure to know that we are in social demand.

And then there's the physical attraction. With our opposable thumb and keen eyesight, intricate hand-held devices are a natural for humans. As the *toolmakers*, humans have a long history of adapting items for special purposes, for labour saving or for weapons. BlackBerrys and mobile phones have an uncanny resemblance to one of the most useful and enduring tools of all time—the humble hand axe. Hand axes, chisel-shaped stones often the size of a palm, endured predominantly unchanged for 1.8 million years. To hold a mobile phone and run your thumb over its surface and caress the side of the implement no doubt gives us the same feeling that early humans felt as they toyed with their hand axes.

Leisure and waste

There are sophisticated ways in which we display our social standing. The philosopher, Thorstein Veblen, wrote *The Theory of the Leisure Class* in 1899. His thesis was that we display our social standing and seek to impress others through the use of:

- conspicuous consumption and
- conspicuous leisure.

We don't have access to each other's bank accounts in order to compare our wealth and relative standing. Instead, we engage in consumption and leisure pursuits that are *conspicuous*. The attribute that connects both strategies, according to Veblen, is *waste*—a person is wealthy enough to be able to waste either time or goods. He writes, 'In order to gain and to hold the esteem of (others) it is not sufficient merely to possess wealth or power. The wealth or power must be put in evidence, for esteem is awarded only on evidence.'

Conspicuous leisure is achieved through the reduction, and ultimately the avoidance of, manual labour. People who are relatively wealthy engage others to do their manual tasks. This occurs because positions involving less manual labour hold greater social status, and so powerful people delegate labour-intensive work to others. The highest power people in organisations might not even write their own emails. Luxury holiday destinations and expensive golf club memberships are other indicators of wealth and affordability to which is attached social prestige.

Consumable goods provide more opportunities to display our social standing. What we buy—from the location and appearance of our house to our brand of car to the label on our clothes—allows a basis of comparison 'which prompts us to outdo those with whom we are in the habit of classing ourselves'. Objects of beauty and decoration, such as precious stones, owe their value to the attribute of conspicuous waste—not everyone can afford them. Elegant dress, Veblen says, serves its purpose partly because it is expensive and also because it is 'the insignia of leisure'. Marketers appeal to this instinct in humans by frequently changing the make or model of an item such as a motor car, clothing or phones, where people seek to own the latest—signifying that they are not falling behind.

IMPLICATIONS OF THIS INSTINCT FOR LEADERS

Here's a snapshot of what we have learned about the instinct of *contest and display*.

1. We use various means in order to get ahead.
2. Social equity or inequity affects national health and wellbeing outcomes.
3. The methods of 'looking good' are different for both genders.
4. Merely holding powerful poses increases feelings of power over others.

There are significant practical implications of *contest and display* which, if incorporated into your toolkit, will make managing people easier.

Implication 1. Elite and 'second-class' citizens

Given our inclination to contest and display in order to improve our social standing, we can expect that people and groups will seek to distinguish themselves at work. There will be a tendency for an elite group to emerge. Often these are sales or the so-called 'work winners', while the 'second-class citizens' are known as overhead or support staff. You quickly get to know which group you are in, and if you aren't sure, the elite group is there to tell you. The high status group often forgets that, like the human body, it's difficult to run a business unless all the functions are working. The lower bowel might not be the most glorious part of the body, but the rest of the body and the glory organs get a nasty reminder of its importance if it doesn't deliver.

If you are part of the elite group in your organisation, understanding *contest and display* helps you realise that it's best not to throw your weight around and diminish others—if for no other reason than it's self-defeating to do so. You can also clamp down on anyone else on your team who seeks to improve their own position by diminishing others.

If you are a manager of a low ranking group, knowing about social positioning helps you and your people avoid *feeling* like second-class citizens. If you are at a supervisor level, you might not have the power and influence to stop prestigious groups diminishing your people. What you can do is control your reaction and influence your team's reaction. You only become a second-class citizen if you concede this view in your own mind, or if you concede power and status to another group. You can choose to hold pride in your own position and truly know that the elite group could not function for long without you.

If you are the CEO you can certainly influence the culture of the organisation and insist that colleagues don't treat others as first- or second-class citizens. And your own actions will demonstrate this to be the case.

Implication 2. Egalitarian leadership

The social equality findings in relation to health and wellbeing are compelling, both in terms of demonstrating the importance of social standing and as a guide to effective leadership of social animals.

First, the findings remind us of the importance of social standing that people have in their social group. At work this includes our standing in our team and in our department and those with whom we most closely compare. A team leader has the greatest impact on the level of acceptance and prestige that people experience in their team. Every team member should feel that they are playing a significant role.

Second, the findings urge managers to lead with an egalitarian style—to help ensure social equity. This means in practice that the leader:

- values the job of all staff irrespective of their function or their level
- gives people significant control over their work
- avoids differentiation through benefits, conditions of employment and badges of office
- values social events and opportunities to interact with staff
- is friendly and approachable
- distributes resources equitably
- ensures that people are valued in the eyes of others
- pays well with no extreme difference between the highest and lowest ranked staff members.

From the social research we know that social *inequity* establishes conditions for distrust, poor staff collegiality and poor health and wellbeing.

Implication 3. Meetings are for display

Meetings are a fact of work life. But there's more to meetings than meets the eye! They aren't merely for functional reasons—not just for communication and decision making. There's an underlying subtext to meetings where part of their purpose is display.

Take, for example, the annual strategic planning workshop. There are community signals as to who gets invited—and who doesn't. Sure, the big bosses are there (which gives them a chance to display). Then some of the up-and-comers will get asked along. For them, they'll get some bragging rights among their peers—not that they'll want to boast too strongly in case they get ostracised for their inflated ego. The young invitees might drop a line into a conversation beforehand: 'Oh, if you're after me next week I'll be at The Vines for the strategic planning workshop.' (The !Kung people of Southern Africa have deliberate ways to avoid what author Boehm calls 'upstartism'. Apart from not coming home as a braggart for making the kill, credit for a large kill goes to the owner of the first arrow to hit the game. Arrows have been randomly assigned. So it's not the person who shot the arrow, it's the owner of that arrow who might not even have been present who gets the credit. 'In effect, it is a way of removing the temptation to dominate'.)

Then there are the weekly management meetings. Everyone knows the managers are in the conference room. There's a signal in that. Some non-managers might get invited to come in and *present* to the meeting—they are being afforded display rights. Some non-managers might be invited to join the managers for a light lunch or dinner that evening. That's socially sensible, to allow the young aspirants to rub shoulders with the higher status people, and to feel socially affirmed at the opportunity to do so. The younger folks will find it worthy to announce at home with a hint of pride, 'Oh, I won't be home for dinner Tuesday evening. I've been invited to dinner with the top team.'

A new manager knows they've made it when they get to their first management meeting. In case you're about to go to your first managers' meeting, here's a word of warning that you will probably be able to anticipate, given that you have almost finished this book: Expect contest and display from your colleagues to keep you in your place. A new manager recently told me about his first meeting where he received a torrid reception. As the new kid on the block he was picked on—put in his place. The big boss, knowing what was happening, let it run a little while. He wanted to let the managers get the contest out of their system and see how the new manager coped. The boss and the new manager debriefed afterwards. The young manager had done well in finding a balance between maintaining his composure and being appropriately firm without being defensive and combative. By the second meeting he was one of the team and the induction ritual was over.

Leaders at every level should use meetings to their advantage—they are subtle but important rituals. Only the leader can call the team together. The meeting then provides a means for the leader to appropriately assert their standing. The way the leader runs the meeting is a way to constructively demonstrate their authority.

Implication 4. Spotting contest and display

As a budding organisational anthropologist you'll become expert at spotting *contest and display*. In many ways, *contest and display* can be constructive. One form is the pride people take in their work. I once consulted to a manufacturing firm where the engagement level of staff was chronically low—unlike anything I'd seen. The low motivation was mostly driven by frustrations with the systems of work and lack of maintenance on basic equipment, resulting in a chronic inability for employees to do their job. Despite this, there was pride in how the employees were regarded by their work mates. In my meetings with the employees they often used the expression, 'We know who the gun operators are.' If they weren't a gun operator they wanted to be one, and if they were one, they wanted to retain that prestigious standing in the eyes of their colleagues *despite* the organisational obstacles put in their way.

A negative form of *contest and display* is the underhanded way a new person might (not always) denigrate the prior incumbent. Another is when leaders take the view that there is no one to replace them. In my years involved in succession planning, most incumbents insist that no one is 'yet ready' for the role. A third example is when a leader goes on leave and their nominated delegate throws their weight around for the time they are in the prestigious role of manager. Their peers may well become frustrated at their competitive display and upstartism.

Contest and display explains why 'pilot' programs are almost always 'deemed' successful. People sponsoring and implementing the program have an investment in its success, even at the pilot stage. They want to look good and to be associated with a *winner*. (Gaining approval to an initiative via a pilot program is an effective use of *loss aversion* as the risks are less for decision-makers when they sign-off on 'just a pilot program'.)

'Being busy' can also be a means of display. A full calendar is a proxy for being in social demand, and vice versa. Even people who aren't busy claim to have a full calendar or are evasive in their language so as not to reveal a lack of social demand.

Another tell-tale sign of *contest and display* is the reluctance of senior people to change a bad decision. Perhaps the executive made a strategic growth call that is not going well, or they acquired a business that is draining the organisational resources, or they invested in a major technology tool that is proving to be a disaster. Generally, there will be a lack of preparedness to admit the mistake and the executive stays with the bad decision—they don't want to look bad. Often the change is only made when a new CEO comes in who was not part of the prior decision.

You might look afresh at how email is used. Emails are a natural for humans, and can be used constructively or destructively for contest and display—who you respond to and with what speed. Constructively, a quick reply from a high-power to a low-power person can have an energising effect. A staff member who once worked with me had completed a review of employment contracts and emailed the executive team with her recommendations. The CEO sent a one-line acknowledgement: 'Hi Cath, great job. Thanks for completing this critical review.' The effect was electrifying on Cath's motivation—high leverage for the ten seconds taken by the CEO to send his email.

We can't let the subject of emails pass without acknowledging the number of instincts that appear in the subtext of how email is used.

- Social belonging—bringing people together and who gets included or excluded.
- Gossip—the sharing of social chitchat.
- Hierarchy—possibly having a go at people (from a safe distance).
- Empathy and mind reading—we miss out on face so we can easily misread people.
- Emotions before reason—reactions to carelessly worded emails (or perhaps deliberately worded to cause insult or hurt).
- Social standing—to let people know of your achievements.
- Loss aversion—covering your backside.

Implication 5. Job titles

Within our work community, titles are the most significant way people display their position in the hierarchy and their worth to the group. Titles are public—that's their purpose. Hence the reason why a) people are so touchy about their title and b) some will walk over hot coals for a promotion (title elevation). Whereas a salary increase is usually known only to the boss and the person, a new title is known to all.

The significance of title as a display ritual is not limited to groups at work. It also works as a display tool to a person's family and peer group. I once worked on an assignment for a legal firm where staff engagement amongst the young lawyers was low and the rate of attrition was high. One of the complaints among the young lawyers was that the firm didn't use the common title of Senior Associate for people at their level. They felt diminished when drinking in the pub with their ex-university peers who boasted about the advances they were making in their careers.

The point of contest within our social group is that we can't take the display factor out of work life. Some organisations attempt to do this by removing job titles. This can't be enduring and is not the answer to the importance and sometimes distraction placed on job titles—we can't take hierarchy out of human systems. People know how they compare. Job titles codify what we suspect to be the case and seek to ensure fairness.

So leaders should handle titles carefully. Be generous enough, consistent and also appreciate that the subject is legitimately important to others. Job titles just happen to be one of our contest and display methods in the habitat of the modern workplace. And when you do promote someone, make a point of announcing it to your team. If you are a department manager, announce promotions to your department. Be sure to acknowledge the reasons for the person's elevation. Being specific about the reasons makes the announcement uniquely personal to the individual. In composing your announcement, apply the gossip test: will this person be proud to share what I am about to say about them with their family tonight?

Implication 6. Power poses

Let's return to the Dana Carney research into power poses—the implications of two minute high-power or low-power poses. Here are the key implications to help with life in organisations:

1. The poses were maintained for just two minutes. Imagine the impact on our personal projection of power and control if we habitually use open and expansive postures as opposed to closed and hunched postures.

2. If we carry ourselves in more powerful displays rather than hunched or constricted ones we will be more active and less inactive. Thus, our personal effectiveness should be enhanced by consistently adopting high-power stances.

3. Those who display openly, occupy more space and hence feel more powerful may be perceived by others as being more powerful and impressive. As a result they might be more inclined to be appointed to positions of power. Yet in making decisions about others we should

remind ourselves to look at them objectively and not become dazzled by their displays.

4. People who hold high-power body poses might win a greater share of scarce organisational resources than people who are inclined to hold low-power poses.

5. If we are in positions of power, such as a manager role, take care not to adopt poses that might intimidate and make others feel less powerful and inhibited. Yet the contrary is also true; that if we are in positions of power we need to display appropriate power in order to carry the required influence in our role. Adopting low-power poses as a manager will inhibit your leadership. It's a fine balance.

6. When facing a difficult confrontation you can prepare by holding an exaggerated power pose for a moment (out of sight). This may sound a bit theatrical, but if it helps to make you feel more powerful, to be more in control and to boost your testosterone, then why not?

7. Take care not to show that you are intimidated by more powerful people. Low-power poses will accentuate your disadvantage and the other person's dominance. But then again, sometimes it's the smart thing to be submissive. Chimps submit by showing hunched, closed postures and often extend a hand to the mouth of the dominating individual. The benefit of submission is that it tends to placate the intimidator.

What happens to ex-alphas?

So what happens to the alpha male chimp when he loses his top ranking? Dr Goodall's description aptly applies to many human leaders who lose their powerful position: 'They become a shadow of their former selves.' Their physical bearing is diminished. They are more constricted in their postures and they lose their aura.

Mostly, the future for the deposed alpha depends on his personality. Some go to the 'back bench' and might make a run for the top job some time later. (The aggressive Frodo was alpha at Gombe several times.) Some take it hard and slip to the edge of their community and live the rest of their lives in relative isolation, often in physical danger in being alone. Others seem happy to relinquish the top job and remain with the adult males albeit lower in the pecking order. Some become confidants of the next alpha and hence retain significant influence.

Alpha males Mike and Goliath are a case in point. Initially there was tension between the two after Mike, aided by his kerosene cans, replaced Goliath. Goliath fought to retain his position, and on one occasion Dr Goodall observed the display and charging go on for nearly half an hour. The contest was mainly through hitting one another with the ends of branches and screeching at each other. As is usually the case between males within their community, neither chimp actually attacked the other. 'Unexpectedly, after an extra long pause, it looked as though Goliath's nerve had broken. He rushed up to Mike, crouched beside him with loud, nervous pant-grunts, and began to groom him with feverish intensity. For a few moments Mike ignored Goliath completely. Suddenly he turned and, with a vigour almost matching Goliath's, began to groom his vanquished rival. There they sat, grooming each other without pause for over an hour. That was the last real duel between the two males. From then on it seemed that Goliath accepted Mike's superiority, and a strange intense relationship grew between the two. They often greeted one another with much display of emotion, embracing and patting one another, kissing each other in the neck and afterwards grooming each other. Although a male chimp is quick to threaten or attack a subordinate, he is usually equally quick to calm his victim with a touch, a pat on the back, an embrace of reassurance.'

One thing a male chimp can't do is to leave his community. He spends his life in the group to which he is born. If he is caught alone by the border patrols of the neighbouring males he is likely to be brutally murdered. He doesn't have the option of resigning to take his chances in another 'organisation'.

Organisational Behaviours that Now Make More Sense

UNDERSTANDING THE INSTINCTIVE behaviours of humans allows us to deal with the reality of the species. This book has uncovered why people behave the way they do at work so we can make more informed leadership choices. To continue your journey with instincts you are welcome to subscribe to our free monthly newsletter via www.hardwiredhumans.com. Prior newsletters are archived on the site. Also available on our website are Leadership Instincts Aids covering extra tips in how to apply instincts to people leadership.

Knowing about natural behaviour allows us both to use instincts and also not to be limited by our instinctive urges. The framework helps explain behaviour in organisations and how we can use that knowledge constructively. When we take business leaders and HR executives to the zoo to learn about and apply human instincts, we ask them to complete a brainstorm exercise. The exercise follows the explanation of the 9 human instincts and a visit to the apes to see our social instincts in the context of the bigger zoological picture. In the exercise we ask participants to reflect on:

1. How are we similar to chimps?
2. How we are different?
3. What organisational behaviours now make more sense?

All groups find the first question easy, the second hard, and the third revealing.

Here's a snapshot of the answers to Question 3 brainstormed by groups from different organisations. Thanks to the leaders from hundreds of organisations, including Bankwest, Cerebos, Chevron, Flight Centre, GE, Guild Group,

Hospira, ING Direct, Mars, Metro Trains Melbourne, Parsons Brinckerhoff, Philips, Schneider, Starlight Children's Foundation, Symantec and Thales who have contributed to this list.

Workplace Behaviours That Now Make Sense		
Group dynamics	Efficient group size	Desire to be accepted
Fight for territory and turf protection	Politics	Orientation of new members
Understanding anti-social behaviour	Competitive language	Working in silos
Team—sense of belonging	Efficiency of small teams	Rituals and routines
Stability from a good leader	Bad leaders ousted	New people need to be introduced
Hierarchy	Unwillingness to challenge hierarchy	Alpha males now seem more obvious
Positioning in the hierarchy	Dominance of males in the hierarchy	Organisations are boys' clubs
Overall figurehead	Leadership can be a learned behaviour	Resource allocation is a status symbol
Displays are sometimes a challenge	How the spoils are shared	Some leaders and some followers
Succession planning tensions	Take organisational cues from alpha	No leadership without support of group
Earn your right to be leader	Some folks fine to be subordinates	Takeover of other organisations
One clear leader per team/ division	Importance of coaching/ mentoring	Change causes conflict and tension
Dealing with/avoiding conflict	Managers become defensive when threatened	Grapevines
Gossip and cliques	How word spreads in an organisation	Alliances change with changes in the organisation
Gossip generates support or sabotage	Leadership depends on network	Positioning/grooming of each other
Making and breaking alliances	Alliances for personal benefit	Looking after Number 1
Political positioning	Greasing/grassing the boss	People who network seem to get ahead
Mixture of personalities	People learn through mimicry	Demonstrating self-worth
Manipulation	Importance of social interaction	Everyone has a role to play
Resistance to outside	Challenge authority	Male display
Status symbols (e.g. job title, office)	Youth challenge the established order	Those who make the most noise get most status

There's one downside to having read this book. You are now no longer able to claim ignorance on the subject of people leadership! From now on, it's a matter of choice. If as a leader you don't spend time with a new employee the first morning they join your team, you will be choosing a path of self-destruction in terms of the first impression you make. If you don't bring your team together for regular team meetings and a mix of social interactions, you will block the formation of constructive team dynamics. If you attempt to manage a team beyond around nine, you now know you will be testing the laws of nature. If you don't set aside time at least every couple of weeks for individual reviews with your people then you will distance yourself from them, diminishing their energy and contribution and sacrificing an important vehicle for leading people. If you are misunderstood or lack persuasion, it might mean that people couldn't quickly classify your meaning. If you are overly aggressive in your use of power, you won't be surprised when people retreat from you—yet if you under-use your power your team will be equally dysfunctional.

But now that you know about instincts, human behaviour should be less of a mystery and, excitingly, leadership of people will be significantly easier—at least nine times so.

Appendix
The 9 Human Instincts Defined

SOCIAL LIVING – How Humans Live	
Social Belonging	Humans desire strong bonds within family-sized groups of around 7 people and a sense of belonging in clans of up to 150.
Hierarchy and Status	Humans seek superiority or security in hierarchical systems. We seek status symbols, recognition and elevation within the hierarchy.
THINKING AND FEELING – How Humans Think and Feel	
Emotions Before Reason	Humans trust their emotional instincts above all else and use emotions as their first screen for all information received. We hear negative news first and loudest.
First Impressions to Classify	Humans quickly classify people, situations and experiences into categories (good or bad, in or out) based on first impressions and gut feelings rather than engage in time-consuming analysis.
Loss Aversion	Humans seek to avoid loss and risky situations but fight frantically when feeling threatened. We explore and are curious about the world around us when we feel safe.
Gossip	Humans seek and share information. We share information with others we like and use it to build alliances. We love to tell and hear stories.
Empathy and Mind Reading	Humans utilise empathy and mind reading to build relationships, be friendly and gather information.
Confidence Before Realism	Humans radiate confidence to move forward in the world, often denying what is realistic. We allow confidence to conquer realism to get what we want.
Contest and Display	Humans seek to impress others and to demonstrate their worth as a means to gain advantages. We spend inordinate amounts of time and energy making ourselves look good in various ways.

Source: Nigel Nicholson, *Managing The Human Animal*, Texere Publishing, UK, 2000 and Nigel Nicholson, 'How Hardwired is Human Behavior?' in *Harvard Business Review*, July 1998

Acknowledgments

I AM INDEBTED to many people for their support in the journey leading to this book.

I owe special thanks to Professor Nigel Nicholson, who years ago triggered my interest in the significance of human instincts for explaining and solving people challenges in the workplace. In 1998 I was pondering the pattern of people-related issues that occurred persistently in organisations I had worked for, and for which I didn't have a satisfactory explanation. Then I read Professor Nicholson's *Harvard Business Review* article and his book. It was an 'Ah hah!' moment. Suddenly so much made sense, and in the HR teams I was with at the time we began to apply our interpretation of Nigel's work. We designed a performance appraisal system that managers and staff loved. We implemented restructures smoothly and completed mergers and acquisitions with minimal disruption to services and with high staff engagement and retention. Years later I met Nigel and he has been a generous supporter and encourager of my work.

The HR teams I have worked with were instrumental in the development of my thinking and with the ways we first applied human instincts theory: teams at IBM Global Services (which just predated the crystallisation of the implications of human nature for leadership but demonstrated our instincts were correct), Cable & Wireless Optus and Sinclair Knight Merz.

Polly Cevallos of the Jane Goodall Institute of Australia holds a special place in this journey. When we take clients to zoos to learn and apply human instincts, Polly leads the discussion on chimpanzee behaviours, with the support of the wonderful zoo keepers who share their knowledge and experiences. It's a joy to work with someone with Polly's positive outlook, motivation and generosity. Thanks to Dr Jane Goodall who first inspired me as a kid—reading in the *National Geographic* of her research and adventures—and then years later I heard her speak and had my second light-bulb moment when I saw the connection to our own human nature as social animals. Dr Jane is a generous supporter of my work and one of the most beautiful people you could ever hope to meet.

Thanks to the wonderful and inspiring zoo keepers who share their insights and stories with our clients. I never tire of both the stories and the jaw-dropping reactions of business leaders and HR professionals as they see the similarities of the apes' behaviour to our own and how they are then able to apply that insight. Thanks to Louise Grossfeldt and Allan Schmidt at Taronga Zoo, Damian Lewis at Melbourne Zoo and Leif Cocks at Perth Zoo. I am very grateful to the management of Taronga Zoo for their support in sharing the stories of their chimps and for their wonderful facility, which, quite deservedly, is one of Sydney's top tourist attractions.

I founded Hardwired Humans (the company) with Cathy Wilks. We had great fun, stimulation and satisfaction in bringing the services to market and adding value to client organisations. To Cathy I extend my sincere gratitude.

We get to work with wonderful clients. The client champions are too many to mention. I'll limit the specific thanks to the clients involved in a PhD research study being conducted by Tamzyn Dorfling at Macquarie Graduate School of Management under the supervision of Professor Richard Badham: Andria Wyman-Clarke and Paul Bowles of Thales, Jo Hilyard of Philips, Kit Middleton of Symantec, Michael Murphy of Flight Centre, Nicole Sullivan of Metro Trains Melbourne and Yvonne Villinger of DB Schenker.

There is one other client person who deserves a special mention! When Cathy and I took the Hardwired Humans services to the market, the first person who signed up to our first public program was Ken Pattemore, then of Colonial First State now with Challenger. In sporting parlance, we call Ken our 'No. 1 ticket holder'!

Many organisations have been generous in bringing the implications of instincts to the attention of their members: AGSM Executive Programs, Australian Human Resources Institute, the CEO Forum and HR Director Forum, Macquarie Graduate School of Management and Mt Eliza Executive Education.

Thanks to the energetic and professional book production team. Thanks to Jeff Higgins and his colleagues at Dennis Jones & Associates for their expertise and guidance, Deb McInnes and her team for the expert promotion campaign and the creative Sheila Parr and Matt Donnelley and their colleagues at Greenleaf Book Group for the cover design and layout. Thanks to Robert Stapelfeldt at McPherson's Printing Group and to Peter Kanellopoulos, Alex Kane and Renee Anderson at Packforce for their distribution service.

At the risk of sounding corny I thank my Mum and Dad. Among many things to be grateful for, from Mum I acquired my love of the humanities and from Dad I had the best career advice you could ever hope for—which is worth sharing as it may help parents and leaders give career advice. At the end of high school I didn't know what I wanted to study at university. Dad never suggested what I should do and didn't even mention options. He helped me in the form of a question: 'Of all the work subjects I talk about at home, what do you enjoy most?' Oh, that was easy—industrial relations! I always loved Dad talking about union matters and the people-related challenges he faced as Chief Engineer at Broken Hill's major mine. Dad's point in asking the question to help me identify what I most enjoyed was that I would be 'choosing a subject that stimulated my curiosity and hence I would always want to know more about'.

Last, and most importantly, thanks to my wife, Jude. She is amazingly supportive of the hours I have devoted to writing this book, she encourages my passion for the subject and adds to my thinking as we bounce ideas around. Jude is the one who set the focus of this book, suggesting that it should be written as a practical guide for managers to help them with the people dimension of their role.

Notes

WHY WE BEHAVE THE WAY WE DO

From an evolutionary view, *Homo sapiens* emerged on the plains of Africa I first read the description of the recent transition of humans into the industrial world stated like this in Nigel Nicholson, 'How Hardwired is Human Behavior?' in *Harvard Business Review*, July 1998.

And early *Homo sapiens* were shaped by their pre-human ancestors From British Natural History Museum exhibit. See also Winston R, *Human Instinct*, Bantam Press, UK, 2002.

Even the transition to agricultural communities occurred only around 10,000 years ago Diamond J, *Guns Germs and Steel: The Fates of Human Societies*, W.W. Norton and Company, 2005.

The definition of instincts Winston R, *Human Instinct*, p. 5.

The key source and inspiration for the human instincts Nicholson N, *Managing The Human Animal*, Texere Publishing, UK, 2000 and Nicholson N, 'How Hardwired is Human Behavior?' in *Harvard Business Review*, July 1998.

INSTINCT 1. SOCIAL BELONGING

Upon Flo's death Flint stopped eating Goodall J, *Through a Window—Thirty Years with the Chimpanzees of Gombe*, Phoenix, UK, 1990, p. 165.

In April 1846, the Donner party Dunbar R, *The Human History, A new history of mankind's evolution*, Faber and Faber, UK, 2004, pp. 178–179.

James Bain spent 35 years in a Florida gaol (http://www.youtube.com/watch?v=indhkHcfJyM)

In a study by physicist Peter Kline *The Australian*, 12 January 2009.

The Economist magazine asked Facebook 'Primates on Facebook', *The Economist*, 26 February 2009.

human societies and a freeloader in its ranks Boehm C, *Hierarchy in the Forest; The Evolution of Egalitarian Behavior*, First Harvard University Press, 2001 e-book 852.

Group size is related to the size of the human brain Dunbar R, *Grooming, Gossip and the Evolution of Language*, Harvard University Press, USA, 1996.

The ex-global CEO of Proctor & Gamble Lafley A, 'What Only the CEO Can Do' in *Harvard Business Review*, May 2009.

The prehistoric Tonga navy Diamond J, *Guns Germs and Steel: The Fates of Human Societies*.

Genghis Khan used family-sized groups Weatherford J, *Genghis Khan and the Making of the Modern World*, Three Rivers Press, USA, 2004.

INSTINCT 2. HIERARCHY AND STATUS

One of the most constructive leaders of the Gombe chimps was Figan Goodall J, *Through a Window*, p. 48.

He was so clearly dominant Goodall J, *Through a Window*, p. 52.

They listed the attitudes and behaviours typical of powerful people Keltner D, Gruenfeld D and Anderson C, 'Power, Approach and Inhibition' in *Psychological Review*, 2003, Vol 110, No 2.

Milgrim explained Cialdini R, *Influence, Science and Practice*, Allyn & Bacon, USA, 2001.

In my book O'Keeffe A, *The Boss*, Greenleaf Book Group, USA, 2009.

INSTINCT 3. EMOTIONS BEFORE REASON

Assuming the worst will tend to keep us out of harm's way Damasio A, *Descartes' Error—Emotion, Reason, and the Human Brain*, Penguin, USA, 1994 p. 267.

As Damasio describes Elliot Damasio A, *Descartes' Error—Emotion, Reason, and the Human Brain*, pp. 37–38.

He lost his job   Damasio A, *Descartes' Error—Emotion, Reason, and the Human Brain*, p. 50.

Damasio suggested two possible dates   Damasio A, *Descartes' Error—Emotion, Reason, and the Human Brain*, pp. 193–194.

In short, it appears a collection of systems in the human brain   Damasio A, *Descartes' Error—Emotion, Reason, and the Human Brain*, p. 70.

Damasio describes the basic experiment   Damasio A, *Descartes' Error—Emotion, Reason, and the Human Brain*, pp. 212–214.

Individuals like Elliot with frontal lobe damage   Damasio A, *Descartes' Error—Emotion, Reason, and the Human Brain*, p. 216.

A second step of the experiment was introduced   Damasio A, *Descartes' Error—Emotion, Reason, and the Human Brain*, pp. 220–221.

Amabile and Kramar had 238 people keep a daily diary of work   Amabile T and Kramer S, 'Inner Work Life' in *Harvard Business Review*, May 2007.

INSTINCT 4. FIRST IMPRESSIONS TO CLASSIFY

We do so in order to *classify*   Nicholson N, *Managing the Human Animal*.

'Mummy, Mummy, I have good news!'   A friend, Christopher Macdonald, shared with me that he used this example in coaching a senior executive in how to clearly communicate his message.

Mike Smith is the CEO   *The Australian*, 20 December 2008.

There was one male called Prof   Goodall J, *Through a Window*, p. 104.

Two Harvard researchers   Ambady N and Rosenthal R, 'Half a Minute: Predicting Teacher Evaluations From Thin Slices of Nonverbal Behavior and Physical Attractiveness' in *Journal of Personality and Social Psychology* 1993, Vol 64. No 3, pp. 431–441.

In a recent study (2007), Dr Dana Carney   Carney D, Colvin R and Hall J, 'A thin slice perspective on the accuracy of first impressions' in *Journal of Research in Personality* 41 (2007) pp. 1054–1072.

In another study, one morning 55 college students   Kelley H, 'The Warm-Cold Variable in First Impressions of Persons' in *Journal of Personality* Vol 19 No 4, pp. 391–418 (June 1950). See also Brafman O and Brafman R, *Sway*, Doubleday, USA, 2008.

we have the capacity to process seven   Miller G, 'The Magical Number Seven, Plus or Minus Two: Some Limits on Our Capacity for Processing Information' in *The Psychological Review*, 1956, vol 63, pp. 81–87.

He is an expert in gut feelings   Gigerenzer G, *Gut Feelings: The Intelligence of the Unconscious*, Viking, 2007 p. 16.

a fire chief who, based on a sixth sense   Klein G, *Sources of Power, How People Make Decisions*, MIT Press, USA, 1999 p. 32.

INSTINCT 5. LOSS AVERSION

he can't imagine an individual being wired for anything other than first screening for pain and danger   Damasio A, *Descartes' Error—Emotion Reason, and the Human Brain*, p. 267.

When the price of eggs drops   Brafman O and Brafman R, *Sway, the Irresistible Pull of Irrational Behavior*, Doubleday, USA, 2008, p. 18.

The research took place in a Chinese high-tech manufacturer   Hossain T and List J, 'The Behavioralist Visits the Factory: Increasing Productivity Using Simple Framing Manipulations', National Bureau of Economic Research, December 2009.

Participants in the study were asked to taste a chocolate chip cookie   Cialdini R, *Influence, Science and Practice*, pp. 219–223.

Ariely knew that basketball tickets at Duke are greatly sought after   Ariely D, *Predictably Irrational – The Hidden Forces That Shape Our Decisions,* Harper Collins, USA, 2008, p 133.

If your manager did not appoint you, you are less likely to receive a good rating   Pfeffer J and Sutton R, *Hard Facts, Dangerous Half-Truths & Total Nonsense*, Harvard Business School Press, USA, 2006, p. 92.

Neuroscientist Joseph LeDoux lists aggressively defending oneself   LeDoux J, *The Emotional Brain, The Mysterious Underpinnings of Emotional Life*, Simon & Schuster, USA, 1996, p. 131.

INSTINCT 6. GOSSIP

The definition of gossip   Dunbar R, *Grooming, Gossip and the Evolution of Language.*

The capability of language   Dunbar R, *Grooming, Gossip and the Evolution of Language.*

Writing systems were invented around 3,000 BCE   Diamond J, *Guns, Germs and Steel*, e-book 3753.

In organisations, managers tend to have more gossip connections   Labianca G, 'It's Not "Unprofessional" to Gossip at Work' in *Harvard Business Review*, September 2010, p. 28.

Goblin was a young aspirant   Dr Jane Goodall speaking to a business audience, Wellington, New Zealand, 17 October 2008.

INSTINCT 7. EMPATHY AND MIND READING

Gombe chimp Mel was a little over three years old when he lost his mum   Email communication with Dr Goodall.

In an early study back in 1964   Kierein N and Gold M, 'Pygmalion in work organizations: a meta-analysis,' in *Journal of Organizational Behavior*, 21 (2000), pp. 913–928.

The setting was an Israeli Defence Force training camp   Eden D and Shani A, 'Pygmalion Goes to Boot Camp: Expectancy, Leadership and Trainee Performance,' in *Journal of Applied Psychology*, 1982, Vol 67, No 2, pp. 194–199.

Dr Goodall was observing him as a youngster trying to get a share of food   Goodall J, *In the Shadow of Man*, Phoenix, UK, 1999, p. 94.

The classic experiments demonstrating fairness to others is the ultimatum game   Lehrer J, *The Decisive Moment, How the Brain Makes Up Its Mind*, Text Publishing, Melbourne, 2009, p. 175.

There's power in an apology   Ariely D, 'The End of Rational Economics' in *Harvard Business Review*, July-August 2009, p. 78.

it only takes five hours of face-to-face contact   Vedantam S, *The Hidden Brain—how our unconscious minds elect presidents, control markets, wage wars, and saves our lives*, Scribe, Melbourne 2010, p. 61.

Our skill of reading faces emerges at an early age   Gigerenzer G, *Gut Feelings, The Intelligence of the Unconscious*, pp. 63–64.

a newcomer can quickly figure out the social status   Gigerenzer G, *Gut Feelings, The Intelligence of the Unconscious*, p. 63.

An incident involving a group of chimps on a border patrol   Boehm C, *Hierarchy in the Forest*, e-book 429.

The significance of eye movement can also help a young chimp get his share of food
Goodall J, *In the Shadow of Man*, pp. 93–94.

facial expressions displaying the key emotions of humans are the same all around the world. That's a remarkable discovery   see for example Ekman P and Friesen W, *Unmasking the Face, A guide to recognizing emotions from facial clues*, Malor Books, USA, 2003

inference of competence based solely on facial appearance predicted the outcomes of US congressional elections   Todorov A, Mandisodza A, Goren A and Hall C, 'Inferences of Competence from Faces Predict Election Outcomes' in *Science*, Vol 308, 10 June 2005.

They conducted a series of studies to determine the exposure   Willis J and Todorov A, 'First Impressions—Making Up Your Mind After a 100-Ms Exposure to a Face' in *Psychological Science*, Vol 17 – No 7, pp. 592–598.

One study looked at the impact of stereotyping associated with attractiveness   Snyder M, Tanke E, Berscheid E, 'Social Perception and Interpersonal Behavior: On the Self-Fulfilling Nature of Social Stereotypes' in *Journal of Personality and Social Psychology*, 1977 Vol 33, No 9, pp. 656–666.

the part of the brain that controls the facial muscles in a 'true' smile   Damasio A, *Descartes' Error—Emotion, Reason, and the Human Brain*, p. 141.

INSTINCT 8. CONFIDENCE BEFORE REALISM

On 15 January 2009 flight 1549 left New York's LaGuardia airport   Sullenberger C, *Highest Duty, My Search for What Really Matters*, Harper Collins, Australia, 2009, p. 207.

'Once I turned back to LaGuardia, it would be an irrevocable choice.'   Sullenberger C, *Highest Duty, My Search for What Really Matters*, p. 224.

an email from a BP engineer   'Blood, Oil & Money', *The Weekend Australian Magazine*, 2-3 October 2010, p. 10.

The pilots survived and in late July 2008 appeared in court for the first time   *The Australian*, 25 July 2008.

Humans are wired to radiate confidence in order to move forward in the world   Nicholson N, *Managing the Human Animal*.

Illusory superiority is why 87% of MBA students   http://en.wikipedia.org/wiki/Illusory_superiority

Lawyers often have an inflated belief http://en.wikipedia.org/wiki/
Illusory_superiority

Gamblers, unfortunately for them, overestimate the probability of success Larwood
L and Whittacker W, 'Managerial Myopia: Self-Serving Bias in Organizational Planning'
in *Journal of Applied Psychology* 1977, Vol 62, No 2, pp. 194–198.

Business managers view themselves as being more able than the typical manager
Kruger J and Denning D, 'Unskilled and Unaware of it: How Difficulties in Recognising
One's Own Incompetence Lead to Inflated Self-Assessments' in *Journal of Personality and
Social Psychology*, 1999, Vol 77, No 6, pp. 1121–1134.

In the managerial study   Larwood L and Whittaker W, 'Managerial Myopia: Self-
Serving Bias in Organizational Planning'.

They conducted four studies to paint a comprehensive picture of inflated self-views
Kruger J and Denning D, 'Unskilled and Unaware of it: How Difficulties in Recognising
One's Own Incompetence Lead to Inflated Self-Assessments.'

One of the individual leaders he has studied is Henry Ford   Tedlow R, *Denial, Why
Business Leaders Fail to Look Facts in the Face—and What to Do About It*, Portfolio, USA,
2010. See also Tedlow R, 'Leaders in Denial' in *Harvard Business Review* July-August
2008, p. 18.

Tedlow explains the reason and elements of denial.   Tedlow R, *Denial, Why Business
Leaders Fail to Look Facts in the Face—and What to Do About It*, p. 33.

He says that if something is too terrible to be true we can deny it   Tedlow R, *Denial,
Why Business Leaders Fail to Look Facts in the Face—and What to Do About It*, p. 175.

Then came the radial revolution through the 1970s and 1980s   Tedlow R, *Denial, Why
Business Leaders Fail to Look Facts in the Face—and What to Do About It*, pp. 39–42.

In one study on work teams, the interactions of 60 teams were observed   Fredrickson
B and Losada M, 'Positive Affect and the Complex Dynamics of Human Flourishing' in
American Psychologist, October 2005, pp. 678–686.

Tedlow reveals the statements that are likely to reveal a state of denial   Tedlow R,
Denial, Why Business Leaders Fail to Look Facts in the Face—and What to Do About It, p. 36.

we can arm ourselves against denial   Tedlow R, *Denial, Why Business Leaders Fail to Look
Facts in the Face—and What to Do About It*, p. 38.

But let's give it to Captain Sullenberger   Sullenberger C, *Highest Duty, My Search for
What Really Matters*, p. 119.

INSTINCT 9. CONTEST AND DISPLAY

Take Mike, for example   Dr Goodall in conversation with a business audience October 2008 and see also Goodall J, *In the Shadow of Man*, p. 118.

Professor Robert Wilkinson has solved an interesting puzzle   Wilkinson R, *The Impact of Inequality—How to Make Sick Societies Healthier,* The New Press, USA, 2005.

To change a monkey's social standing will significantly affect its health   Wilkinson R, *The Impact of Inequality—How to Make Sick Societies Healthier,* p. 73.

In Europe only nine of the top 500 companies are led by a female CEO   http://www.catalyst.org/publication/285/women-in-europe

In Australia only four (2%) of ASX200 companies   http://www.eowa.gov.au/Australian_Women_In_Leadership_Census/2008_Australian_Women_In_Leadership_Census/Media_Kit/EOWA_Census_2008_Publication.pdf

In the general American population only 3.9% of adult men   Gladwell M, *Blink—The Power of Thinking Without Thinking,* Allen Lane/Penguin, Australia, 2005, pp. 86–87.

A study in the UK found that women   Chesterchronicle.co.uk http://www.chesterchronicle.co.uk/entertainment-chester/chester-cheshire-women/chester-fashion/fashion-news/2009/07/09/fashion-women-spend-one-year-of-their-lives-deciding-what-to-wear-59067-24114116/

Power is expressed through specific body language   Carney D, Cuddy A and Yap A, 'Power Posing: Brief Nonverbal Displays Affect Neuroendocrine Levels and Risk Tolerance' in press but available at http://www.columbia.edu/~dc2534/Power.Poses.pdf

Hand axes, chisel-shaped stones often the size of a palm   Winston R, *Human Instinct.*

There are sophisticated ways in which we display our social standing   Veblen T, *The Theory of the Leisure Class,* Bibliobazaar, 2007, first published 1899.

The wealth or power must be put in evidence   Veblen T, *The Theory of the Leisure Class,* p. 33.

Elegant dress, Veblen says   Veblen T, *The Theory of the Leisure Class*, p. 121.

The !Kung people of Southern Africa   Boehm C, *Hierarchy in the Forest: The Evolution of Egalitarian Behavior,* e-book 666.

From then on it seemed that Goliath accepted Mike's superiority   Goodall J, *In the Shadow of Man*, p. 118.

References

Amabile T and Kramer S, 'Inner Work Life' in *Harvard Business Review*, May 2007

Ambady N and Rosenthal R, 'Half a Minute: Predicting Teacher Evaluations From Thin Slices of Nonverbal Behavior and Physical Attractiveness' in *Journal of Personality and Social Psychology* 1993, Vol 64. No 3, pp. 431–441

Ariely D, *Predictably Irrational—The Hidden Forces That Shape Our Decisions*, Harper Collins, USA, 2008

Ariely D, 'The End of Rational Economics', *Harvard Business Review*, July-August 2009

Boehm C, *Hierarchy in the Forest; The Evolution of Egalitarian Behavior*, First Harvard University Press, USA, 2001

Brafman O, and Brafman R, *Sway, the Irresistible Pull of Irrational Behavior,* Doubleday, USA, 2008

Carney D, Colvin C, and Hall. J, 'A thin slice perspective on the accuracy of first impressions' in *Journal of Research in Personality* 41 (2007) pp. 1054–1072

Carney D, Cuddy A, and Yap A, 'Power Posing: Brief Nonverbal Displays Affect Neuroendocrine Levels and Risk Tolerance' in press but available at http://www.columbia.edu/~dc2534/Power.Poses.pdf

Cialdini R, *Influence, Science and Practice*, Allyn & Bacon, USA, 2001

Damasio A, *Descartes' Error—Emotion, Reason, and the Human Brain*, Penguin, USA, 1994

Diamond J, *Guns Germs and Steel: The Fates of Human Societies*, W.W. Norton and Company, 2005

Dunbar R, *Grooming, Gossip and the Evolution of Language*, Harvard University Press, USA, 1996

Dunbar R, *The Human History, A new history of mankind's evolution*, Faber and Faber, UK, 2004

Eden D and A Shani, 'Pygmalion Goes to Boot Camp: Expectancy, Leadership and Trainee Performance,' in *Journal of Applied Psychology*, 1982, Vol 67, No 2, pp. 194–199

Ekman P and Friesen W, *Unmasking the Face, A guide to recognizing emotions from facial clues*, Malor Books, USA, 2003

Fredrickson B and Losada M, 'Positive Affect and the Complex Dynamics of Human Flourishing' in *American Psychologist*, October 2005, pp. 678–686

Gigerenzer G, *Gut Feelings: The Intelligence of the Unconscious*, Viking, 2007

Gladwell M, *Blink—The Power of Thinking Without Thinking*, Allen Lane/Penguin, Australia, 2005

Goodall J, *In the Shadow of Man*, Phoenix, UK, 1999

Goodall J, *Through a Window—Thirty Years with the Chimpanzees of Gombe*, Phoenix, UK, 1990

Hossain T and List J, 'The Behavioralist Visits the Factory: Increasing Productivity Using Simple Framing Manipulations', National Bureau of Economic Research, December 2009

http://en.wikipedia.org/wiki/Illusory_superiority

http://www.chesterchronicle.co.uk/entertainment-chester/chester-cheshire-women/chester-fashion/fashion-news/2009/07/09/fashion-women-spend-one-year-of-their-lives-deciding-what-to-wear-59067-24114116/

http://www.eowa.gov.au/Australian_Women_In_Leadership_Census/2008_Australian_Women_In_Leadership_Census/Media_Kit/EOWA_Census_2008_Publication.pdf

http://www.catalyst.org/publication/285/women-in-europe

http://www.youtube.com/watch?v=indhkHcfJyM

Kelley H, 'The Warm-Cold Variable in First Impressions of Persons' in *Journal of Personality* Vol 19 No 4, pp. 391–418 (June 1950)

Keltner D, Gruenfeld D, Anderson C, 'Power, Approach and Inhibition' in *Psychological Review*, 2003, Vol 110, No 2

Kierein N and Gold M, 'Pygmalion in work organizations: a meta-analysis,' in *Journal of Organizational Behavior*, 21 (2000), pp. 913–928

Klein G, *Sources of Power, How People Make Decisions*, MIT Press, USA, 1999

Kruger J and Denning D, 'Unskilled and Unaware of it: How Difficulties in Recognising One's Own Incompetence Lead to Inflated Self-Assessments' in *Journal of Personality and Social Psychology*, 1999, Vol 77, No 6, pp. 1121–1134

Labianca G, 'It's Not "Unprofessional" to Gossip at Work', *Harvard Business Review*, September 2010, p. 28

Lafley A, 'What Only the CEO Can Do' in *Harvard Business Review* May 2009

Larwood L and Whittaker W, 'Managerial Myopia: Self-Serving Bias in Organizational Planning' in *Journal of Applied Psychology* 1977, Vol 62, No 2, pp. 194–198.

LeDoux J, *The Emotional Brain, The Mysterious Underpinnings of Emotional Life*, Simon & Schuster, USA, 1996

Lehrer J, *The Decisive Moment, How the Brain Makes Up Its Mind*, Text Publishing, Melbourne, 2009

Miller G, 'The Magical Number Seven, Plus or Minus Two: Some Limits on Our Capacity for Processing Information' in *The Psychological Review*, 1956, vol 63, pp. 81–87.

Nicholson N, 'How Hardwired is Human Behavior?' in *Harvard Business Review*, July 1998

Nicholson N, *Managing The Human Animal*, Texere Publishing, UK, 2000

O'Keeffe A, *The Boss*, Greenleaf Book Group, USA, 2009

Sullenberger C, *Highest Duty, My Search for What Really Matters*, Harper Collins, Australia, 2009

'Primates on Facebook', *The Economist*, 26 February 2009

Pfeffer J and Sutton R, *Hard Facts, Dangerous Half-Truths & Total Nonsense*, Harvard Business School Press, USA, 2006

Snyder M, Tanke E, Berscheid E, 'Social Perception and Interpersonal Behavior: On the Self-Fulfilling Nature of Social Stereotypes' in *Journal of Personality and Social Psychology*, 1977 Vol 33, No 9, pp. 656–666.

Tedlow R, *Denial, Why Business Leaders Fail to Look Facts in the Face—and What to Do About It*, Portfolio, USA, 2010.

Tedlow R, 'Leaders in Denial' in *Harvard Business Review* July-August 2008, p. 18

The Australian, 12 January 2009

The Australian, 20 December 2008

The Australian, 25 July 2008

The Weekend Australian Magazine, 2-3 October 2010

Todorov A, Mandisodza A, Goren Amir and Hall C, 'Inferences of Competence from Faces Predict Election Outcomes' in *Science*, Vol 308, 10 June 2005

Veblen T, *The Theory of the Leisure Class*, Bibliobazaar, 2007, first published 1899

Vedantam S, *The Hidden Brain—how our unconscious minds elect presidents, control markets, wage wars, and saves our lives*, Scribe, Melbourne, 2010

Weatherford J, *Genghis Khan and the Making of the Modern World*, Three Rivers Press, USA, 2004

Wilkinson R, *The Impact of Inequality—How to Make Sick Societies Healthier*, The New Press, USA, 2005

Willis J and Todorov A, 'First Impressions—Making Up Your Mind After a 100-Ms Exposure to a Face' in *Psychological Science*, Vol 17, No 7, pp. 592–598.

Winston R, *Human Instinct*, Bantam Press, UK, 2002.

Index

Note: page numbers in *italics* refer to illustrations.

A

Accenture, 98
aggressiveness read in faces, 159
alliances and cliques. *See also* gossip
    favouritism, avoiding, 124–125
    the gossip map and, 121–123, *122*
    grooming and, 112–115, 125–126
    networking and, 126–128
altruism, 139, 145–146
Amabile, Teresa, 52–54
Ambady, N, 63–64, 65
Anecdote (company name), 117
apologies, power of, 146–147
Ariely, Dan, 100–101, 146–147
Armstrong, Bill, 128
attractiveness, 160–161, 164–165

B

Bain, James, 7
Behr, Gerard, 84–85
body postures, 194–196, 204–205
Boehm, Christopher, 19, 156, 200
border protection behaviours, 74
Bowra, Tony, 116–117, 151
BP, 168–169
Brafman, Ori, 90
Brafman, Rom, 90
brain, human
    classification and, *60*

    emotions and decision making, 47–52
    face reading and, 155
    loss aversion and, 52
    number seven and, 9
    seven items of data and, 68
brain size and clans, 20

C

Campling, David, 152–153
Carney, Dana, 64–65, 194–196, 204
catch-ups, 150–152
CEOs. *See* senior executives and CEOs
change. *See also* loss aversion and assum-
    ing the worst
    chimpanzees and, 93–94
    gossip and, 133–136
    individual-level implications, 96–99
    management of, 103–106
    myth of resistance to, 92–96, 104–106
chimpanzees
    alliances and cliques, 123
    border protection behaviours, 74
    brain size and clans, 20
    classification and, 62–63
    contest and display, 192–194
    emotion, 5–6, 46–47
    empathy and altruism, 139, 145–146
    face reading, 156
    family bonds, 5–6, 7–9, 18

chimpanzees (continued)
  grooming, 114–115, 125–126
  hierarchy and power, 1, 28–30, 58,
      205–206
  hunting, 38
  inter-group conflict, 22
  leadership competition, 16
  loss aversion, 93–94
  morning greetings, 154
  motivation to lead, 35
  networking, 126–128
  self-interest, 144–145
  sense of self and mirror test, 138–139
  sex, 192
Cialdini, Robert, 91–92
clans, 6, 20–25, 75
Clason, Patricia, 76–77
classification. *See* first impressions to
      classify
Clinton, Hillary, 32
cliques. *See* alliances and cliques
communication and language, 59, 75–78,
      172. *See also* gossip
competence, 157–159, 169–173, 182–183
confidence and self-esteem, 152–153
confidence before realism
  airplane crashes and, 167–169
  balance, 179–180
  benefits of self confidence, 176–177
  defined, 212
  denial, 173–176, 178–179, 182
  focusing on vital few, 180–181
  inflated self-view and overconfidence,
      169–173, 182–183
  leader's own self-estimation, 185
  positivity ratio and, 177–178
  simplistic solutions, 181–182
confirmation bias, 66
conspicuous consumption, 197–198
contest and display
  overview, 187–188
  defined, 212
  elite and second-class groups, 198–199
  ex-alphas, 205–206
  gender strategies, 191–194

income equity, effects of, 188–191
  job titles, 203–204
  leisure and waste, 197–198
  meetings and, 200–201
  power poses, 194–196, 204–205
  recognising, 201–203
  technological devices as, 196–197
cortisol, 194–195

D

Damasio, Antonio, 44, 47–52, 90, 163
decision making, 47–52, 72–73, 87–88,
      167–169, 202
denial, 173–176, 178–179
Donner party, 7
Dunbar, Robin, 112–113
Dunning, David, 171, 185

E

egalitarian leadership, 199–200
Ekman, Paul, 157
email, 75–76, 202–203
emotion
  concealment of, 164
  negative feedback and, 84, 151
  positivity ratio, 177–178
  readability of, 162–163
  universal facial expressions, 157
emotions before reason
  agreement, disagreement and, 57
  brain, decision making, and, 47–52
  defined, 211
  email and, 203
  enabling management and, 57
  the 'five word' test, 56
  jumping to conclusions, 43–44
  laughter, power of, 57–58
  meaning and imprinting, 44–47, 55
  performance appraisals and, 107–108
  proactively using positive emotion,
      55–56
  work output and enabling management,
      52–54, 57
empathy. *See also* mind reading and face
      reading

altruism, 139, 145–146
apologies, power of, 146–147
birthdays, 153–154
catch-ups or one-on-ones, 150–152
chimps and, 139, 144–146
defined, 212
hiring and newcomers, 150
knowing individuals, 142–144, 148–150
leader expectations, 139–142
managing individually, 147–148
morning 'hello', 154
self-esteem and confidence, 152–153
self-interest, 144–145
theory of mind, 138–139
employee retention, 17–18, 116–117
enabling management, 53–54, 57
equity, 188–191, 199–200
Evans, John, 57
Evdokimov, Nick, 130–131
evolution, human, 2–3, 20, 60, 177
expectations as self-fulfilling, 139–142

F
Facebook, 9–10
facial expressions. *See* mind reading and
    face reading
fads, 181
family. *See* social belonging and family
favouritism, 123, 124–125
fear, 22, 58
feedback, 81–85, 100–101, 109, 151–152
fight/flight response, 109, 190
First 7 Words technique, 69–71, 75–78,
    81–82, 83–84, 134
first impressions to classify
    anxiety when can't classify, 73
    bad news and, 80
    binary, 59, 67
    change and, 92–99, 106
    chimpanzees and, 62–63
    decision making and, 72–73, 87–88
    defined, 211
    face reading and, 159
    feedback, giving, 81–85

First 7 Words and, 69–71, 75–78,
    81–82, 83–84, 134
gut feelings, 61–62, 72–73
judgment on 7 items of data, 68
meeting for the first time, 78
negative and positive classifications,
    62–63
new role and, 86
news, being first with, 79
new team members and, 87
positive first actions, 78–79
purpose of, 60–62
recruiting and, 85–86
speed of, 63–68
suspending judgment, 86, 88
them and us dynamic and, 74–75
the 'five word test', 56
Flight Centre, 15, 23
Ford, Henry, 173
Ford Motor Company, 173–174
Frederickson, Barbara, 177
freeloaders, 19
Friesen, Wallace, 157

G
the Gambling Experiments, 49–52
gender strategies of contest and display,
    191–194
General Motors, 173–174
Genghis Khan, 24–25
Gigerenzer, Gert, 72, 155–156
Gladwell, Malcolm, 191
Gombe chimpanzees. *See* chimpanzees
Goodall, Jane, 5–6, 111, 127, 139,
    144–145, 156, 188, 205–206. *See also*
    chimpanzees
Gore Associates, 23
gorillas, 12–13, 18, 39
gossip
    asking the gossip question, 129–130
    change management and, 133–136
    defined, 212
    don't try to stop it, 124
    email and, 203
    the gossip test, 119–121, 131–134

gossip (continued)
  influencing, 116–117, 130–133
  networking, 126–128
  positive, 115–116
  purpose and definition of, 112
  reciprocity, healthy, 125–126
  small groups, 113, 128–129, 134–136
  social settings for, 128
  stories and, 117–119, 133
  team dynamics and, 121–123, *122*,
    124–125
  technological devices and, 196
  vocal capability and, 111–112
  as vocal grooming, 112–115
the gossip map, 121–123, *122*
greetings, 154
Grossfeldt, Louise, 7, 192
growth beyond clan size, 21–22, 75
gut feelings, 61–62, 72–73, 85. *See also*
    first impressions to classify

H

hardwiredhumans.com, 207
'hello' in the morning, 154
hierarchy, status, and power. *See also* alli-
    ances and cliques; contest and display
  allocation of resources, 38
  chimpanzees, 28–30, 35, 38, 127–128
  controlling anti-social behaviour and,
    39
  defined, 211
  email and, 203
  face reading and, 163
  first-class and second-class citizens,
    198–199
  gossip and, 134
  imbalance within a team, 24
  licence to lead, 36
  managing up and down, 41–42
  matrix structure and, 40–41
  motivation to lead, 35, 36–37
  overuse or underuse of power, 37–38
  positive and negative indicators of
    power, 32–34
  progression up the hierarchy, 127–128
  review meetings, regular, 40
  social standing and position, 30–32,
    39–40
  systems to manage and constrain power,
    34
  visual and facial clues, 155–156
HIH, 175
Hilyard, Jo, 105
hiring and recruiting, 80, 85–86, 150, 182.
    See also newcomer integration
Hossain, Tanjim, 90–91
humour, 57–58, 171

I

IBM, 116–117, 148
identity, 6, 7, 118, 142–144, 148–149
illusory superiority (inflated self-view),
    169–173, 182–183
imprinting, 44–47, 62
income inequity, 188–191
incompetence, 169–173, 182–183. *See also*
    poor performers
individuals. *See also* empathy
  change response and, 96–99, 106
  leader expectations of, 139–142
  managing individually, 147–148
  one-on-one meetings, 150–152
  self-esteem and confidence, 152–153
  self-interest, 144–145
  valuing identities of, 142–144, 148–149
inflated self-view, 169–173, 182–183
Ingvall, Ludde, 137–138, 142–143, 144
instincts (overview), 1–3. *See also specific*
    instincts
interviews. *See* recruiting and hiring
Israeli Defence Force, 140–141

J

job titles, 31, 203–204
Jones, Steve, 143–144

K

Klein, Gary, 72
Komar, Marwoto, 169, 185
Kornetsky, Rachel, 45-46

Kramar, Steven, 52–54
Kruger, Justin, 171, 185
Kwik Kopy, 119

L

language, 59, 75–78, 172. *See also* gossip
laughter, power of, 57–58
leadership implications of instincts
    confidence before realism, 176–185
    contest and display, 198–206
    emotions before reason, 54–58
    empathy and mind reading, 147–154,
        162–165
    first impressions to classify, 75–88
    gossip, 124–136
    hierarchy and status, 36–42
    loss aversion, 103–110
    social belonging, 10–11, 14–19
LeDoux, Joseph, 109
Lehrer, Jonah, 145
leisure, 197–198
Lewis, Damian, 12-13, 39
licence to give feedback, 84–85
licence to lead, 36
List, John, 90–91
Loechel, John, 165
Losada, Marcial, 177
loss aversion and assuming the worst
    actual loss and, 99–100, 106–107
    brain and, 52
    classification and, 73, 92–99, 106
    defined, 212
    email and, 203
    feedback and, 100–101, 109
    gossip and, 134, 135
    at individual level, 96–99, 106
    logic of, 90–92
    performance appraisals and, 102–103,
        107–109
    pilot programs and, 202
    resistance to change, myth of, 92–96,
        104–106
    response to change, 103–104
    safe environment, establishing, 107
    technological devices and, 196
loyalty, 17–18, 41, 126

M

managing up and down, 41–42
Marks, Andrew, 142
Marks, Isaac, 109
Marlow, Cameron, 10
matrix reporting structure, 40–41
McGibbon, Graham, 149–150
Meat and Livestock Australia, 125
meeting for the first time, 78
meetings as display, 200–201
Metro Trains (Melbourne), 128, 143–144
Milgrim, Stanley, 34
Miller, George, 68
mind reading and face reading
    chimps and, 156
    concealing emotions, 164
    defined, 212
    email and, 203
    emotional readability, 162–163
    hierarchy and, 155–156
    inferences from faces, 157–159
    power and, 163
    remote staff and, 165
    skill in, 155
    stereotyping from attractiveness,
        160–161, 164–165
    universal expressions of emotion, 157
mobile phones, 113, 196–197
morning 'hello', 154
motivation
    to lead, 35, 36–37
    perception-emotion-motivation-output
        cycle, 53
    pride in one's work and, 201–202
Murphy, Michael, 15

N

names, knowing, 142
negativity, appropriate, 178
networking and gossip, 126–128
newcomer integration, 11–13, 18–19, 87,
    150
new role or position in management, 86
news and first impressions, 79, 99–100

Newton, Brad, 132–133
Nicholson, Nigel, 3, 35, 191, 212

O

Obama, Barack, 32
O'Keeffe, David, 45–46
O'Keeffe, Heather, 45–46
O'Keeffe, Paul, 98
Optus, 120, 134–136, 153–154
organisational structure
  clan formation and, 22–25
  family-sized teams, 9–10, 14–15
  restructuring, 105–106, 130–131
  silos, 21–22, 74
organisation charts and loss aversion, 105
output. *See* productivity
overconfidence. *See* confidence before
  realism

P

pecking order. *See* hierarchy, status, and
  power
perception-emotion-motivation-output
  cycle, 53
performance appraisals and reviews
  classification and, 76
  loss aversion and, 102–103, 107–109
  regular, 40
  self confidence and, 176
performance outcomes. *See* productivity
persuasion and First 7 Words technique,
  69–71
Philips Healthcare, 105–106, 130–131,
  149–150, 152–153
pilot programs, 202
political parties, 31–32
poor performers
  agreement not needed from, 183–184
  denial by managers, 175, 182
  incompetence from inflated self-view,
    169–173
  negative feedback and, 81–84, 109
  silverback three-step warning process,
    39
  social rejection and, 19

positivity ratio, 177–178
power. *See* contest and display; hierarchy,
  status, and power
power poses, 194–196, 204–205
pride in one's work, 201–202
productivity
  emotion and, 52–54
  incentives and, 90–91
  leader expectations and, 140–142
  loss aversion and, 91
  team size and, 14–15

Q

Qantas, 115–116

R

realism. *See* confidence before realism
reason and rationality, 44, 47–52, 57,
  171–173. *See also* emotions before
  reason
reciprocity, 125–126
recruiting and hiring, 80, 85–86, 150, 182.
  See also newcomer integration
relocation of offices, 97–98, 133–134
remote staff, keeping in touch with, 165
resources
  allocation of, 38
  clans and, 22
  denial about, 175–176
  matrix and control of, 40–41
reviews. *See* catch-ups; performance
  appraisals and reviews
Richardson, Mark, 87–88
Rosenthal, R, 63–64

S

safe environment, establishing, 107
Schenck, Mark, 117–119
Schmidt, Allan, 7, 126, 193, 194
'second-class' citizens, 198–199
self-esteem, 152–153, 183. *See also*
  confidence before realism
self-interest, 144–145
senior executives and CEOs
  automotive CEOs in Washington, 27

clans and, 23
denial by, 175–176
first-class/second-class rankings and,
    199
gender and, 191
morning 'hello', 154
power imbalances and, 24
reluctance to change a bad decision,
    202
simplistic solutions and, 181
team size and, 14–15
silos, 21–22, 74
simplistic solutions, 181–182
Smith, Mike, 61–62, 72
social belonging and family
chimpanzee family bonding, 5–6, 7–9
clans, 6, 20–25, 75
defined, 211
elements of social belonging, 13
email and, 203
the family paradox, 10–11
family size, 9–10, 14–15
freeloaders and social rejection, 19
Genghis Khan and, 24–25
identity, sense of, 7
'in-group' language and, 74
as instinct, 6
knowing about someone's family, 129,
    142, 144
leader protection of, 18
loyalty to leaders, 17–18
newcomer dynamics, 11–13, 18–19
reproductive strategy and, 6–7
team leader role and, 15–17
technological devices and, 196
social boundaries, 11, 74
social chitchat. See gossip
social rejection, 19
social settings, 128, 149–150
social standing. See also contest and dis-
    play; hierarchy, status, and power
email and, 203
hierarchy and, 30–32, 39–40
income inequity and, 188–191
performance appraisals and, 108

status. See contest and display; hierarchy,
    status, and power
stereotyping, 160–161, 164–165
stories, 117–119, 133
strangers, fear of, 22
strategic planning workshops, 200
stress and social standing, 189–190
Strong, James, 115
submission, 109, 188, 205
Sullenberger, Chesley, 167–168, 185
Sullivan, Barry, 116–117
Sullivan, Nicole, 128
Symantec, 132–133

T

Taronga chimpanzees. See chimpanzees
Tasker, Jude, 89–90, 163, 191
team leaders. See leadership implications
    of instincts
Tedlow, Richard, 173–174, 178–179
testosterone, 195
them and us dynamic, 22, 23, 74–75, 123
theory of mind, 138–139
Thompson, Glen, 125
Todorov, Alexander, 157–159
'Tonga test', 45–46, 55
training, incompetence and, 172–173, 183
trust, 99–100, 106, 159, 189

V

values, 132–133
Van Dyk, Harry, 105–106
Veblen, Thorstein, 197–198
Vedantam, Shankar, 155
vocal grooming, 113

W

Wilkinson, Robert, 188, 190
Wilks, Cathy, 120, 153–154
Willis, Janine, 158–159
Winston, Robert, 3
Wolsely Partners, 87–88
work output. See productivity
Wyman-Clarke, Andria, 86